THE BANDEIRANTES

✷

The Historical Role of the Brazilian Pathfinders

Borzoi Books on Latin America

General Editor,
LEWIS HANKE,

COLUMBIA UNIVERSITY

THE
BANDEIRANTES

❋ ❋ ❋

The Historical Role of the

Brazilian Pathfinders

<small>EDITED WITH AN INTRODUCTION BY</small>

Richard M. Morse

<small>YALE UNIVERSITY</small>

19 65

New York: Alfred·A·Knopf

NOTE: *All but one of the selections in this book, as indicated in the source footnotes, were unavailable in English translation. These have been translated by Richard M. Morse with the assistance of Russell Hamilton.*

L. C. catalog card number: 64-23728

THIS IS A BORZOI BOOK,
PUBLISHED BY ALFRED A. KNOPF, INC.

FIRST EDITION

Dedicated to

SÉRGIO BUARQUE DE HOLANDA

Acknowledgments

I am deeply indebted to Lewis Hanke for suggesting that I do this book and for offering warm encouragement and thoughtful criticism at each step of the way. I have also profited from the searching comments and corrections of the students in Professor Hanke's Colloquium on Latin American History at Columbia University (fall semester, 1963-1964), and in particular an extended critique by Mrs. Jane Meskill. Professor Russell Hamilton, formerly of the Department of Romance Languages and Literature, Yale University, and now of the University of Minnesota, gave me the benefit of his intimate knowledge of Portuguese and Spanish by preparing working drafts of ten of the twelve translated selections. The map I owe to the kindness of Professor David E. Snyder, Department of Geography, Yale University.

Insertions appearing in brackets in quoted or translated texts have been supplied by me.

R. M. M.

Woodbridge, Conn.

Contents

_____

III THE EIGHTEENTH CENTURY

IV THE BANDEIRAS IN HISTORICAL PERSPECTIVE

THE BANDEIRANTES

The Historical Role of the Brazilian Pathfinders

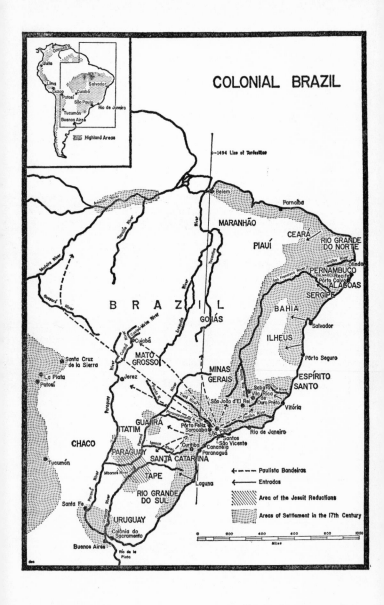

COLONIAL BRAZIL

1494 Line of Tordesillas

Belém
Parnaíba
MARANHÃO
CEARÁ
RIO GRANDE
DO NORTE
PIAUÍ
PALMARES Olinda
PERNAMBUCO
Pôrto Calvo Recife
ALAGOAS
SERGIPE
B R A Z I L
GOIÁS
BAHIA
Salvador
ILHEUS
MATO
GROSSO
Cuiabá
Santa Cruz
de la Sierra
Jerez
La Plata
Potosí
MINAS
GERAIS
Sabará
Vila Rica de
Ouro Prêto
São João d'El Rei
Pôrto Seguro
ESPÍRITO
SANTO
Vitória
GUAIRÁ
ITATIM
Pôrto Feliz
Sorocaba
São Paulo
Rio de Janeiro
CHACO
PARAGUAY
SANTA CATARINA
Curitiba
Santos
São Vicente
Cananéia
Paranaguá
Tucumán
TAPE
Laguna
Mbororé River
RIO GRANDE
DO SUL
Santa Fe
URUGUAY
Colônia do
Sacramento
Buenos Aires
Rio de la
Plata

Amazon River
Tapajós River
Madeira River
Guaporé River
Tocantins River
Araguaia River
São Francisco River
Cuiabá River
Paraguay River
Paraná River
Uruguay River
Paranapanema River
Igoaco River
Tietê River

←--- Paulista Bandeiras
←--- Entradas

▨ Area of the Jesuit Reductions

▨ Areas of Settlement in the 17th Century

0   200   400   600   800   1000
Miles

Orinoco River
Quito
Lima
Cuzco
Potosí
Tucumán
Salvador
Cuiabá
São Paulo
Rio de Janeiro
Buenos Aires
▨ Highland Areas

INTRODUCTION

If one were to propose the following figures as representative frontiersmen or pathfinders of the four great areas of European settlement in the New World—the Spanish American conquistador, the American pioneer, the Canadian *coureur de bois,* and the Brazilian bandeirante—it is certain that the last named would be the least familiar to an English-speaking audience. In fact the whole saga of the exploration and settlement of colonial Brazil might be a blank page for such a group—and this despite the fact that the modern Brazilian nation, with its 3.3 million square miles and nearly eighty million inhabitants, contains virtually one half the land and population of the South American continent. How many educated Americans, one wonders, think of Teddy Roosevelt and Colonel Fawcett as the first explorers of Brazil?

It is not for lack of mythopoeic inventiveness on the part of Brazilians themselves that the exploits of the bandeiras, and the bandeirantes who composed them, have failed to become legend abroad. The phrase "bandeirante spirit" is as fully charged for Brazilians as "pioneer spirit" is for Americans, although each phrase has its own tonalities. Hundreds of volumes of narratives, studies, and documents pertaining to the bandeirantes have been published in Portuguese. They have been celebrated in poetry, fiction, sculpture, and painting. Indeed, they lend themselves to such commemoration.

The bandeirantes were not, to be sure, conquistadors in all that that term implies, although from a Brazilian standpoint they enjoy a certain sentimental advantage over the Spanish conquistadors. For the conquistador was an invading European upon whom latter-day descendants have projected their ambivalent feelings toward the mother country. The bandeirante, characteristically part Indian, was emphatically a New World creature harboring vigorous local loyalties.

If the bandeirante was not a conquistador, neither was he primarily a colonist. True, an archipelago of settlements of bandeirante origin stretches across the face of Brazil. But the bandeirantes were themselves descended from colonists and had their roots in a region of Brazil. On occasion they went "homesteading" in far-off virgin lands, but more frequently their colonizing was a byproduct of some other pursuit. In any case, once they permanently colonized new lands, they ceased being bandeirantes.

Finally, although the bandeirantes roamed a poorly mapped half-continent for more than a century, they are not properly called explorers; for exploration implies rationalized service in a scientific or political cause which, with possible exceptions (see Document 6), had no place in their round of life. "Pathfinders" seems a more appropriate term.

Along with pathfinding, the usual activities of the bandeirante were those of slaver, of prospector, and of informal militiaman. The dominance of one or another of these roles varied with time and circumstance. None of the roles, certainly not that of slaver or prospector, lends itself to the ideal image-building that can be performed for conquistador, colonist, or explorer. In explaining the vitality of the bandeirante legend in modern Brazil, however, we cannot isolate naked economic or military function from its cultural framework.

The bandeirante leader was the headman of a vigorous family system, a man who feared God and who was himself the arbiter of a severe patriarchal code of equity and honor. He was also a telluric man. His life and lore were keyed to the soil from which he wrested a living. His rich Iberian, Catholic heritage had been stripped down to meet the flow and thrust of life in a wild hinterland. He made little attempt to re-create European airs and pageantry. From the plateau of his south Brazilian homeland—long the only real inland settlement of Portuguese America—he turned his back upon the Atlantic, angered by foreign marauders, scornful of royal bureaucrats, ill supplied for maritime trade. Looking westward, he was drawn not to another, distant ocean but to the heartland of a continent which might providentially redeem him from penury. As he began to penetrate this wilderness he learned from and traveled with the Indian, and the unique society and culture of the bandeirantes took shape. Fernão

Dias Pais, one of the most commanding bandeirante figures, has been likened by Jaime Cortesão (p. 112 below) to "one of those terrifying Biblical patriarchs who sacrificed their sons to Jehovah; who endured, like Job, the devastating torrent of scourge and catastrophe inexorably faithful to their Law."

If the bandeirante is so eminently the creature of an American wilderness, ranking in dramatic value with the conquistador and pioneer, why has he so successfully escaped notice in English? First we must recognize that the larger history of Brazil has been rendered only fragmentarily in our language, for reasons too complex to rehearse here. Beyond that, the bandeirantes themselves left no such literary monuments as the letters of Cortés or the chronicle of Bernal Díaz del Castillo. The Brazilian historian Afonso d'E. Taunay observed: "The documentation surviving from the essential activities of *bandeirantismo* is most summary and all, so to speak, of a juridical nature." [1] There is a large amount of such material in print—the meticulous inventories and wills of the bandeirantes, the municipal records of São Paulo, a few dispatches (see Document 7) and itineraries. But it is terse and crabbed; it sheds light on only certain aspects of the bandeirantes' round of life, and the historical vision of an Alcântara Machado (Document 3) is required to reconstruct from it an image of the society. As for literary expression, the only survival is four stanzas of an epic written in 1689 and ascribed to one Diogo Grasson Tinoco, possibly himself a bandeirante. Cast in the verse form of Camoëns's *Lusiads,* it celebrated the great "emerald hunter," Fernão Dias Pais.

Only late in the nineteenth century did Brazilian historians, notably João Capistrano de Abreu, begin to pay serious attention to the bandeirantes. It is therefore not surprising that the chapter on Brazil by the American sociologist Albert G. Keller in his *Colonization, a Study of the Founding of New Societies* (Boston, 1908) should have focused on the seventeenth-century sugar plantations and the eighteenth-century gold rush, with only passing reference to the "disgraceful reputation" of the slavers from São Paulo and their "manhunts." Even a generation later Keller's disciple James G.

---

[1] *História das bandeiras paulistas* (2 vols.; São Paulo, 1954), II, 320.

Leyburn published a comparative study of frontier societies, *Frontier Folkways* (New Haven, 1935), in which the Brazil chapter dealt merely with the coastal plantations.

The appearance in 1946 of the first English edition of the now classic *The Masters and the Slaves* by the Brazilian social historian Gilberto Freyre perpetuated for English-speaking readers the image of colonial Brazil as a sugar-based plantation society of the coast, an indolent, lubricous, tropical, partly permissive, partly authoritarian version of ol' Virginny. Some Brazilians indeed accuse Freyre of representing the whole of Brazil through a part. He replies, however, that his purpose was to examine "the patriarchal system based upon a latifundiary and slave-holding monoculture in that part of the country where the system found its most characteristic and forceful expression." Moreover he views Brazilian social development as "a process of balancing antagonisms," among the many being that between bandeirante and planter. Pernambuco in the Northeast and São Paulo in the South were "the two great foci of creative energy in the first centuries of colonization." The Pernambucans' line of action was a "vertical" one which effected a:

> . . . regional concentration of effort in the establishment of sugar-raising and the sugar industry, the consolidation of a slave-holding and agrarian society, and the expulsion of the Dutch, who disturbed this effort and this process of forming an aristocracy. This is in contrast to the activity of the Paulistas, or . . . the horizontal mobility of the slave-hunters and gold-seekers, the founders of the backland cattle-ranches, and the missionaries.[2]

The distinction between a vertical and a horizontal pattern of settlement is frequently made by Brazilian historians. This book is concerned with the many-sided historical role of the bandeirantes, who were the most conspicuous agents of the settlement process in its horizontal, or extensive, aspect.

---

[2] *The Masters and the Slaves* (2nd ed.; New York, 1956), p. 16. See Freyre's fuller discussion in *New World in the Tropics* (New York, 1963), pp. 67-76.

THE CONQUEST OF BRAZIL

The discovery of Brazil is commonly attributed to Pedro
Álvares Cabral, who made landfall in 1500 while looping
widely around Africa en route to India. Portugal did not immediately attempt to colonize in America, for the small nation's limited resources were already heavily committed to
the enterprise described in the title of its king as "the Conquest, Navigation, and Commerce of India, Ethiopia, Arabia,
and Persia." During the next three decades semi-permanent
coastal trading posts were established in Brazil for shipping
out dyewood (the brazilwood for which the land was named)
hewn by the Indians. A coast guard operated intermittently
to oppose similar activities by the French. The first permanent settlers were groups of survivors, deserters, and exiles
who mixed with the Indians and took to their ways. One of
these squaw men, João Ramalho, established an inland village toward the South on the plains of Piratininga, reached
only by treacherous ascent of the 2,400-foot coastal range.
This was to become the homeland of the bandeirantes, and
Ramalho, who took as concubine the daughter of an Indian
chieftain, was the ancestor of their mestizo breed.

In 1530 João III of Portugal dispatched the most formal
expedition yet sent to Brazil. Its commander, Martim Afonso
de Sousa, was empowered to drive the French from Brazilian
waters and to explore the coast, placing markers to assert
Portugal's sovereignty over territory it claimed by the Tordesillas Treaty of 1494. Martim Afonso was the first to spon-
sor officially any serious reconnoitering of the interior. From
Rio de Janeiro four men were sent inland on a journey of almost five hundred miles; they returned two months later with
some crystals and bearing reports of the River Paraguay and
of plentiful gold and silver deposits.

Farther south, at Cananéia, the flotilla encountered a small
settlement of castaways, among them the squaw man Francisco de Chaves. Chaves had been a member of the expedition of Juan Díaz de Solís, who was killed by Indians while
seeking a westward strait in 1516. He had also marched with
Aleixo Garcia (a fellow survivor of the Solís expedition),
killed while leading hundreds of Guarani Indians from Brazil
across Paraguay to the Incan empire, a decade before Pi-

zarro, pursuing rumors of a white king and a mountain of pure silver. Encouraged by Chaves's promise to return this time in ten months with four hundred Indian slaves laden with silver and gold, Martim Afonso sent an eighty-man force inland led by Pero Lôbo. It was annihilated by Carijó Indians at the mouth of the Iguaçu River.

Martim Afonso set the official precedent for the coastal as well as the inland appropriation of Brazilian territory. In 1532 he established the first formal Portuguese settlement in Brazil at São Vicente. Favorable geographic and climatic factors influenced his choice, as did the proximity of João Ramalho's plateau village of Piratininga, which would mediate between the new port and the Indians of its hinterland. In 1534 São Vicente was made the seat of one of twelve Brazilian captaincies, a free enterprise system of settlement under *donatários,* or proprietary landlords. Of the twelve captaincies four were never settled; four were settled briefly; and only four, including São Vicente, produced permanent communities.

In 1549 the captaincy system was replaced by a central government under Governor Tomé de Sousa who was sent to Bahia that year. This was a moment when strategic withdrawals and consolidation were occurring elsewhere in the far-flung Portuguese empire. It was also a time when news of the Spaniards' discovery of the Potosí silver mines (1545) had rekindled the hope of reaching quick wealth via the route of Aleixo Garcia across southern Brazil. The new governor, however, gave no signal for a westward migration. He restricted settlement to the coast and required persons making inland journeys to obtain a special license. His purpose, which reflected the crown's, was to create a maritime settlement strip that was unified, militarily defensible, and easily served by seaports. The later action of the bandeirantes directly opposed this design.

Over the years some have criticized Portugal for paying belated, reluctant attention to its American empire. Others have congratulated the crown for devising a realistic, carefully staged Brazilian policy that did not overcommit the slender resources of a mother country whose population was only a fraction of Spain's. Some have endorsed the charge made in 1627 by the historian Frei Vicente do Salvador that the Portuguese were neglectful: "though they are great conquerors of lands they do not take advantage of them but are content to move along the seacoast scratching at them like crabs." [3] Others have called this neglect a salutary one which was to allow the natural, organic growth of an indigenous Brazilian civilization that would be largely spared the separatism and tumult of its Spanish American neighbors.

The episodic nature of Brazilian settlement, however one evaluates it, was described as follows by an early historian of Portuguese expansion:

> The conquests of the Portuguese in the New World are not as pleasing on a broad view as the conquests of Mexico and Peru. In the latter we see a single Conqueror who . . . successfully conquers a mighty State in a short space of time with few men to establish himself solidly on the ruins of a great Empire. As in the epic Poem, it appears as a single action embellished by a few Episodes. With the former, on the contrary, it is a long period of years, a multitude of different lands, an infinite number of actions, many Chiefs who succeed one another with different ideas, an assemblage of disparate things which have neither unity nor sequence, and a kind of chaos from which a single whole emerges only because it is the same nation which acts everywhere and to which all is related.[4]

Spanish colonization soon became an imperial enterprise, a full-scale transplantation of metropolitan institutions and hierarchy. Advanced Indian civilizations, offering a disciplined labor supply in zones of mineral wealth and developed agriculture, determined the deployment of Spanish settlers from the outset. Spain struck directly to the inland plateaus at what was then for Europeans the economic jugular of the hemisphere. Occupation of the mountain backbone from Mexico to the southern Andes was achieved four centuries ago. One need except only the surge of immigrants to the Plata region during the past one hundred years to say that

---

[3] *História do Brasil (1500-1627)* (4th ed.; São Paulo, 1954), p. 46.

[4] Joseph François Lafitau, *Histoire des découvertes et conquestes des Portugais dans le Nouveau Monde* (2 vols.; Paris, 1733), I, xv.

the population pattern of Spanish America has remained un-
changed since then.

The English colonies in America were, like the Portuguese,
coastal settlements. The westward movement in the United
States got fully under way only in the nineteenth century,
and a westward drift of the country's population center still
continues. For Brazil the eventual settlement pattern cannot
even now be predicted. The national capital has just been re-
located deep in the interior, the second move in two centuries.
In the southern states a multiple push to the West is occurring,
frequently along "hollow frontiers" that leave behind zones
of unstable settlement. Whether and in what ways the Amazon region of the North (twice the area of Mexico) will become more than a token segment of the human geography of
Brazil still continues a subject of lively conjecture and debate.

THE PAULISTA PLATEAU: HOMELAND OF THE BANDEIRANTES

The bandeirantes' homeland and base of support was a region
that fanned out from the town of São Paulo and its adjacent
plains of Piratininga. São Paulo is only thirty miles from
Santos, which soon eclipsed São Vicente as the captaincy's
main seaport. Yet its location over the crest of the coastal
escarpment places it on the rim of a vast plateau that tilts
westward and drains its waterways inland into the Paraná-
Plata system. (Document I discusses the geographical determinants of the bandeirante movement.)

São Paulo is today Brazil's largest city, with a population
approaching five million. In 1600, at the start of the bandeirante period, it had at most 2,000 inhabitants, including all
races, freemen and slaves. The bandeirante movement
caused a steady outflow of settlers to other parts of the plateau and to the rest of Brazil, so that a century and a half
later, after the decline of the bandeirantes, São Paulo's population had not reached 4,000.

São Paulo did not grow out of João Ramalho's straggling
mud-and-thatch village but was founded about nine miles
from it by a group of Jesuits. Before leaving Brazil in 1553
Governor Tomé de Sousa had opposed this Jesuit venture. He
erected Ramalho's settlement into the town (*vila*) of Santo

André, hoping to secure the allegiance of his people and use them as a barrier against the inland migration of coastal settlers. Under the leadership of Father Manuel da Nóbrega the Jesuits persisted in their decision to found a *colégio* (combined school and mission) on the plateau, where the land and climate were more favorable than on the hot seacoast, where they would be more independent of civil authority, and where they would have direct access to large numbers of Indians. Their mission was consecrated in 1554. It is supremely ironic that São Paulo, founded as a Jesuit spearhead toward the West, was to hurl devastating raids against the Jesuit missions in Paraguay, and to become the main base from which the eastward advance of the Order from Spanish lands would be intercepted and thrown back. This twist of fate resulted from the merging of São Paulo and Santo André in 1562.

Although the Jesuits reproached the Portuguese and mamelucos (as mestizos were known in Brazil) of Santo André for their pagan and licentious ways and their bad example for the Indians, the two communities showed cooperation and mutual respect. Ramalho and his father-in-law, Chief Tibiriçá, had helped to build the Jesuits' stockade; they admired the fathers' discipline and their wisdom in choosing a good location for defense. The Jesuits recognized in Santo André a valuable reserve of manpower and practical experience. Before long Santo André petitioned the governor general for a transfer to the more secure site of São Paulo. This was ordered in 1560, and the merger of the two communities was completed in 1562, on the eve of a fierce attack by the Tamoio Indians.

The rest of the century saw the consolidation of the impoverished, virtually autarckical plateau settlement. Attacks by the Tamoio from Rio de Janeiro continued, and European freebooters periodically threatened the coast. The settlers had come to the plateau without resources. A few had hereditary titles of nobility; a larger number were petty nobles, fidalgos through personal merit. All had migrated in straitened circumstances. The majority were plebeians. Of the settlers whose origin is known, 60% were from Portugal and 15% from the Portuguese Atlantic islands, the Azores and Madeira. The rest were from other countries: 19% from Spain, and 6% from the Low Countries, Italy, France, England, and Germany.[5] The occasional claim that many of these immigrants were criminals—in the modern definition—seems exaggerated.

The plateau settlement pattern was of mixed rural-urban character. The amount of free land available, the extensive nature of cattle herding and of the agriculture practiced, and the Indian workers on each estate who served as a defensive soldiery were all centrifugal forces upon the town nucleus. São Paulo became an appendage of the country. The self-sufficiency of the estates, the sluggish pace of capital accumulation, and the shortage of currency limited the urban professionals to perhaps ten artisans. What gave continuity to town life, once the threat of Indian attack was lessened, were hardy Iberian traditions of religious observance and civic responsibility. At least five yearly religious processions brought family heads and their dependents into town from their rural residences. Normal sessions of the town council (*câmara*) and, for urgent matters, extraordinary assemblies of the electorate of "good men" (*homens bons*) assured the planters' participation, however irregular, in municipal government. Until the eighteenth century the Paulistas enjoyed considerable autonomy in such areas as defense, Indian policy, ecclesiastical administration, commodity and price control, public works, and municipal services. As a rule the dual rural-urban allegiance of the family head was marked by his possessing a town dwelling in addition to his rural estate.

Some have stressed the "democratizing" effect of living conditions on the plateau (see Document 13). If the term is at all useful, it is so only within strict limits, political and social. The *homens bons* who controlled town government were generally Christian men of property, and not Jews, foreigners, artisans and laborers, exiles from Portugal, or broadly speaking the common people. Typically an *homem bom* was a seignorial patriarch who commanded the allegiance of a large extended family and retinue.

> The family group, an organization for defence, requires a head who leads and governs militarily, in the Roman manner. Hence the incontestable authority of the family father over the mother, the offspring, the

---

[5] Alfredo Ellis Júnior, *Capitulos da história social de São Paulo* (São Paulo, 1944), pp. 127-31.

slaves, and also the *agregados* or *familiares,* free workers who seek the protection of his fortune and prestige,
calling to mind the *clientela* of the patriciate. In all
matters his is the decisive vote. It is generally he who
gives the husband to his daughter or wife to his son,
without consulting their inclinations or preferences, so
that sometimes marriages occur without the betrothed
ever having corresponded or seen each other.[6]

Ten or twelve legitimate children were normal for a marriage, and given the precarious conditions of life multiple
marriages were common. In addition Indian and later Negro
slave women regularly bore their masters children who
were almost as regularly recognized in the wills which have
survived. Few testators, however, were as permissive as the
one who acknowledged: "There remain some bastards. . . .
I do not know precisely how many are mine. . . . It shall be
as the mothers declare." [7]

The social system was complex and hierarchical. A man's
position within it was defined by his birth and family ties, occupation, property holdings, and personal qualities of prowess and endurance. Clearly this was no static equation, and
the social structure itself was in many ways not prescriptive.
Distinctions between "nobles" and artisans (or *mecânicos*)
were difficult to sustain in the face of generalized poverty,
the ease with which land and an Indian work force might be
acquired, the common perils which periodically united the
community, and the tests of leadership imposed by the bandeiras.

The common workers were a plebs at the base of the structure. Here there was no sharp distinction between the Indian
slave and the freed Indian or the mameluco. And in the early
years at least, biracial origin did not disqualify a man from a
role of leadership. The genealogies of many bandeirante leaders and many aristocratic Paulista families can be traced to
plebeian or mestizo beginnings in the sixteenth century.
Moreover the Indians did not become a permanent rural
proletariat.

---

[6] José de Alcântara Machado, *Vida e morte do bandeirante*
(2nd ed.; São Paulo, 1930), p. 146.
[7] Ibid., p. 158.

[The] way in which native labor was utilized did not lead to any kind of specialization on an ethnic or racial basis. Therefore when the conditions which obliged the white to exploit native labor disappear, the native element itself is removed from the rural economy: a situation in reverse of what [Robert] Redfield supposed to be characteristic of Latin America, namely, the regular transformation of the native into a peasant.[8]

Negro slaves first appeared in São Paulo in the late sixteenth century, but their high cost restricted the number imported. From the colonial inventories Ellis calculated the ratio of Negroes to Indians in service as one to 34 for the whole bandeirante era.[9] Negroes gradually became more numerous in the bandeiras, and in the eighteenth century they showed themselves to be of great use as miners.

In the late sixteenth century the town of São Paulo contained about 120 dwellings clustered on a hilltop. At distances of four and eight miles were two affiliated Indian settlements (*aldeias*). The Paulistas lived without luxury, and their inventories eloquently confirm the scarcity of imports. The occasional imported armchair, embroidered pillowcase, or plumed hat was as valuable as a horse or a cow. A European petticoat or four old mattresses were worth a house in town. Mirrors are not mentioned until 1619. Indian hammocks and leather cots were generally used, and in 1620 the only decent bed in town had to be requisitioned, over the owner's protests, for a visiting judge. The town council met in private homes until 1575, when a leaky one-room structure was erected to serve as town hall and jail.

The freedom with which livestock roamed the town, knocking down walls and damaging houses, signalized the primacy of rural life. The farm house was the dwelling, the town house simply a lodging for temporary visits. Cotton and sugar were basic crops; each farm generally had its own looms and its distillery for *aguardente*. Wheat was widely grown and locally ground into flour. Many fruits were cultivated, including the quinces that provided the community's

---

[8] Florestan Fernandes, *Mudanças sociais no Brasil* (São Paulo, 1960), p. 184.

[9] Ellis Júnior, *Capítulos da história social*, p. 405.

main export in the form of marmalade. Livestock were soon plentiful.

By the early seventeenth century the captaincy of São Vicente had a modest export trade in salt meat, hides, fruit preserves, and flour. It supplied both the coastal cities of northern Brazil and Buenos Aires to the South. Trade with the latter was often conducted in roundabout fashion via Bahia, although one Paulista will mentions direct commerce with a merchant in Buenos Aires and Spanish pesos and reales are known to have circulated on the plateau.[1] In 1622 the Spanish crown, to which Portugal was then subject, suspended the Brazil-Plata trade. Since this was also a time when Dutch corsairs were threatening South Atlantic shipping, the main artery between Brazil and the Peruvian viceroyalty shifted to the overland route via Guairá (modern Paraná) and Paraguay. This development virtually coincided with the thrust of the Paulista slave hunts into that region and suggests the possibility of some commercial basis for or corollary to the bandeirantes' activities (see Document 6).

The Paulista plateau, however, was far from being a commercial emporium. Its economic base was essentially subsistence agriculture. The scarcity of coinage made payment in kind customary for exchange, wages, and local taxation. Cotton cloth, wax, hides, cattle, poultry, sugar, in fact any foodstuffs might serve as tender. Transactions or loans were frequently consummated without any documentation. Such phrases in the wills as "he owes me whatever he may declare as the truth" or "whatever he finds in his conscience" imply a pre-commercial regime of mutual trust and natural law.

The society and economy of the Paulista plateau tell us much about the organization and economic objectives of the bandeiras. Penury and subsistence agriculture, however, do not sufficiently explain the magnitude and persistence of the exploits of the bandeirantes. One is led to speculate about other orders of motivation and the dreams and legends which gave them force.

---

[1] Alice P. Canabrava, *O comércio português no Rio da Prata* (*1580-1640*) (São Paulo, 1944), pp. 100-01.

THE VISIONS OF THE BANDEIRANTE

The European migrant to São Paulo underwent various selective processes. The voyage to sixteenth-century Brazil, where there were few sinecures or sources of certain wealth, tended to attract marginal and restless types. To continue to São Paulo required particular fiber. The plateau offered no agricultural possibilities to match the sugar culture of the North, and to reach it one had to make the arduous ascent of the coastal escarpment, clutching at roots of trees along sheer precipices. A third selective process was survival on the plateau itself in the face of Indian attacks, famine, plague, and a climate which, although generally warm-temperate, might reach freezing in winter.

The Paulistas who in their words "sought their life" or "their remedy" in the backlands obeyed historic cultural imperatives as well as immediate economic ones. In Document 11 Mario Góngora sees the bandeira as a mestizo variant of the warrior band or company which originated in the medieval Reconquest of the Iberian peninsula from the Moors and was later deployed to two continents. This comparative view causes one to suspect that the large contingent of Spaniards in São Paulo gave the bandeiras certain affinities to the "cabalgadas" of Spanish America.

The yearnings and visions of the bandeirantes are difficult to reconstruct. Of some 450 inventories examined by Alcântara Machado only fifteen mention books. The majority of the fifty-five items listed are books of devotions and sermons. The sprinkling of didactic and literary works includes Hernando Pérez del Pulger's chronicle of the life of the "Great Captain," Gonzalo de Córdoba; a volume by the Portuguese traveler to the Orient, Fernão Mendes Pinto; and a copy of Cervantes's *Novelas ejemplares.* Not even the Portuguese epic of overseas expansion, Camoëns's *Lusiads,* is mentioned, although part of a will executed in the backlands in 1616 is written on the back of a sheet on which some of the verses are copied.[2]

Sérgio Buarque de Holanda has studied an "Edenic" vision that was widely shared by the Portuguese in Brazil. From the Middle Ages the Iberian peoples had inherited the belief

---

[2] Alcântara Machado, pp. 90-92.

that a Terrestrial Paradise or garden of delights existed in a hitherto undiscovered corner of the world. This belief gave impetus to the conquest of America, where it borrowed new guises from aboriginal tales and from reported discoveries. Joaquim Ribeiro lists the following legends which were current among the bandeirantes, most of them in several versions:[3] Legend of the Shining Mountain (a mountain of emeralds or other precious stones); Legend of the Golden Lake (related to the famous El Dorado legend); Legend of the Valley of the Impious (in the mountains between Brazil and Peru, where the wicked were punished); Legend of Upabuçu (a region prohibited for white men); Legend of the Mountains of Martyrdom (a range on whose highest peak giant bars of gold were arranged to represent the crown, spear, and nails of Christ); Legend of the River of Death (various versions); Legend of the Abandoned City (probably related to the famous legend of the Seven Cities); Legend of the Amazons (one of many mythical tribes). Document I conveys the aura of the fabulous which invested the Brazilian interior.

Buarque de Holanda draws a nice distinction between the "Edenic" psychology of the Spaniard and that of the Portuguese. Portuguese expansion he describes as "a vast enterprise of exorcism." That is, the practical effect of exploration, trade, and settlement was to purge away the fantasies and demons of *terrae incognitae*. If the Portuguese share with the Spaniards the myths of El Dorados, silver mountains, magic lakes, and fountains of youth, these tend to "thin out, lose color, or grow dim" as they penetrate Brazil. The eleven apparitions of St. James to the Spaniards during combat with the Indians, or the six of the Virgin, are not matched in Brazil. The Portuguese chronicler relays fabulous tales, but generally with reserve and a sense of "plausible attenuation." Yet this is not to say that the Portuguese was prosaic and utilitarian. "On the contrary, is not one of his most constant traits precisely a fund of emotions which, for being extremely rich, scarcely permits that minimum of detachment necessary for their becoming objectified in fantastic images or miraculous creations that come, so to speak, from a state of appeased wonderment?" [4]

---

[3] *Folklore dos bandeirantes* (Rio de Janeiro, 1946), pp. 44-58.
[4] Sérgio Buarque de Holanda, *Visão do paraíso, os motivos*

For all his critical realism, the Portuguese, or the Paulista bandeirante, stood ready at least to acknowledge the supernatural and the prodigious. Nature challenged his reason with "hieroglyphs" which kept ever present the ambiguities and shifting meanings of the mortal world.[5] If this Nature concealed somewhere a Garden of Delights, it was a garden not created by human agency, a garden ringed with treacherous byways, a garden perhaps forbidden to man. The myth was Janus-faced, a compelling incentive and a sober warning. It was a far cry from the cheerful, bourgeois Garden of the World—the placid agrarian empire to be won by an industrious free yeomanry—which Henry Nash Smith describes in his book *Virgin Land* as a master myth for the Western movement in the United States.

THE ABORIGINAL INHERITANCE

Discrepancies between the Iberian and North American visions of Eden may be ascribed to differences of historical era as well as of cultural tradition. Yet from another perspective the bandeirante movement and its myths may be viewed as sequels to the prehistory of America itself, and not wholly as projections of European energies upon a "virgin" continent. In this light the story of the bandeirantes becomes one of the rare episodes of New World history in which the line of aboriginal history was not cut short and there occurred a merging of two lines of historical action beyond a mere fusion of culture traits.

This argument has been developed as follows by Jaime Cortesão.[6] Aboriginal South America included three broad culture areas: the advanced and sedentary Incan civilization along the Andean cordillera to the West, the plains culture of the southern pampas, and the nomadic or seminomadic forest culture covering the vast area from Venezuela and the Guianas south through Brazil to Paraguay and northern Argentina. These last were stone-age peoples who used neither metal for tools nor rammed earth for their dwellings. They

---

edênicos no descobrimento e colonização do Brasil (Rio de Janeiro, 1959), pp. 15, 148-49, 166, 268-71.

[5] Ibid., p. 243.

[6] *Rapôso Tavares e a formação territorial do Brasil* (Rio de Janeiro, 1958), pp. 9-25. See also Document 6.

employed neither the wheel nor the sail nor domestic animals. They were hunters, fishers, and gatherers; using slash-
and-burn methods they planted manioc, maize, cotton, and
tobacco. Their villages, generally four to eight large com-
munal houses, were moved every few years as the soil became exhausted or the house thatching rotted.

Yet for all the geographic diversity and tribal fragmentation of this third culture area, it harbored certain latent uni-
ties. The enormous Atlantic hump of the continent which
contains it is set off from the other areas by two great river
systems, the Amazon system to the North and the Plata-
Paraná-Paraguay to the South. These systems almost meet—
to make Brazil an immense island—and they provide a network of lateral and vertical fluvial communication throughout the continental heartland. If the geographic unity of
Brazil was to be perceived, it had to be from this indigenous,
inland, or *mediterranean* point of view, not from an imping-
ing European or *littoral* one.

The river systems were in fact utilized by the Arawak
groups migrating south from the Orinoco and Amazon and
by the Tupi-Guarani groups migrating north from the Plata-
Paraná. One motivation for these movements, apart from
demographic or economic ones, was the pursuit of an Indian
version of the Terrestrial Paradise.

> Peoples gifted with a great capacity for expansion,
> did not the Tupi-Guarani and the Arawak possess a
> geographic culture, even if rudimentary, which corre-
> sponded to the area into which they were displaced?
> And might they not have communicated among them-
> selves and, as in cases of ethnic and cultural fusion,
> transmitted to the Europeans a notion of territorial
> unity that was incompatible with the Treaty of Tordesil-
> las? [7]

This imputed aboriginal vision of a "Brazil" was analogous
to a popular image of an Island of Brazil long current in
Europe. According to Cortesão, the notion that the country
might be an island was not fully put to rest in Brazil itself
until the mid-seventeenth century.

---

[7] Ibid., p. 21. Also: René Ribeiro, "Brazilian Messianic Movements" in Sylvia L. Thrupp, ed., *Millennial Dreams in Action*
(The Hague, 1962), pp. 55-58.

The question raised in Document 6 as to whether one objective of the bandeira movement was the political one of re-
vising Tordesillas may be left for discussion. The point made
here is that in spite of the "backwardness" of the Brazilian Indians—their stone-age technics, social fragmentation, and
political divisiveness—their legends and geographical notions
may have reinforced and extended the expectations with
which the Portuguese arrived. If this was the case the bandeirante differed from the American trapper or the Canadian
coureur de bois in that he inherited something of the Indian's
cosmography, beyond merely adopting his hammock and
canoe or learning his tongue or using his women.[8] On this as-
sumption the bandeirantes' extensive borrowings of Indian
artifacts, methods, and culture traits seem more than a series
of practical decisions enforced by a straitened environment.

Buarque de Holanda has studied the nature of such borrowings. To begin with, the *lingua franca* of the Paulistas
was Tupi, or a version thereof. As late as 1698 the governor
of Brazil complained that "most of those People express
themselves in no other language, especially the feminine sex
and all the servants; and this lack causes irreparable loss, as
can be seen today in São Paulo with the new Vicar who was
supplied for that Church and who needs an interpreter."[9]
Some bandeirantes bore Indian nicknames: Apuçá (Tin Ear),
Jaguaretê (Jaguar), Tamarutaca (Mantis Shrimp). Or else
Portuguese names might be indianized by a Tupi suffix.
Buarque de Holanda concludes that "the process of effective
integration of the Paulista people into the Portuguese-
speaking world may be said to have occurred, in all probabil-
ity, during the first half of the eighteenth century."[1]

---

[8] There were Frenchmen in Canada who abandoned themselves
to Indian or backwoods life, but they scarcely formed so coherent
a society as that of the bandeirantes. (See Richard M. Saunders,
"The Emergence of the Coureur de Bois as a Social Type,"
Report [Canadian Historical Association] [Toronto, 1939], pp.
22-33.) Also the Canadian fur trade placed the Indians in more
immediate contact with a specialized, industrial economy than did
bandeirismo. The Canadian-Brazilian parallel, however, deserves
attention.

[9] Cited in Sérgio Buarque de Holanda, *Raízes do Brasil* (3rd
ed.; Rio de Janeiro, 1956), p. 175.

[1] Ibid., pp. 183-84. Ribeiro (*Folklore dos bandeirantes,* pp.
95-98, 163-84) discounts the prevalence of Indian nicknames and

The bandeirantes generally traveled on foot, using the rivers more as route markers than as means of transit. Often they proceeded single file along Indian or animal trails, especially those of the tapir. A bandeira normally covered five or six miles a day, but under pressure could move at four times this speed. One presumes that the bandeirante developed much of the Indian's sensory perception. The latter was able to tell time and to "navigate" through forests by the sun and stars. On one occasion two Tupinambá who were captured and sent by sea from Bahia to Rio de Janeiro made their escape and returned home across twelve hundred miles of backlands. The modern Caingang, it is said, can tell a snake's presence by its smell. Such powers were undoubtedly shared by the mameluco of São Paulo along with a roster of indigenous crops, artifacts, and skills.[2]

River navigation was practiced on a significant scale only by the eighteenth-century "monsoons," successors of the bandeiras; and even they were heavily indebted to Indian methods (see Document 10). Similarly, horses played little role in either the agricultural or the nomadic life of the bandeirantes. They began to come into general use for transportation in about 1720, at the same time as the pirogues of the monsoons. The mule was particularly suited to conditions of the Brazilian interior. For almost a century and a half, until the advent of the railway, the mule team continued the work of the bandeira in knitting together the diverse hinterlands of Brazil. It also introduced a new way of life that helped to "de-indianize" the culture of the Brazilian backlands.

THE BANDEIRANTE MOVEMENT

There is no need to present here a full synopsis of the bandeirante movement. Document 2 outlines the chronology and phasing of the bandeiras as well as their origins, functional types, and historical consequences.

As one might expect, there has been controversy as to what constituted a bandeira. João Capistrano de Abreu used the term for nearly all the significant expeditions into the inte-

---

claims that the bandeirantes spoke a local dialect of Portuguese rather than Tupi.

[2] Sérgio Buarque de Holanda, *Caminhos e fronteiras* (Rio de Janeiro, 1957), pp. 15-159 *passim*.

rior, which he classified by place of origin (Paulista, Bahian, Pernambucan, Maranhense, and Amazonian bandeiras).[3] Others differentiate between the entrada (entry) and the bandeira. They define the former as a small-scale expedition engaged in peaceful prospecting for minerals or in expansion of land holdings, defensively organized, conducted under official auspices, and characteristically based in the coastal region north from Espírito Santo. The bandeira is defined as an expedition large in numbers, organized under local auspices for offensive warfare (mostly for capture of Indians), generally based on the Paulista plateau, and marked by regional culture traits.[4] This distinction, in some ways helpful, has the drawback of placing the prospecting expeditions of the late seventeenth century, notably the famous bandeira of Fernão Dias Pais, in a marginal category.

Cortesão asked us to examine the word "bandeira" itself. At least three origins for the term in this use have been advanced: *bandeira* (flag or insignia) around which expeditionaries rallied;[5] *bandeira,* "band" of men captained by a caudillo; and *bandeira,* small assault group or raiding party detached from a body of troops. Of these, Cortesão held, only the third approaches the proper derivation. The bandeira was a medieval Portuguese military unit of thirty-six men; a certain number of them comprised a "company" of armed men. By the sixteenth century the distinction between bandeira and company had disappeared. Governor Francisco de Sousa officially organized the fighting men of São Paulo into military companies in the early seventeenth century. Since both whites and Indians were recruited, "the *bandeira* of militia comes to have a Luso-Tupi structure." These military units were strengthened after 1624 under threat of invasion by the Dutch. At the same time the expeditions to the interior be-

---

[3] *Caminhos antigos e povoamento do Brasil* (2nd ed.; Rio de Janeiro, 1960), pp. 215-16.

[4] Alfredo Ellis Júnior, *O ouro e a Paulistânia* (São Paulo, 1948), pp. 28-34; Alfredo Gomes, "Entradas, bandeiras e moncões: característicos," *Anais* (IV Congresso de História Nacional) (13 vols.; Rio de Janeiro, 1950-52), V, 13-23, and "Do bandeirismo e suas formas," *ibid.,* XI, 483-512.

[5] See below (p. 83) in the 1629 Jesuit account: ". . . their captains and other officers of war hoisted their flags (*vanderas*) as if they had arisen and mutinied against your Royal Crown."

came bolder and more persistent. A document of 1624 speaks of the "companies which went to the sertão." [6] By 1635 the word "bandeira" was being used in this same sense, to designate a company of backlands militiamen.[7] The term "bandeirante" came into use later; the earliest written appearance found by Taunay is in a document of 1740.

Although many bandeiras were *sui generis,* it is hard to make a firm distinction between the Paulista bandeira and the Bahian entrada on the grounds of size, military objective, economic function, or sponsorship (official or local). During the seventeenth century the expeditions from São Paulo ran the gamut on each of these counts. What distinguished the Paulista bandeira was first, in Cortesão's phrase, its "Luso-Tupi structure." As a patriarchal, mameluco variant of an Iberian military unit it shared the cultural characteristics of a unique frontier society. Second, for the inhabitants of the Paulista plateau "bandeirismo" became a way of life for a century or more; this gave their expeditions a funded reserve of expansive energy that was unmatched elsewhere.

Taunay called Francisco de Sousa the "true promoter" although not the initiator of the bandeirante movement. First as governor general of Brazil and then as governor of the southern captaincies he organized both military and prospecting expeditions in São Paulo in the first decade of the seventeenth century. After this early period of official sponsorship, the bandeirante movement is customarily divided into two cycles: a slave-hunting cycle which gives way after 1640 to a prospecting cycle. Actually both pursuits continued through-

---

[6] In this book "sertão" (plural, "sertões") generally designates the backlands or interior of Brazil, although the term also applies specifically to the arid hinterland of the Northeast. A "sertanista" is a pathfinder of the backlands, and a "sertanejo" is an inhabitant of them.

[7] Cortesão, pp. 70-77. See below p. 74 for other designations of the bandeira. A bandeira was not composed wholly of males. "At first an occasional woman accompanied the bandeira, wearing 'a heavy cotton sack with three holes for the head and arms.' Later many Indian and mameluco women go as servants of the sertanistas. At the end women in great number and of all sorts go along, as in the era of the gold strikes." Cassiano Ricardo, *Marcha para Oeste* (3rd ed.; 2 vols.; Rio de Janeiro, 1959), I, 138 *n.*

out the bandeirante era; the phasing simply identifies the main thrusts of the movement.

While Francisco de Sousa was still in São Paulo, the Paulistas embarked upon the large-scale capture of Indians for their own labor needs and for export to the northern plantations. These expeditions were locally planned and organized. Although they seized large numbers of forest Indians, their favorite prey were the disciplined, partly acculturated Indians of the Spanish Jesuit missions, or "reductions," to the Southwest. Document 4 is a classic account of one such raid, written by two Jesuits who accompanied their wards back to São Paulo with the bandeirantes in 1629. It is followed in Document 5 by a defense of the Paulistas written in the next century by a Benedictine friar, who absolves them of lawlessness and irresponsibility, and accuses the Jesuits themselves of tyrannizing the Indians. On anthropological grounds one can indeed argue that the nomadic life of the hundreds, even thousands of Indian slaves and servants who might accompany a bandeira conformed more closely to their aboriginal ways than did their regulated existence in the Jesuit stockades, engaging in intensive agriculture, learning the catechism, and, it is said, being awakened at night by the church-bell to perform their conjugal duties.

Alfredo Ellis Júnior calculated that the Paulistas took more than 350,000 Indian prisoners in the sixteenth and seventeenth centuries, of which some 80% were shipped to other parts of Brazil.[8] His total may be exaggerated, however, and others might virtually reverse his ratio for retention and export.

The dramatic clash of bandeirante and Jesuit obscures the fact that the overland route between São Paulo and Paraguay had been used for peaceful traffic since the arrival of the Europeans. Paraguay was the way station for Portuguese, known as *peruleiros*, who went in quest of the wealth of Peru and Potosí. And there is the case of a Spanish governor of Paraguay who in 1628 proceeded to his post via São Paulo, traveling for a time with a bandeira that was en route to attack the Jesuit missions. Subsequently he quarreled with the Jesuits and, it seems, connived with the bandeirantes to obtain slaves for the plantations of his Brazilian wife. Here is

---

[8] *Panoramas históricas* (São Paulo, 1946), pp. 19-21.

strong evidence for what Cortesão terms in Document 6: "the enormous importance of the clandestine Luso-Spanish exchange that transcended the imaginary boundaries of the two crowns in America, uniting interests and transmitting mutual influences and patterns of culture." It may even be that except for its Jesuit missionary enclaves the Paulista-Paraguay region had a roughly homogeneous society and culture in colonial times.

The image of the ferocious, mission-raiding bandeira has been partly displaced by recent studies of the prodigious bandeira of Antônio Rapôso Tavares (1648-51). Cortesão maintains this to have been an imperial, geopolitical enterprise and not simply a slave- or gold-hunting probe of a straitened local community (Document 6). It was in this period, moreover, that the Paulistas sent an expedition against the Dutch, who occupied Northeast Brazil from 1630 to 1654. In the second half of the century they sent several expeditions against the Indians of Bahia, Rio Grande do Norte, and Ceará who were impeding inland settlement from the coast. In the 1690's Paulista troops under Domingos Jorge Velho besieged Palmares, the "republic" of runaway Negroes in the northern interior. Document 7, which relates to this episode, affords many clues to the motivations and way of life of the bandeirantes.

The prospecting bandeiras gathered impetus in the third quarter of the seventeenth century, after the decline of slave-raiding, encouraged by fresh assurances of royal prizes and honors. Buarque de Holanda observes that Indian legends and the image of Peruvian riches led the bandeirantes to search for silver and emeralds rather than those minerals which were in fact to constitute the windfall, gold and diamonds. "In other words, what was expected to be discovered in Brazil was Peru, and not Brazil." [9] Document 8 is a famous contemporary account of the gold strike in Minas Gerais and the methods of exploitation. In Document 9 an American scholar compares this rush with that of California; he also describes the war between the Paulistas and the *emboabas,* the "outsiders" who flocked from the coast and from overseas to jump the Paulistas' claims.

The search for minerals continued in the western lands of

---

[9] *Visão do paraíso,* p. 118.

Goiás and Mato Grosso. Here, prospecting and later commerce were conducted by the eighteenth-century successors
to the bandeiras, the *monções* or monsoons described in
Document 10. These differed from the bandeiras in significant respects. Not only were they riverborne, with all the in-
novations that this implied, but also: "Profits were no longer
shared as in the seventeenth-century expeditions. Each man
worked for himself, having nothing to do with his neighbors." [1]

The accounts of mining in Minas, Goiás, and Mato Grosso
focus attention on the colonizing function of the bandeira,
for the discovery of gold or diamonds tended to turn prospector into settler. If the slaving phase of bandeirismo has been
called a cycle which "depopulated" the sertão, the mining
phase has been called one which "repopulated" it. Many
were the Paulista mining camps (*arraiais*) that developed into
permanent towns and cities. As Taunay makes clear in Document 12, the mineral strikes bled the Paulista plateau of its
most enterprising inhabitants, leaving its society and economy nearly stagnant. The outflow need not have been nu-
merically large to have produced this effect, for in 1700 the
captaincy of São Paulo[2] had only about 15,000 people: 3,000
in São Paulo, 1,500 in Santos and São Vicente combined, the
rest scattered in towns or clusters of 30 to 500 souls.

Another activity leading to Paulista colonization was stock
raising. By 1700 an appreciable number of Paulistas, including many who had come as Indian fighters, were established
as cattlemen in the upper valley of the São Francisco, the
important river flowing north from Minas to empty into the
Atlantic just below the Brazilian bulge. The market for their
oxen and beef, originally limited to the plantation settlements of the coast, now expanded as mining towns mush-
roomed in the interior. "In the southern sector of the cattle
zone," wrote Basílio de Magalhães, "the permanent occupation of the land was largely a mere extension of the Paulista
bandeira movement." And, reminding us of the "mediterranean" as opposed to the littoral sources of Brazilian unity,
he observed that this settlement was mostly effected "not inland from the ocean but from the hinterland moving toward

---

[1] Ellis Júnior, *Capitulos da história social,* p. 96.

[2] The town of São Paulo had become the seat of the captaincy
in 1681.

the Atlantic coast." [3] One of the letters in Document 7 confirms the Paulistas' interest in colonizing the North and contains their appeal for government support.

The other great cattle domain was the southernmost region of Rio Grande do Sul and Uruguay. Although it had been visited time and again by bandeiras attracted by the Spanish Jesuit missions, its colonization by Brazilians was long in coming. In 1676 Pedro II took advantage of Spain's war with France to assert Portuguese sovereignty over the lands "to the mouth of the River Plata." In 1680 the governor of the southern captaincies founded the Nova Colônia do Sacramento opposite Buenos Aires. Although later a trump card in boundary negotiations with Spain, Colônia was an artificial settlement, and many of its founders were Paulistas who had virtually to be dragooned into an enterprise of so little benefit to them.

A better rooted community was Laguna, established farther north, in Santa Catarina, by a Paulista expedition under Domingos de Brito Peixoto in 1684. This served as a staging area where the Paulistas shifted from farming and fishing to pastoral pursuits. It was some forty years before there occurred a large-scale migration of Lagunistas south to the sweeping plains of Rio Grande. Thenceforth southern Brazil responded to the quickening need of the mining region and other parts of Brazil for its cattle, and its economic integration with the rest of the country was under way. Celso Furtado points out that cattle raising in the Northeast, along the São Francisco, was called into being by the economic requirements of the sugar zone, while in Rio Grande a modest cattle industry had existed for years on little more than a subsistence basis before finally the demand of the mining regions forced it to intensify production.[4]

The following conclusions, adapted from Alfredo Ellis, help us to summarize at this point the principal effects of the whole bandeirante movement:

1.—Exploration of the interior of South America.

2.—Depopulation of Indians and settlement by Europeans in large areas of the continent.

---

[3] *Expansão geographica do Brasil colonial* (2nd ed.; São Paulo, 1935), pp. 178, 349.

[4] *The Economic Growth of Brazil* (Berkeley and Los Angeles, 1963), pp. 84-85.

3.—Miscegenation between Indians and whites on the Paulista plateau to produce an "American" population.

4.—Creation of sources of income for the plateau population and a source of forced Indian labor for the plantations of the Northeast.

5.—Extension of Brazilian territory far west of the Tordesillas boundary, placing large areas under Portuguese rather than Spanish domination.

6.—Discoveries of wealth that attracted heavy immigration for the settlement of Brazil.

7.—Export of Brazilian bullion to Portugal, much of which found its way to England under the terms of trade prevailing between the two countries. Thus Brazilian gold discovered by the bandeiras and monsoons is said to have hastened England's Industrial Revolution, and with it the decline of French industry and the advent of the French Revolution.[5]

BRAZILIAN FRONTIERS

Theories of both the European and the aboriginal antecedents of the bandeiras were mentioned above. As our résumé of the bandeirante movement makes clear, this genetic view should be complemented by a functional one which draws attention to processes of change and innovation occurring in the Brazilian sertão. The term "frontier" comes to mind in this connection. Developed by Frederick Jackson Turner as a leading hypothesis for American history, the frontier concept has in recent years been broadened and applied to many other historical examples of conquest and settlement. Extending it to the Brazilian case is useful above all for the questions which this leads us to pose.

The master image projected by the Turner school is that of a society securely postholed along the Atlantic seaboard which, at the proper moment, begins to expand steadily westward behind the cutting edge of the "frontier." California gold causes a premature leap to the Pacific, but the unsettled western spaces are soon methodically "filled in." Each

---

[5] Ellis Júnior, *Panoramas históricas,* p. 26. The seventh point is developed in an essay by Júlio de Mesquita Filho, "O Brasil e a revolução industrial da Inglaterra," in his *Ensaios sul-americanos* (São Paulo, 1946), pp. 135-92. See also Document 12.

new frontier zone is battened down in logical sequence by a predictable succession of trappers, ranchers, miners, farmers, and urban types.

A number of Turner's sub-theses yield promising leads for studying the confrontation between the bandeirante and the Brazilian sertão. These include: the disintegrative or regressive effect of the frontier on transplanted institutions; the "safety valve" effect of empty land upon settled areas; democratizing influences of backlands life; and the loyalty to a national government which a moving frontier is said to produce. The readings in this book allow comparative interpretation on all of these points, and those by modern writers generally show familiarity with Turner's work.

What needs to be kept in mind is that the American frontier thesis, in its classic formulation, carries nationalistic and even Protestant, evangelical overtones. From the vantage point of latter-day industrial America it harks back to the invigorating, self-refreshing action of a chosen "civilization" along the retreating line of a wilderness. When Walter P. Webb expanded his theory of the American "great plains" to a global "great frontier" theory, he found that it "does not seem to apply to Latin America as well as it does to those countries taken over by northern European groups. . . . It seems that the rigid character of the Catholic structure was too much for the disintegrative forces which were so successful with the more mundane institutions." [6] Similarly Ray Allen Billington, because he uses the frontier in a normative sense, forces several northern preconceptions upon the southern societies. According to him: Pioneers of New Spain were "handicapped" by their traditions and culture patterns; individual enterprise was powerless to combat nature's forces in Latin America; colonial Latin America was prey to a "martial spirit"; Indian workers "monopolized jobs on farms and in mines which could otherwise have been opened to Spanish immigrants." [7]

---

[6] *The Great Frontier* (Cambridge, 1952), p. 87.

[7] "The Frontier in American Thought and Character" in Archibald R. Lewis and Thomas F. McGann, eds., *The New World Looks at Its History* (Austin, 1963), pp. 78-80. For an informed statement by an American historian see Arthur S. Aiton, "Latin-American Frontiers," *Report* (Canadian Historical Association) (Toronto, 1940), pp. 100-4.

A decade before Webb's *The Great Frontier* appeared, George W. Pierson had criticized Turner's thesis as culture-bound. He called for "less emphasis on the concept 'frontier' and a deeper comparative study of migrations around the earth." Such comparisons, he felt, might be extended "from migration to the *whole story of settlement* or environmental adjustment in South America, Australia, and Africa." [8] This judgment is confirmed by two Spanish American historians, Belaúnde and Zavala, who have found the term "frontier," as Turner defined it, either inapplicable or of limited relevance to Latin America.[9]

The frontier concept is still attractive, however, to many Brazilian historians, one of whom has suggested lines for reformulating it:

> "Frontier" of course [applies in Brazil] among landscapes, peoples, habits, institutions, techniques, even dissimilar languages which met here. Sometimes the frontier fades away, giving rise to mixed or symbiotic products; sometimes it persists, at least until such time as it may yield to the final triumph of those elements which are shown to be more active, more robust, or better equipped. In this meaning the word "frontier" already appears in texts contemporary with the first phase of the colonization of Brazil, and it can well be used here independently of any relations to the meaning it acquired in modern historiography, in particular the American since the now classic works of Frederick Jackson Turner.[1]

In Brazil, that is, the frontier is not a line or limit, or an advance of civilization, or a process either unilateral or

---

[8] "The Frontier and American Institutions, a Criticism of the Turner Theory," *The New England Quarterly,* XV, 2 (June 1942), 229, 251.

[9] Víctor Andrés Belaúnde, "The Frontier in Hispanic America," *The Rice Institute Pamphlet,* X, 4 (Oct. 1923), 202-13; Silvio Zavala, "The Frontiers of Hispanic America" in Walker D. Wyman and Clifton B. Kroeber, eds., *The Frontier in Perspective* (Madison, 1957), pp. 35-58.

[1] Buarque de Holanda, *Caminhos e fronteiras,* p. vi. Professor Charles W. Anderson of the University of Wisconsin develops many comparative aspects in his unpublished paper, "The Image of the Frontier Tradition in Brazil and the United States."

unilinear. We must in fact speak not of a frontier but of multiple, complex frontier experiences, transactions, and mutations. We can draw no fixed line between white man and Indian, civilization and primitivism, settled and unsettled areas, imperial outpost and autonomous community. Settlement occurred and still occurs in an archipelago pattern. For a bandeira the frontier was protoplasmic. Two thousand persons transport their community, their *genius loci,* on a sweeping incursion into the hinterland. At times they present a phenomenon of sheer mobility.[2] The group may settle for months in the wilderness, hundreds of miles from home, long enough to plant and harvest a crop. It may spin off one or more permanent mining, pastoral, trading, or subsistence settlements. It may be lost and never more be heard from. It may return home, after months or years, leaving the wilderness as it was before the journey.

To understand the Brazilian settlement process means to perceive the frontier more as interpenetration than as advance, more as relation to than as projection upon environment, more as intermittent quest for a garden of delights than as systematic construction of one. These considerations are in turn bound up with propositions that are fundamental to the sociology of a Catholic civilization.

HISTORICAL ECHOES

After the close of the bandeirante epoch the Paulista plateau entered a long era of quiescence. One would be tempted to call it a time of lethargy and decadence, were it not that commercial relations continued to develop along the now well-established routes, north to Minas, northwest to Cuiabá, south to Rio Grande do Sul, and northeast by ocean to the new capital of Rio de Janeiro. Some modest fortunes were accumulated. A spirit of commercial enterprise persisted; so too did a sense of regional identity, despite the administrative centralization of the eighteenth century. In 1821-22 events in São Paulo affected the course of Brazilian independence, which was declared by Prince Regent Pedro on the banks of the Ipiranga, not far from the city. A few years later

---

[2] Cassiano Ricardo carefully calls his book on the bandeirantes *Westward March* rather than the more explicit *March to the West* (Document 13).

one of Brazil's first two law academies was established in São Paulo, which helped to make it a center of cultural and political importance for the rest of the century.

The popular connotations of the term "bandeirante" or "bandeirante spirit" in modern Brazil are understandable only in relation to the surge of economic and demographic growth which has occurred in the Paulista region during the past hundred years. Elsewhere I have told part of this story[3] and will not try to synthesize it here. The key ingredients are: 1) the appearance of a coffee frontier west of São Paulo city in the mid-nineteenth century which moved steadily inland till today its pioneer fringes have reached Paraná, Mato Grosso, and even Paraguay; 2) the industrial development of São Paulo city and its region, which began in the late nineteenth century and has produced what is reputedly the largest industrial concentration in Latin America; 3) an influx of millions of immigrants from all parts of Europe, from the Near East, from Japan, and more recently from all of Brazil, lured by economic opportunity in São Paulo.

The exaltation of the bandeirante tradition, however, predates the economic transformation of São Paulo by several generations. It begins perhaps with the genealogist Pedro Taques de Almeida Pais Leme (1714-77), a descendant of bandeirantes, who aristocratized the bandeirante leaders and nostalgically commemorated their heroism in his *Paulista Peerage*.[4] One should also mention the poet Cláudio Manuel da Costa (1729-89), who committed suicide after his involvement in the patriotic conspiracy (Inconfidência) of Minas Gerais. His epic poem "Vila Rica," which celebrates the founding of Vila Rica de Ouro Prêto, accords the Paulistas a role in Brazilian history similar to that of the Portuguese explorers glorified by Camoëns:

> Though you, nymphs of the Tagus, may sing
> Full-throated of the Lusitanians
> And the noble deeds of their great Gama,
> Of my Paulistas I will celebrate the fame,
> Who suffer pains of hunger and of thirst,

---

[3] Richard M. Morse, *From Community to Metropolis, a Biography of São Paulo, Brazil* (Gainesville, 1958).

[4] *Nobiliarquia paulistana histórica e genealógica* (3 vols.; São Paulo, 1953).

Who drag their bodies, broken and in rags,
Ravaged by diseases without cure,
Knowing the face of misery on every hand.
Yet no other spirit animates their zeal
Save love of king in measure surfeited.

It would be a stimulating exercise in cultural history, and a
task of fresh research, to trace the shifting versions of the
bandeirante legend through two centuries of Brazilian lore
and literature. Here we must limit ourselves to some contemporary manifestations.

The French geographer Pierre Monbeig writes of a "bandeirante psychology" that combines a gambling spirit, zest
for fresh experience, pride in creation, hunger for empty
lands, and a yearning for fortune and political prestige. One
finds it particularly among the coffee planters of São Paulo
and Minas Gerais.

When one wishes to celebrate a planter, a clearer of forests, a founder of cities, there is no more handsome title
to bestow upon him than that of "bandeirante." . . .
In the dynamism of the planter-pioneer the mass of the
people rediscovers what it had retained from the bandeirante legend: penetration deep into the sertão, ag-
grandizement of São Paulo and of Brazil.[5]

Paulistas themselves invoke the bandeirante spirit as a cry
of autonomy for their economically powerful state when
they challenge the political control of the central government (as in the Paulista Revolution of 1932) or when they
protest fiscal exploitation that is alleged to make São Paulo
the locomotive for a line of "empty freight cars." On the
other hand an astute Brazilian president can invoke the bandeirantes in an appeal for national unity. Speaking in São
Paulo in 1939, Getúlio Vargas called the bandeiras "the first
nationalizing expeditions." "With them Brazil began to exist."
He then exhorted São Paulo's "modern bandeirantes" to take
their place in a "new crusade of national expansion." [6]

Gilberto Freyre identifies the bandeirante spirit with the
cultural and artistic as well as the economic development of

[5] *Pionniers et planteurs de São Paulo* (Paris, 1952), pp. 107-10.
[6] Getúlio Vargas, *A nova política do Brasil* (7 vols.; Rio de
Janeiro, 1938-40), VI, 283-85.

modern São Paulo. He finds it to provide an ethos of experiment and innovation for migrants from the rest of the nation and from the whole world. Once they are steeped in bandeirante traditions, the newcomers "spread their triumphant influence throughout all Brazil." Thus the bandeirante personality becomes transregional, to form part of a larger "Brazilian personality." [7]

Clodomir Vianna Moog also takes a transregional view of the bandeirante heritage, although a much less sanguine one than Freyre's or than that of the poet-historian Cassiano Ricardo in Document 13. Contrasting the bandeirante with the American pioneer, he calls the former's way of life unstable and extractive, and the latter's progressive and constructive. The pioneer, a permanent emigrant, creates an "organic" image; the bandeirante, who roams and returns, creates a "predatory" one. Since the start of its coffee boom, according to Vianna Moog, São Paulo is the state which has profited most by a pioneer spirit yet which has most vociferously celebrated the bandeirante spirit. By now the whole of Brazilian civilization is contaminated by the predatory style:

> In ideas, hopes for quick wealth, obsession with the sudden coup, social instability, adhesion to the coast, economic xenophobia, poverty of social organs to deal with collective and not simply class and caste interests, public and private life—there is no sector in which vestiges of the bandeirante's style of life and the imprint of the bandeira may not be found.[8]

It might be difficult to sustain that the bandeirante was more exploitative than the pioneer in his slashing attack on the forests and Indians of North America. In any case the contrasting views of Freyre and Vianna Moog are less valuable for their illumination of the past than for the reminder that the memory of the bandeirantes deeply influences the modern search for Brazilian national identity.

---

[7] "A propósito de paulistas" in *Problemas brasileiros de antropologia* (3rd ed.; Rio de Janeiro, 1962), pp. 40-83.

[8] *Bandeirantes e pioneiros, paralelo entre duas culturas* (2nd ed.; Pôrto Alegre, 1961), pp. 235-50. Translated as *Bandeirantes and Pioneers* (New York, 1964).

SOME QUESTIONS

The readings that follow are in part documentary, in part expository, in part interpretive. On many points of interpretation neither they nor the whole of bandeirante historiography can furnish conclusive answers. Alice Canabrava has observed: "In spite of the fruitful results of research in this century, the study of bandeirismo as the combined process of political, economic, and social evolution of the colony has not yet been attempted." [9]

These readings do at least set out points of departure for reflection, further study, and fresh research. Although the chronology and geography of the bandeiras have by now been fairly well pieced together by scholars, most other aspects of their history still lie open to speculation. What were the structure and composition of the representative types of bandeira? What were the patriarchal, municipal, and military aspects of their organization? What was the relative social and cultural importance of the Indian, Portuguese, and Spanish influences? Were other influences, such as Jewish and African, of sociological consequence?

What were the leading motivations of the bandeirantes at different periods? How do we weigh geographic and economic determinants? Was there a special mystique which explains the force and longevity of the movement? Was the movement essentially an expression of local energies? Or did it at times obey imperatives of a metropolitan or national order? Or again, are certain of its phases best considered in the context of a transnational economic region that lay athwart the southern part of the continent?

Finally, what were the processes of colonization and adaptation as the bandeirantes settled diverse sections of the Brazilian interior? How and to what extent did they establish social and economic connections among far-flung hinterlands, or between these and the coast? Are they partly responsible for the political unity of modern Brazil? What impact did their discoveries have, not only upon Brazil but upon the economy of the Western world?

---

[9] "Bandeiras" in William Berrien and Rubens Borba de Moraes, eds., *Manual bibliográfico de estudos brasileiros* (Rio de Janeiro, 1949), p. 501.

As we address these and other questions we must be wary of Vianna Moog's insistence upon the "predatory" action of the bandeiras. The modern thirst for "development" should not make us impatient with history, or insensitive to the limits which define, indeed make possible, cultural achievement. Colonial Paulista history was one of the most notable New World episodes of accommodation between European and Indian. It produced a tough, resistant society, or family of communities, in which passions, dreams, practical sense, and vigorous traditions were interpolated along a common moral base. To study the complex, shifting patterns of Paulista loyalties—to personal enterprise, to family, to social group, to town or region, to a Brazil in formation, to a distant king, and to a common faith—is to lay bare in microcosm the logic and architectonics of a Catholic, Iberian frontier society which, in important respects, endure to our own day.

I
* * *

CONSPECTUS
OF THE
BANDEIRANTE
MOVEMENT

1

TEODORO SAMPAIO

❦

The Sertão before the Conquest

The Brazilian scholar Teodoro Sampaio (1855-1937)
made important contributions to the ethnography,
linguistics, and history of his country. In this essay
he identifies some geographical determinants for the
Brazilian settlement process and for the bandeirante
movement. He also evokes the spirit of mystery, en-
chantment, and terror which brooded over the interior
on the eve of the great incursions inland.

The sixteenth century was ending, and with it the vacillations,
the half-heartedness, even the disbelief with which the ventures of discovery into the sertões of the colony had been
regarded until then. Along the coast, almost completely occupied but very sparsely settled, a whole century of obscure
struggles had elapsed, what with the resistance of the
heathen, the surprise attacks of the corsairs, and the oppres-
sion of a tropical climate which neither the beauty nor the
fertility and abundance of the land was able to soften for
the European. . . .

In spite of the many forays already made into it, the

From Teodoro Sampaio, "O sertão antes da conquista (seculo
XVII)," *Revista do Instituto Historico e Geographico de São
Paulo,* V (1899-1900), excerpts from pp. 79-94. Translated; and
printed by permission of the Instituto.

sertão remained unknown and as if veiled by a mysterious penumbra of charms, which delighted the imagination and fed the naive credulity of the men on the coast. Of the first abortive expeditions, some already forgotten, there were left only confused legends describing the treasures and beauties of the sertão, whose immense valleys few had penetrated but whose hidden riches were instinctively sensed by all. . . .

Popular imagination, however, continued its propaganda in favor of the sertões, producing fantastic tales and spreading marvelous accounts of the western lands, which were painted as a region of incalculable riches. Astounding things were related. The few doubtful clues furnished by the Indians were interpreted as positive and true, and these added substance to the superstitions of a people already predisposed to believe. . . .

The historians [of the time] speak enthusiastically of the land's inexhaustible fish and game. They describe the great resources with which bountiful nature surrounded enraptured man on all sides. They tell of the abundance of the manatee in almost all the estuaries and rivers of the coast, of the large and numerous whales, and also of the sea lions and porpoises which bred on both land and sea. Frei Vicente do Salvador reports that in the seas of Brazil there even appeared men known as Hipupiaras who had been seen on land pursuing the Indians, whose eyes and noses they were fond of eating. This same historian tells us with the disarming simplicity and credulity of Herodotus that there were snakes in this country that came at night to suckle the breasts of ladies, as gently and softly as if they were their own children. The historian Gandavo relates the wonders of the *giboiuçu* (boa constrictor), which would swallow a whole deer and then burst open from glutting itself, whereupon all the meat on its body rotted, leaving only the spine, the head, and the end of the tail intact; and, the historian goes on, "after it has remained for a time in this condition, little by little the flesh begins to grow again, until it is covered anew with flesh, as completely as before." [1]

Of the country's interior contemporary historians leave us

---

[1] Pero Magalhães de Gandavo, *The Histories of Brazil* (2 vols.; New York, 1922), II, 176. [Ed.]

the most mysterious and fantastic accounts. The same Gandavo writes that some men assured him that in this land they had seen serpents with large and terrifying wings (although they were rather rare monsters) and also enormous lizards whose testicles smelled sweeter than musk. Another contemporary historian cites among the many riches of the vegetable kingdom the "soap tree" and the "glass tree." "The whole sertão seems like a woodland in bas-relief, sculpted by nature itself with its waters," said [Simão de] Vasconcelos.

This false notion clearly demonstrates how unknown that part of the country was even as late as the mid-seventeenth century, when the Jesuit chronicler [Vasconcelos] was writing. His impression can probably be ascribed to the early crossing of the continent along the Amazon valley and to early entradas, made precisely in the region where the coastal forest was widest. . . . Here indeed the forest becomes very dense and is the leading trait of this region whose swollen rivers, cutting the land at frequent intervals, are joined by trunks or mainstreams like the Amazon and the Tocantins, or the Jequitinhonha and the Pardo, or else receive, as the Doce does, the continual flow of many broad lakes. . . .

Extending behind the maritime zone at a varying distance from the coast, the sertão presents a very different physical appearance in each of the two main natural regions of the country: the north and the south, separated at approximately 18° south. In both regions the physical characteristics of the sertão depend closely upon the relief and structure of the mountains, the constitution of the soil, and the degree of humidity of the continental climate.

Toward the north the relief of the country is much less rugged. The land, less varied in its geological composition, rises without large or abrupt differences in level. The mountains thus have the appearance of elevated plains or steep-edged plateaus, which the intermittently flowing river currents cut into and traverse, leaving behind broad ridges shaped by age-old erosion. Here and there on the plain that stretches until lost from sight there rise low, pointed hills which reflect the sun on their bare slopes, white and barren with quartz.

The landscape is generally dry and monotonous. Over a vast region the vegetation has always the same rachitic,

spiny, twisted form, characteristically accentuated in the spe-
cies that constitute the type of *catinga* where acacias, ju-
jubes, and a great variety of cacti flourish in hot, rocky soil.
The rains are sparse in their annual season, and sometimes
they stop completely for successive years. On the moisture-
less earth, under a burning sky, the vegetation then seems
to die. Stripped of their foliage the trees seem scorched by
fire. The springs go dry; the rivers are mere gulleys where
signs of the water which once ran there are barely percepti-
ble. The large rivers which come from afar and whose
sources are found in other climates flow across this parched
land as strangers, announcing their passage by long rows of
greener vegetation like an oasis in the desert plain. Here and
there the salt marshes, mantled by carnaubas in handsome
arrangement, break the wearisome monotony of the landscape and mark the site of a small settlement under the
arching shade of the palms.

The catinga, however, is not an impenetrable barrier. Its
unique vegetation makes it more like a labyrinth, with a
multitude of paths and clearings, always alike, and transformed as if by magic, to revive for a day, only when a
chance rain fills the merciless sky. If the peril of virgin
forest is solitude without trails or egress, the terror of the
catinga is the bewilderment which their multiplicity never
fails to cause. The beast, led by instinct, can range to
the uttermost parts and reach his destination without stray-
ing; but once a man enters the catinga and his memory
falters in choosing a trail, he is a victim whom only a miracle will save. . . .

The southern region is quite different. Here the coastal
forest narrows. The mountains come down to meet the
ocean, and more than once their steep cliffs project into
its waters as promontories. The topography is more varied
and therefore more beautiful. The mountain ranges multiply, and some raise their summits more than two thousand
meters above the sea. . . .

Here the bare fields, whose mournful tranquility is broken
only by the woodlands of araucaria, are open regions leading deep into the continental interior. Here in fact are the
gateways to the western sertões. The rivers have their
source almost in sight of the sea, then plunge into the unknown to serve the insatiable ambition of the conquerors

through endless plains whose level, sweeping horizons suggest the mute surrender of the unknown before the audacity of the newcomers.

The North of Brazil was one of the most forbidding theaters for the historic action of the New World conquerors. Had it not been for the Amazon, Brazilian expansion in this region would have come to a stop in the valley of the São Francisco. The South, on the other hand, provided a geographical basis to assure almost half the continent for the Portuguese realm in the eventual partition of America. . . .

Given the nature of the conquest, then, the future of each half of the colony was fully prefigured in the geographic structure of its respective territory. By virtue of his habitat, the Paulista had to be the bandeirante par excellence. The conquest of the sertões was his historic destiny.

Note well that in the whole hydrography of the southern continent no large river has its headwaters nearer the ocean than does the Tietê, and none permits broader access to the interior through an ample river system such as the one to which it was the key. This fine route which the Tietê made available for the thrust of invasion can be compared for efficacy only with the Amazon in the North and the Plata in the South. But neither of them surpassed the Tietê in offering the preconditions for militant expansion of the kind that the Paulistas would later effect. Thus the Amazon settler goes upstream without meeting resistance, and he stops or lingers only because he has wearied of the trip. There is no other explanation. The Spaniard ascends the Plata and stops at the falls or the swamplands; he does not go beyond Guairá, just as he fails to penetrate above Lake Xarayes. Later, he must give ground before the victorious bandeiras which conquer Guairá, cross the swamps of the Paraguay, reach the Guaporé, and from there continue to the Amazon, finally linking across the sertões the two extremes of the conquest initiated along the coast.

At the beginning of the seventeenth century, however, this hydrography, these sertões, as we have described them, were no more than a myth for the settlements expanding along the seacoast.

The falsest of notions were spread concerning the source and direction of the great rivers that poured fresh water as far as twenty leagues out to sea, as did the São Francisco according to Gandavo. This river was then the most celebrated of all those known in the colony. It was said to have its source in a famous lake fed by mountain waters from the ranges of Chile and Peru, whence the Grão Pará and Plata also flowed. On the shores of this lake there were alleged to exist many settlements whose inhabitants owned large amounts of gold and precious stones. This body of water was called Dourada, which brings to mind El Dorado at the headwaters of the Orinoco.

The river had an enormous sinkhole twelve leagues wide, ninety leagues from the sea, with more than three hundred islands between the hole and the harbor. Its banks were inhabited by several Indian nations, some of which used strips of gold as ornaments. . . . Rare woods were in abundance there, as were brazilwood and cassia fistula. Its meadows were like the Elysian Fields, fertile, enchanting, and overflowing with native fruits. This river ran through mineral lands, rich in gold, silver, and nitrate, with larger deposits the further one entered the sertão. . . .

The strangest legends circulated about the multitude of heathen who lived in the sertões. The Guaiasi of the far West were so dwarfish that they seemed a parody of men. The Matuiú had their feet reversed. The Corugueana were fifteen-foot giants who decorated their lips and nostrils with pieces of gold. A tribe in Ceará was reported to devour its aged to save them the travail of living. A tribe of the southern pampas had legs like those of birds. Most of these outlandish heathen were indescribably ferocious. No one dared enter their domains without a large and competent following.

The great treasures of the sertão were thus guarded by the highest mountains, by immense and unfordable torrents, by ferocious tribes, and by monsters of terrifying aspect. That there might exist treasures unprotected by creatures of dread never occurred to men's imagination. In America as in Colchis, the golden fleece or El Dorado is guarded by monsters—three-tongued dragons or winged serpents—but always monsters. It was a popular belief among the settlers that a mysterious "something" impeded the discovery of the riches of the sertão, and that death was the inevitable punishment for anyone so imprudent as to dare reveal the secret. . . .

Aleixo Garcia never returned from his journey, which was so daring that for many it was legendary. In 1531 Pero Lôbo and the whole of his large party were slaughtered on the banks of the Paraná. The expedition in which Father Aspilcueta Navarro took part in 1532 had no success. The galley commanded by Miguel Henriques, which [Governor] Tomé de Sousa sent to explore the São Francisco River, never returned. If Sebastião Tourinho managed to reach the mountain of emeralds he never brought back conclusive proof. Antônio Dias Adôrno, who visited the same sertões, fared no better. Sebastião Álvares in the sertões of São Francisco; Luís Alves de Espinha in those of Ilhéus; Francisco de Caldas in Pernambuco; Diogo Martins Cão, nicknamed Indian-Slayer, and Marcos de Azeredo in Espírito Santo suffered similar failures.

Nonetheless, the sixteenth century, which ended without having revealed the treasures of the sertão, left the new one no legacy of disbelief or discouragement, as might have been expected after so many misfortunes. Instead the quests were redoubled.

Before 1580 João Coelho de Sousa had spent three years exploring the sertões of the headwaters of the Paraguaçu; during this unfortunate journey he died at an unknown place. The capital which he bequeathed to his brother Gabriel Soares was not gold, which he never found, but experience for undertaking new and more daring attempts at discovery. Possessing charts which were to have opened for him the secrets of the mines which his brother did not manage to explore, Gabriel Soares sails for Europe and goes to the Court of Castile, where he solicits favors which he promises to repay with valuable discoveries. He obtains grants and awards and finally the promise that arms, ammunition, and men will be sent him. He then returns to Brazil.

However, the illustrious author of the *Roteiro do Brasil* [2] was not more fortunate. Gabriel Soares . . . finds signs of gold and silver at Pedra Furada and from there, mounting

---

[2] Gabriel Soares de Sousa, *Tratado descriptivo do Brasil em 1587* (3rd ed.; São Paulo, 1938). [Ed.]

the plateau, he penetrates the high plains of the upper valley of the Salitre River and thence proceeds to the Morro do Chapeu, whose sertões he had begun to explore in all directions when he and most of his party met their death at a place still unknown.

From the memory of this ill-fated enterprise remained the vague tradition which the years ennobled and transfigured into the most famous legend of our history: "the mines of silver" . . . mines mightier than those of Potosí itself, richer than the iron mines of Bilbao, and with whose output all the streets of Madrid could be paved, according to the claims of the unfortunate adventurer.

Silver was the most generally prized metal of the time. After the conquest of Mexico and Peru, America had showered silver everywhere. Each year stately galleons carried the richest treasures to Europe. The Potosí silver mines, discovered in 1545, were at the height of their production in Upper Peru, from which Brazil was separated by only an imaginary line. Hence the prevalent belief that Portuguese America also possessed abundant silver, and hence the search for signs of it through the sertões. Almost nothing was said about gold. The chronicles and reports of the day, like the tall stories of the people, attached more value to silver. Built of silver was the enchanted city of Manoa, whose reflection at night was like the Milky Way on high. . . . Of silver were the "resplendent mountains" of the sertões of Pôrto Seguro which became legendary under the name Itaberabuçu.

Here is how the historian Gandavo explains the origin of this famous legend: "Certain Indians arrived in the Captaincy of Pôrto Seguro, from the sertão, giving news of the existence of green stones in a mountain range many leagues inland; and they brought some with them as samples; they were emeralds, but not of very great value: the Indians themselves said that they were plentiful, and that this mountain range was beautiful and resplendent." [3] These resplendent mountains, which in the language of the heathen were called Itaberaba-oçu, corrupted by the Portuguese to Taberaboçu or more popularly Sabarabuçu, become throughout the next century the goal of the most daring backlands ex-

---

[3] Magalhães de Gandavo, II, 180. [Ed.]

peditions to leave São Paulo for the São Francisco valley. Many of these scoured the sertões in search of Pôrto Seguro or Espírito Santo, whence the old tradition of the "emerald mountains" had come to them.

The legend of Sabarabuçu will long reverberate among the mamelucos of São Paulo. Here begins the period of search in the sertões of which the 1602 expedition commanded by Nicolau Barreto is one of the first and most memorable examples. . . . Here begins the era of far-ranging expeditions to capture Indians for agriculture, or to discover mines whose treasures will be revealed only after a century of stubborn endeavors. A whole century of beating the sertões in pursuit of a chimera. . . .

2

MYRIAM ELLIS

❁

The Bandeiras
in the
Geographical Expansion
of Brazil

Myriam Ellis, a contemporary Brazilian historian at the University of São Paulo, has written numerous studies of the economic history of colonial Brazil. Here she presents a synthesis of the bandeirante movement: the origins, the principal phases and objectives, the memorable expeditions and leaders, the consequences. The reading serves as a factual and chronological framework for those which follow.

From Sérgio Buarque de Holanda, ed., *História geral da civilização brasileira* (2 vols. in 4; São Paulo, 1960-64), I (Part 1), 283-96. Translated; and printed by permission of Difusão Européia do Livro Ltda.

ORIGINS OF THE BANDEIRA MOVEMENT

Piratininga and defensive bandeirismo

With the suppression of the town of Santo André da Borda do Campo and the transfer of its pillory [i.e., municipal symbol] to the settlement established next to the Jesuit college of São Paulo [1562], whites and mamelucos banded together there to offer greater resistance to expected assaults by the enraged heathen. The Tamoio and the Carijó threatened to attack the incipient nuclei of colonization. The activities of capturing Indians were at that time concentrated in the very modest cluster of settlers at [São Paulo de] Piratininga, and they had originated in a defensive struggle to secure and extend possession of the land and to safeguard the inhabitants of the plateau. This situation obtained until almost the last years of the sixteenth century. That period witnessed countless attacks against the Indian in the valleys of the Paraíba, the Tietê, the Moji Guaçu, and the upper Paranapanema. They included those led by Jerônimo Leitão—captain major of the captaincy of São Vicente (1571-92), one of the region's most efficient and fearless Indian fighters in the sixteenth century—against the Tamoio in Rio de Janeiro, against the Tupiniquim and Carijó who menaced the Tietê valley, and southwest into the region of Guairá, beyond the Paranapanema, whence he brought the first contingent of Indians in 1581. In subsequent years he organized new sorties to the South.

In short, Paulista bandeirismo in the sixteenth century, usually directed by captains major, governors, or the favored officials of these authorities, had a defensive and protective function for the embryonic settlement of the southern plateau. It was actually a preparatory phase for the true slave-hunting period and for Paulista expansion of the seventeenth century, the great century of the bandeiras.

Offensive bandeirismo

The era of offense for bandeirismo was the seventeenth century. It commenced following the operations of Captain Major João Pereira de Sousa in 1596, which established definitive possession of the land. The defeated Indians either took refuge far in the sertão or accepted captivity.

Ownership of Indian slaves served as an index of wealth and power, which were proportionate to the number of Indians possessed. The servile regime was the only one then understood by the mentality of the colonists. Of no effect were the orders issued by the crown guaranteeing the freedom of the natives, such as the royal edict of Dom Sebastião, signed at Évora on March 20, 1570, and influenced by Jesuit principles of protection for the Indian; the law of Felipe II of November 11, 1595, prohibiting the enslavement of the heathen of Brazil; and the decree of July 26, 1596, on the same subject. The king would permit a "just war," with enslavement of the heathen becoming legal only when they attacked the Portuguese and the pacified Indians. But a just war would be easy to provoke! Used as a mere pretext, it became a dead letter among the sertanistas of São Paulo.

Thus all the provisions of the crown were circumvented. The encomiendas of Spanish America corresponded to the "free services" (*serviços forros*) of the Portuguese, exacted from Indians who were free by royal decision but maintained in captivity, "deposited" in the domiciles of the colonists. The opposition of the Jesuits to this general tendency provoked a series of conflicts that culminated in their expulsion from the town of São Paulo in 1640.

The period during which offensive bandeirismo was undertaken on a large scale in São Paulo coincided with the presence of the seventh governor general of Brazil (1591-1602), the illustrious Dom Francisco de Sousa, who arrived in 1599 and whose activities had a powerful influence on Paulista expansion into the sertão. Convinced of the presence of mineral riches in the interior of Brazil, Dom Francisco dispatched a number of prospecting expeditions from many points in the colony in search of precious stones and metals. Under his leadership the backlands expeditions were disciplined and provided with military divisions, traveling judges, notaries, chaplains, and prearranged itineraries. After the voyage of Dom Francisco de Sousa to Lisbon (1605) the Paulistas continued their penetrations into the sertões, having in mind, however, immediate profits from Indian-hunting.

The great century of the bandeiras was ushered in by the expeditions of André de Leão (1601) and Nicolau Barreto

(1602), sponsored by Dom Francisco. The first of these left in search of silver mines, following the valleys of the Tietê and Paraíba and from there climbing the Mantiqueira range to reach the sources of the São Francisco. The second, composed of three hundred whites and mamelucos in addition to peaceful Indians, returned to its point of origin after two years and gave rise to differences of opinion as to the region it had reached, whether the São Francisco basin, the Plata basin, or Peru. We know, however, that one third of the Indians it captured had been set aside for the crown.

These were followed by new bandeiras, those of Diogo de Quadros and Manuel Prêto in 1606, that of Belchior Dias Carneiro in 1607—all headed south with the object of taking Indians—as well as many others. Thenceforth and for more than half a century the enslaving expeditions predominated, unleashing the offensive against the native in an ever widening area.

DEVELOPMENT AND DECLINE OF SLAVE-HUNTING
IN THE SEVENTEENTH CENTURY

The first half of the seventeenth century was the period of the development and apogee of slave-hunting bandeirismo. The town of São Paulo became a crucible for bandeirantes, whose capturing expeditions penetrated the sertão in all directions, passing beyond the meridian of Tordesillas. To the South and Southeast, however, the Paulistas confronted the missionary expansion of the Spanish Jesuits. This was the most active and important sector for Indian-hunting.

The Jesuit reductions

In 1610 the missionaries of the Company of Jesus had established themselves on the left bank of the Paranapanema River to begin the spiritual conquest of the heathen. In that region they erected the first villages of neophytes, known as "reductions": San Ignacio and Loreto. As the proselytizing continued, others were built, spreading over and settling wide areas washed by the main rivers and affluents of the Plata basin. The reductions belonged to the jurisdiction of the Province of Paraguay, created in 1607 and covering an area which corresponds to southern Bolivia,

Paraguay, and Argentina of today; and to the regions of Guairá (between the Rivers Paranapanema and Iguaçu on the left bank of the Paraná, where the first establishments were located in 1610), of Paraná (between the lower reaches of the Paraná and Uruguay Rivers), of Uruguay (to Tape, that is, part of the present state of Rio Grande do Sul), and of Itatí (in southern Mato Grosso). The hundreds of Indians settled in villages, already pacified and acculturated by the Jesuits, were excellent and tempting prey for the slave-hunters. Accustomed to obey, they did not offer the resistance of the savage, whose capture was more difficult and dangerous.

While the fathers were establishing themselves in the Guairá region, and even before, the Paulistas engaged in raids there in pursuit of the Indian: Diogo de Quadros (1606), Manuel Prêto (1606, 1607), Clemente Álvares (1610), Cristóvão de Aguiar and Brás Gonçalves (1610), Pedro Vaz de Barros (1611), Sebastião Prêto (1612), Lázaro da Costa (1615), and others. The zone of Guairá was included in the "sertão of the Carijó," a vague term denoting an extremely vast territory stretching to the Lagoa dos Patos in Rio Grande do Sul. But it was the presence of the reductions which gave sharp impetus to slave-hunting bandeirismo throughout the first half of the seventeenth century. The assaults on the Jesuit missions commanded by Manuel Prêto (1619, 1623) began some time after the establishment of the first reductions of the province of Guairá.

The period of Spanish rule

With Portugal under the rule of Felipe II, III, and IV of Spain after 1580, the union of the two crowns permitted greater rapprochement and contact between the South American colonies, Spanish and Portuguese, which were separated by the boundary meridian [of Tordesillas]. With the greatest facility, therefore, the audacious Paulistas could raid the lands of the Spanish crown, where the military garrisons were few, the distances immense, and the daring and temerity of the bandeirantes increasingly pronounced. Furthermore, Spanish colonization, attracted by the mining area, was directed by preference toward Peru. Nor have we yet mentioned the connivance of the Spaniards of Asunción who joined in the attacks on the reductions, among them the governor of Paraguay himself, Don Luis Céspedes y Jeria. Married to a niece of Martim de Sá, governor of Rio de Janeiro and owner of a sugar mill in that region, Céspedes must have been an accomplice of the bandeirantes because of his ties of interest, giving them full support and extending them full facilities, in exchange for Indians for his sugar plantation in Rio de Janeiro and for his fields of yerba mate in Maracaju which supplied this product to the markets of the Plata.

The principal slave-raiding bandeiras

After 1628 the bandeirante attacks on the Jesuit reductions came in swift and systematic order. Starting with the establishments of Guairá that had already been assaulted, the missions were the target of interest for the principal slave-raiding expeditions which left São Paulo.

Early in 1629 the bandeira of Manuel Prêto and Antônio Rapôso Tavares, Pedro Vaz de Barros, Salvador Pires de Medeiros, and others struck into the region of Guairá. This was the largest of any that had been directed there: 900 mamelucos and 2,000 auxiliary Indians, led by 69 Paulistas. It destroyed many reductions, took their Indians captive, drove the Jesuits down the Paraná, and leveled the Spanish towns of Villa Rica, on the left bank of the River Ivaí, and Ciudad Real, on the Paraná near the mouth of the Pequiri.

During the next three years other bandeiras finished the destruction of Guairá, appropriating land that was incorporated into Brazil through Paulista expansion. Thereafter, in 1632 and 1633, the conquest was extended to the region of Itati, in the southwest of the present state of Mato Grosso, apparently under the leadership not of Rapôso Tavares but of Ascenso Ribeiro and André Fernandes. By 1635 the onslaughts of the bandeirantes against the Jesuit domain had conquered the reductions of San Pedro and San Pablo, Concepción de los Gualachos, San José, Angeles, Santa María Mayor, and others, as well as the Spanish settlement of Santiago de Jerez near the sources of the Aquidauana.

In 1636 came a new thrust toward the South, the southern sertão of the Pato Indians, or Rio Grande, much frequented by Paulista bandeiras during the previous twenty years. This force was led by Antônio Rapôso Tavares and his next in command, Diogo Coutinho de Melo: one hundred twenty Paulistas and a thousand Indians. It had been preceded in 1635 by the famous bandeira of Aracambi, commanded by Luís Dias Leme, which reached Rio Grande do Sul by the ocean and remained there about eight months, possibly assigned to scout the Jesuit positions for the assault launched the following year.

The year 1637 saw another large slave-hunting expedition led by Francisco Bueno with about a hundred Paulistas, among them various members of the Cunha, Bueno, and Prêto families. A new and important bandeira set out in 1638 under the command of Fernão Dias Pais, the future "emerald hunter." By 1641 the regions of Tape and Uruguay were conquered, where the Paulistas managed to take over all the reductions.

The Jesuits continued to fall back, with the plan of consolidating their missions that remained along the banks of the Uruguay and Paraná Rivers. Here they organized their resistance; the Paulistas under Jerônimo Pedroso de Barros and Manuel Pires encountered it head-on in their attack of 1641 and were defeated near the River Mbororé on the right bank of the Uruguay. At Caasapaguaçu in 1638 they had already suffered a reverse at the hands of the Jesuit proselytes and the forces of the governor of Paraguay, Don Pedro de Lugo y Navarra. In answer to the insistent demands of the missionaries, Madrid had granted them full permission to arm the Indians in settlements and to defend themselves *manu militari* against the aggression of the bandeirantes.

Spanish rule over Portugal had ended in 1640. Possibly this fact is related to the stronger reaction of the reductions to the Paulista attacks.

The decline of slave-hunting bandeirismo

The second half of the seventeenth century was the era of decline for slave-hunting bandeirismo. The large expeditions of the previous period, organized for attack on the reductions, ceased to exist. In spite of the blows they had suffered, the Paulistas continued for some time in their labor of enslaving Indians in Jesuit lands beyond the Paraná, and in 1640 with assistance from the Bishop of Paraguay, Don

Bernardino de Cárdenas, who was an enemy of the Jesuits and also governor of the region. While he remained in power he encouraged the activities of the Indian-hunters.

The missions which remained, however, were located in a zone that lay beyond the Paulistas' radius of action, which had already become excessively extended with the expeditions of the third and fourth decades of the century. Therefore the capture of Indians continued in other directions after the Jesuits withdrew and abandoned the large area on the left bank of the Paraná and part of the region east of the Uruguay. What now took precedence were forays into the virgin sertão against the wild Indians beyond the Mantiqueira range, in the regions of Goiás and Mato Grosso, along with others whose object was the search for mineral wealth. Bandeirismo was following new paths.

Besides the extinction of various Jesuit reductions, other factors contributed to diminish the activity of slave-raiding: first, the Portuguese restoration of 1640, which made the boundaries between Spanish and Portuguese America more rigid; second, the eclipse of Dutch power in northeast Brazil and in the Atlantic; third, the reconquest of Angola in 1648 by Salvador Correia de Sá e Benavides, which allowed the Portuguese once again to supply the Negro slave markets in Brazil and therefore to make available African labor for the sugar cane fields in detriment to the Indian slave trade; finally, and at a later time, the ruin of the northeast sugar culture and industry brought on by competition from the Antilles, which also worked toward reducing the possibilities for utilization of slave labor in that region.

For these reasons slave-raiding lost much of its economic importance. The geographic expansion of the Paulistas continued, however, in search of mineral wealth concealed in the sertão.

The consequences of slave-raiding bandeirismo were: the preservation and survival of the Paulista social nucleus; provision of a labor supply for the agriculture of São Paulo, for the sugar region, and elsewhere; the reconnoitering of the interior, which facilitated settlement; the collapse of Spanish expansion toward the Atlantic, carried forward by the Jesuits and brought to a halt by the bandeirantes; the territorial conquest and expansion of Brazil to the South and Southwest through occupation of the broad area which included the left bank of the Paraná and the territory of the present state of Rio Grande do Sul.

BANDEIRISMO IN SEARCH OF RICHES

The slave-hunting crisis did not hold back the expansionist impetus of the bandeirante. On the contrary, the decline of Indian-hunting was compensated for by the prospecting expeditions for precious stones and metals. The product of the same geographic, economic, social, and psychological conditions which gave rise to slave-hunting—ideal conditions for the practice of sertanismo—prospecting bandeirismo was, in the first place, a continuation of the expansion effected in the first half of the seventeenth century, although with new objectives. Second, it was a sequel to the entradas carried out in sixteenth-century Brazil for the purpose of discovering gold and silver mines. . . .

Brás Cubas

If the conquest of Peru contributed to Martim Afonso da Sousa's lack of interest in his captaincy and to the fading out of the Portuguese plans to reach the legendary Mountain of Silver in the remote sertão beyond the Tordesillas boundary, it undoubtedly contributed also to cause the settlers of the São Vicente littoral to devote themselves primarily to the cultivation of sugar, to commerce, and to the capture of Indians. A few years after [its founding] a few modest attempts were made in the captaincy of São Vicente to locate precious minerals, among these the probes conducted along the coastal lowland and in the rivers which fall from the Cubatão range. Here some alluvial gold was discovered, which influenced [Governor General] Mem de Sá to send into the interior Brás Cubas, purveyor of the captaincy of São Vicente, and Luís Martins, a specialist in mining designated by the Portuguese crown to survey the metals to be found in Brazil. Two entradas were made. One in 1560 led by Brás Cubas, whose itinerary is still debated. The other, led by Martins in late 1561 and early 1562, a few leagues from Santos to the region of Jaraguá or to Caatiba, present-day Bacaetava. Gold and green stones seem to have been found, although of limited economic importance. Continuing these first probes for gold in the captaincy of São Vicente, the mameluco Afonso Sardinha, nicknamed "the youth," found alluvial gold in the Mantiqueira range, in Guarulhos, Jaraguá, and São Roque. In 1598 he organized an entrada which reached the area of the sources of the River São Francisco.

Dom Francisco de Sousa

At the beginning of the next year the governor general, Dom Francisco de Sousa, arrived in the captaincy of São Vicente, attracted by the alluvial gold which, although scarce, seemed a probable sign of great riches. In light of these possibilities he transferred his administrative apparatus south from Bahia to install it where he might direct the search for metals already begun by him in the Brazilian interior. Among his officials he brought the miner Jacques Oalte, the engineers Geraldo Beting and Bacio di Filicaia, and others.

He remained fully active in the captaincy of São Vicente until 1605, when he returned to Portugal. In that period he sent to the sertão the expeditions of André de Leão and Nicolau Barreto, already mentioned. Returning from Lisbon in 1606 as governor of the Southern Division of the Colony, and obsessed by the idea of the existence of mineral wealth in Brazil, the Count do Prado e Beringel [Francisco de Sousa] persisted in his arduous task of locating precious metals in Sabarabuçu and Araçoiaba. During his second administration occurred the expedition of Simão Álvares the older, leaving São Paulo in 1610 headed for the River Casca sertão in Minas Gerais.

De Sousa's efforts in this direction were futile until 1611, in which year he died, in isolation and penury. They were effective, however, insofar as they promoted reconnaissance of the land and helped set the lines for Paulista expansion.

Participation of other captaincies in the search for precious metals

Countless expeditions prospecting for precious minerals set out from various points along the Brazilian coast during the sixteenth and seventeenth centuries, from Bahia, Sergipe,

Ceará, Espírito Santo. They were organized directly under official auspices from Lisbon or its representatives and operated within the area stipulated by Tordesillas, where they followed along the rivers. . . .

The entradas originating in Bahia, including the captaincies of Ilhéus and Pôrto Seguro, were undertaken from the early years of the donataries and later received additional support from the central government of Brazil. In search of colored stones and silver, they ranged over a vast area that was drained by the rivers São Francisco, Paraguaçu, Pardo, Jequitinhonha, Araçuaí, Caravelas, Mucuri, and São Mateus, and reached the Diamantinha plateau and the region of Minas Novas. Such was the official support given the Bahian entradas that when the mines of Monomotapa [East Africa] were exhausted their administrative apparatus was transplanted to Bahia under the direction of Dom Francisco de Sousa so that the mineral possibilities of the Brazilian subsoil might be explored. . . .

Until the end of the seventeenth century Sergipe was another important center of radiation into the sertão in the search for silver mines. Among the more notable expeditions, for the time it remained in the interior and for the area visited, was that of Belchior Dias Moréia, grandson of Caramuru,[1] which left the banks of the River Real in 1595 or 1598 and proceeded into the sertão along the Itapicuru, where it stayed for eight years.

To the prospecting operations out of Ceará belongs the expedition of Pero Coelho de Sousa, performed in 1603 by order of Governor General Diogo Botelho. It came to the Ibiapaba range, where it overcame the Indians of the region, and reached the banks of the Parnaíba.

Other enterprises were carried out in the northeast even during the Dutch occupation, among them the expedition of Elias Hercksmans in 1641 at the instigation of [Johan Maurits, Count of] Nassau; that of Niemeyer seeking the mines of Itabaiana; and that of Mathias Beck in 1649.

As for the entradas organized in the captaincy of Espírito Santo, which preferred to seek emeralds, these followed cer-

---

[1] "Caramuru," or Diogo Álvares, was a Portuguese squaw man in Bahia. His Tupi nickname meant "moray" (*i.e.*, electric eel, because of his flashing firearm), for which Moréia, his descendant's name, was the Portuguese equivalent. [Ed.]

tain Bahian itineraries that had already been followed in
the River Doce region and its environs. . . .

In São Paulo de Piratininga the task of the bandeiras of
enslavement concentrated all initiative. Men of practical
realism, the Paulistas preferred the immediate profit of Indian-
hunting. When this activity suffered its crisis, the need for
economic resources drove them once again into the sertão,
this time, however, in search of the legendary Sabarabuçu.

In the second half of the seventeenth century the reduced
number of slave-hunting bandeiras recorded was greatly
surpassed by the expeditions prospecting for precious minerals. These also had economic objectives, but their characteristics differed from those of the private warrior groups
organized for combat and comprised of several hundred
whites, mamelucos, and Indians. The prospecting bandeiras
were composed of much smaller human contingents; they
had no aggressive purposes, and their principal goal was to
discover precious stones and metals, for the exploitation of
which they carried adequate instruments, picks, and washing pans.

Decadence of the sugar industry and its influence on prospecting

Instigated by royal orders sent by the Portuguese crown
to the Paulistas, these entradas were of official and semi-
official character. Prizes and honors were promised to the
sertanistas who discovered precious minerals, which motivated them for adventure. Portugal, just emerged from rule
by the House of Austria, was undergoing in that second half
of the seventeenth century a severe economic and financial
crisis, later accentuated by the decadence of the Brazilian
sugar industry caused by competition from the Antilles.
For Brazilian sugar, now in decline on the European markets, it was urgent to substitute a new source of revenue.
This decline affected the Paulistas' Indian-hunting, diminishing its intensity, but it had the opposite effect on the
prospecting expeditions and served to give them impetus. It
would·be impossible to mention all of them. Many are recorded in documents not yet brought to light. Others were
not even registered in the chronicles. What is really important is that various sertanistas from São Paulo in the seven-

teenth century ranged over the sertões of Minas Gerais, Goiás, and Mato Grosso, such as: Lourenço Castanho Taques the elder in 1668, a pathfinder of the Cataguases region; Luís Castanho de Almeida in 1671; Manuel de Campos Bicudo in 1675, in the north of Mato Grosso; and Bartolomeu Bueno da Silva in 1676, in the region of Goiás. And these were not the first. There were also: the bandeirante Antônio Castanho da Silva, who died in Peru in 1622; Antônio Rapôso Tavares between 1648 and 1652, who went inland along the Paraguay, reached the Andean watershed in search of mines, and later emerged in the Amazon basin [see Document 6], and Luís Pedroso de Barros in 1656, who reached Peru where he died at the hands of the Serrano Indians. And how many references there are in the documents to expeditions which took an unknown and indeterminate route into the sertão!

The prospecting expeditions seeking the legendary treasures of the sertão followed various bandeirante routes converging on São Paulo de Piratininga: along the Paraíba valley and through the pass of Embaú in the Mantiqueira range, leading toward Minas Gerais; along the northern routes, one reaching Goiás via Moji Mirim and the other reaching southern Minas via the region of Atibaia and Bragança; and by the river route of the Tietê which led toward the interior of Mato Grosso. They penetrated the interior, opened trails, set the stage for the discovery of gold in the eighteenth century in Minas Gerais, Goiás, and Mato Grosso, and extended the lands of Portuguese America progressively westward.

The expedition of Fernão Dias Pais

Of all the prospecting expeditions the most outstanding was that of Fernão Dias Pais [see Document 9]. Leaving São Paulo on July 21, 1674, in quest of silver and emeralds, he explored for seven years a large area of the south-central region of Brazil: from the headwaters of the River das Velhas northward to the zone of Sêrro Frio, where lay the gold later discovered by other Paulistas. The backlands leader was accompanied by his next in command, Matias Cardoso de Almeida; his son-in-law, Manuel de Borba Gato;

and his son, Garcia Rodrigues Pais; in addition to thirty-odd Paulistas and many dependent Indians.

Though its search for wealth was fruitless, the expedition was extremely important for the link it provided between the period of the prospecting entradas and the discovery of gold-bearing streams effected some time after. Moreover, the three names mentioned are intimately related to the beginnings of settlement in Minas Gerais: Matias Cardoso de Almeida, for establishing the route connecting the mines with the cattle ranches of the São Francisco in Bahia; Borba Gato, for exploring the sertão of the River das Velhas; Garcia Rodrigues Pais, for opening the route of great historic significance between Minas Gerais and Rio de Janeiro. This last also appears to have been one of the discoverers of gold in the Minas territory, anticipating the finds made there by the expeditions of Antônio Rodrigues de Arzão, who left Taubaté in 1693; of Bartolomeu Bueno de Siqueira in 1694; and many others in the following years— the activities of all of these falling properly within the period of actual mining, which began in the last five years of the seventeenth century.

Paulista expeditions of the eighteenth century

Once gold was revealed in Sabará, Ribeirão do Carmo, Tripuí, Itaverava, Cataguases, Caeté, River das Mortes, and various other sites, discoveries followed throughout almost all the interior of Minas Gerais during the first decade of the eighteenth century. Mining and settlement developed hand in hand in the region. Yet this did not put an end to the geographic expansion of the Paulistas, who were driven westward by their defeat suffered in the War of the Emboabas [war of the "outsiders"; see Document 9]. Following old, previously used itineraries, new entradas were carried out into the sertões of Mato Grosso and Goiás in search of the coveted metal, further extending Portuguese boundaries in America.

Of the earliest expeditions responsible for discovering gold in Mato Grosso, the first that should be mentioned is that of Antônio Pires de Campos, who in about 1716 set out toward Cuiabá in search of the Martírios range. He had already been in those parts as a youth, in 1675, in company with his father, Manuel de Campos Bicudo. In 1718 Pascoal Moreira Cabral Leme, following the same route, found gold in the Coxipó Mirim River, initiating the work of mining and, together with other settlers, the era of the "monsoons." These were river expeditions for commerce and settlement which superseded the bandeiras and entradas in that zone and in which the men of Itu and Sorocaba took the leading role. They would depart from Araritaguaba, or Pôrto Feliz, navigating the Tietê and the network of tributaries of the Paraná and the Paraguay to reach Cuiabá. [See Document 10.]

Paulista expansion into the sertão of Goiás had occurred since the seventeenth century, when the region was frequently crossed by the slave hunters. The conquest and settlement were achieved after the discovery of gold, however, by the expedition of Bartolomeu Bueno da Silva, the Anhangüera.[2] He left São Paulo in July, 1722, leading 152 men, among them 20 Indians for carrying loads, 3 priests, 5 or 6 Paulistas, many Portuguese, and one Bahian, in search of the Martírios range where, according to legend, nature had sculpted the crown, spear, and nails of the passion of Christ. For three years the expedition remained roaming the sertão, suffering every privation, till finally in 1725 it located the precious metal it sought, four leagues from the present city of Goiás.

As in Minas Gerais and in Mato Grosso, there followed new discoveries throughout the territory. With the gold deposits identified, the entradas ended and were followed by settlement proper around the workings, the camps, and the towns, attracted by the benefits yielded by mining and inaugurating a new epoch in the history of Brazil.

.   .   .

Exploring without settling, operating more in extension than in depth, the bandeiras had decisive importance in the geographic expansion of colonial Brazil. In the hunt for Indians and the search for stones and metals they extended the

---

[2] Bartolomeu Bueno da Silva was the second Anhangüera. His father had received the nickname, which meant "Old Devil" in the Indian tongue, because once he set fire to some alcohol, telling the Indians it was water and that whenever he wished he would do the same thing to their rivers. [Ed.]

Brazil defined by Tordesillas; penetrated and conquered the land; broke up the Jesuits' pioneer advance front for proselytizing and colonizing; furnished Indian labor for agriculture in the south and north; established routes; discovered gold; and opened roads for the settlement of Minas Gerais, Mato Grosso, and Goiás, as well as for the effective occupation of Paraná and Rio Grande do Sul.

The territorial area of Brazil was established in the mid-eighteenth century, with only slight deviations from its present geographic configuration. In 1750 the Treaty of Madrid effectively demarcated the boundaries between Portugal and Spain in South America. The Treaty of San Ildefonso in 1777 served to reaffirm and maintain the *uti possidetis* arrangement toward which the bandeiras had contributed the conquest of two thirds of the territory of Brazil.

3

JOSÉ

DE ALCÂNTARA MACHADO

❋

Life and Death of the Bandeirante

From an analysis of some 450 inventories and wills of
sixteenth- and seventeenth-century Paulistas, José de
Alcântara Machado (1875-1941) constructed an image of the life, times, and culture of the bandeirantes
and of the society that produced them. His pages are
studded with words and phrases lifted from these la-
conic, matter-of-fact documents. One of his important
contributions was to prove the relative poverty and
strenuousness of Paulista life; this challenged an assump-
tion of the social historian F. J. de Oliveira Vianna
(1885-1951) that the Paulistas lived in wealth and aristocratic refinement like the sugar planters of the Northeast.

Alcântara Machado was a Brazilian legal scholar,
and most of his publications are in the fields of law
and legal medicine.

From José de Alcântara Machado, *Vida e morte do bandeirante* (2nd ed.; São Paulo, 1930), pp. 245-68.

The sertão . . . regularly, with the tenacity of an obsessive refrain, with the tyrannical insistence of a leitmotiv, the word appears and reappears in the Paulista inventories of the sixteenth and seventeenth centuries, to reveal that the collective soul is turned constantly toward the sertão, like a needle attracted by the magnetic pole. For the sertão is indeed the solar center of the colonial world. All interests and aspirations gravitate around it, enslaved by its influence, nourished by its light and heat. Life is not conceivable without it: "The inhabitants not being able to live without the sertão," declare the officials of the town council in a meeting of 1640.

This is natural. Neither agriculture nor trade, which at that time and place are the most lucrative activities, measures up to the ideals of those who arrive with such impatience at the "somewhat melancholy" settlements of the land of Santa Cruz [Brazil]. They hold much promise, but only in the long run—and of course only for those who have a few thousand *cruzados* at hand. Look in Antonil's little book to see how much wealth is needed to be a "powerful farmer" or sugar-mill owner: slaves for the hoe and scythe, boatmen and overseers, ceramists and calkers, carters and carpenters; farmlands that supply food for all these people; equipment for the work of planting, harvest, processing, and transport; shops for manufacture and repair of tools and vehicles. Practiced on a lesser scale, it is true that trade and agriculture can yield a modest living. But what is a handful of pennies for those who dream of El Dorado?

The sertão, on the other hand, knows the poverty of those who seek Brazil with their minds set on fortune, and it makes demands only upon their abundant vigor and daring; knowing them to be impatient, it tempts them with the mirage of easy and immediate wealth within reach of their avid hands: in the forests full of Indians destined for captivity, in the mines resplendent with gems and rich metals, in the luminous gleam of mountain ranges gilded by fables.

Better to seduce them, the sertão arouses not merely their ambition for gain. It grips their imagination, embodying, as it splendidly does, the unexpected and the mysterious, with all the virile joys of risk and struggle. It is there that one meets the forces of destruction mobilized against the invader by rebellious nature: "jaguars, wild cats, and many other untamed beasts," deserts and miasmas, fevers and poisons. In its caves and shadowy lairs dwell the one-legged devil, the will-o'-the-wisp, the bogy, and the petulant demons of the waters and woods. All this combines to make the sertão a permanent provocation to the imagination and adventurous spirit of the conquerors and inhabitants of the land. For the latter in particular the temptation is irresistible. Was not the blood of a seafaring people mixed in their veins with that of wandering tribes?

Between sailor and sertanista there are obvious affinities, which result from the many which link the sertão and the ocean. There is no need to attempt a parallel already developed in a page by Rui [Barbosa]. Both ocean and sertão produce the same awe, the same impression of the infinite and the eternal, the same giddiness. Immense and empty, they alone can satiate the hunger for the boundless freedom which devours man, the innate nomadism which torments him, the pride of throwing his weak, small self against the unleashed elements and defeating them. In payment for these high raptures, sea and sertão take full and lifelong possession of their devotees. They mold them body and soul. The body acquires the suppleness and strength of sea monsters and wild beasts. Even its gait changes: the seaman's swaying walk reflects the rolling waves; the sertanejo's broken stride copies the rambling course of footpaths and wagon trails. Man of the sea and man of the forest have the same temperament; both are simple and brutal, ingenuous and fearless. The ocean and the sertão pursue them everywhere. Jealous, they interrupt their other loves; domineering, they dictate their destiny. And, almost always, they kill them.

Geographic factors, economic determinants, and psychological motives make a bandeirante of the Paulista. Pervading each moment of the history of São Paulo de Piratininga we feel the presence of the sertão, guardian spirit or evil genius presiding over life and death. At times we lose sight of it when we delve into hidden corners of the past. But no matter how remote these may seem, the landscape suddenly leaps forth at a sharp turn in the road, etching the horizon with the profile of its miraculous mountains: Martírios, Esmeraldas, Sabarabuçu. Or it comes as a gust of wind, wafting unexpectedly the fragrant breath of virgin forest, the dull clap of gunshot, and the harsh whir of feathered arrows.

From early childhood the sixteenth- and seventeenth-century Paulista breathes an air saturated with sertanismo. The sertão is the everyday reality. At the interminable nightly gatherings of the dull little village or the drowsy plantation the topic never varies. The oldest tell what they saw and suffered "in the time of the war of Jerônimo Leitão," on the expeditions of Nicolau Barreto, on other entradas of less renown. A heathen Indian relates the wonders of his native soil, the wars in which his tribe was immersed, the prodigies of the witch doctors, the delicious tales of indigenous folklore. And in the eyes of the little boys flames the desire to experience the same adventures.

From time to time this minute world is thrown into tumult. Someone departs resolutely for the unknown. Someone returns triumphant and exhausted, laden with gold and followed by a train of sullen natives; or he returns empty-handed, "defeated, with no profit whatever." In all that surrounds him—the well being of some, the misery of others, the arrogance of the powerful, the mourning of widows and orphans—the citizen of São Vicente feels the mysterious power of the sertão. He cannot flee from it. For here lies the destiny of his breed.

Scarcely yet a man, the bandeirante readies himself and sets forth "to seek his life, the way to his fortune, and relief for himself and his sisters." Francisco Dias da Silva is only sixteen when, "being of age and capable to set forth," he is taken along by his uncle, the redoubtable Fernão Dias Pais, "to the discovery of silver in the service of His majesty." On the entrada of 1673 against the Serrano Indians, Manuel de Campos Bicudo has his son accompany him, Antônio Pires de Campos, who is no more than fourteen; and the second Anhangüera is twelve or fourteen when he sets out with his father on the expedition in pursuit of the tribes of Goiás which reached the River Vermelho.

The inclusion of children and youths in such risky enterprises caused the authorities to react. For having sent to the sertão one of the minors under his care, "to the great distress of the orphan," the tutor of the children of Manuel Galera is discharged. But generally it is the parents who send out their younger children, first to hunt for slaves and, after the start of the gold cycle, "shipping them off to the mines." Only a mistaken perspective could make one condemn the custom as inhuman. At this time the sertão is the best of schools. Face to face with nature man learns to depend on his own resources, which is essential in a land where the action of the central authority is weak and belated. Besides tempering both body and character in the heat of danger, the sertão prepares youths to exercise the only two attractive callings which the environment offers: slave traffic and mining. An entrada serves as a diploma. Therefore the youth who aspires to his freedom never fails to point to the journey he has made as sufficient proof that he is a "diligent and mature man, not only in age but also in his competence to handle his property."

The youths set out. So too do the aged. Manuel Prêto is about ninety when he dies from an arrow in the heart of the forest. Governor Fernão Dias Pais is sixty-six when he begins his search for emeralds, cut short seven years later with his death at the camp of Sumidouro. They never tire. Manuel de Campos Bicudo went twenty-four times into the sertão.

All go seeking their fortune. The town is depopulated, "evacuated by its inhabitants finding relief in the sertão," said a municipal act in 1623. In 1602 substitutes must be elected for the officials of the town council, "all the others having gone away." Because there is no one to maintain them, bridges and roads fall into ruin. Threatened by the Dutch, the captaincy risks having no one capable of defending it. Thus Father Mansilla is not far from the truth when . . . he writes that the life of the Paulistas in the second quarter of the seventeenth century can be summed up as a constant "going and coming, and bringing and selling Indians," and that in the entire town of São Paulo there can be no more than one or two inhabitants who are not engaged in the traffic of human cattle, either going in person or sending their sons and dependents to the sertão [see Document 4].

But even those who are left behind, restrained by sickness or because of their sex, participate in their own way in the sertão expeditions. They manage to have someone go at their expense. It is a true partnership of capital and labor, or rather, a contract, whereby the wealthy supply the capital and the poor the heroism.

LIFE AND DEATH OF THE BANDEIRANTE ((69

The capitalist, who is called an outfitter (*armador*), gives to the bandeirante what the documents of the period call the equipment (*armação*): Indians, chains, arms, ammunition. There are domesticated Indians who in exchange for a musket offer to lead bandeiras sponsored by others and destined to enslave their brothers. But generally the profits are divided equally. "I give as equipment for the sertão two Indians, a shotgun and six pounds of powder and twelve of ammunition, and all else necessary, on condition that in case of profits I be entitled to half," declares Antônia Ribeiro in her will. On the eve of leaving for Goiás, Captain Antônio Pais receives from Manuel da Fonseca Osório all his necessary supplies of powder, shot, muskets, and other things, to a total value of 107$984, "on condition that, God permitting the return from the sertão of him and his above named son," they deliver to the capitalist a third of the slaves which "God might see fit to give him with their families and, if no slaves be taken, that they pay the debt one month after arriving without raising any doubt on this point."

There are repeated allusions to these contracts with sertanistas. They are common, even between fathers and sons. Only rarely does someone appear who "from love and as a gift" unselfishly gives Indians or arms to a needy relative to help him seek his fortune. For the capitalist the business is quite risky. What can and often does happen is that the adventurer "departs this present life" during the journey or else returns ruined, like that armador of whom one of the inventories speaks who left in the sertão six of the twelve Indians he had brought, along with the Indian woman and the chains. Thirty thousand cruzados is the estimated loss suffered by the captain major, Pedro Taques de Almeida, who advanced the sum—in the phrase of his namesake, the genealogist—with no more security than his judgment of the debtor's word.

Sometimes through a prearranged payment a bandeirante agrees to take along "on the round trip" a partner who is not able to meet the expenses of the venture. This is proven by a clarification appended to the inventory of Martim do Prado: "I hereby declare . . . that I contract with Felipe de Veres to take him in my company on this journey in the entrada of Lázaro da Costa, which obliges me to take him out and back, Our Lord giving me life and health, for the price and amount of ten milréis in cash or property." This same sertanista makes a similar agreement with Francisco Álvares, who in return promises him a slave of ten or twelve years and, in case there are no slaves, six milréis in property or currency. From this one concludes that the sertanista paid for the excursion and issued round-trip tickets . . .

Even the religious orders cannot resist the temptation, especially the Carmelite order. It organizes several expeditions on the grounds that, in view of the monastery's limited means, its solution lies in the service of Indians. Among the documents made public by Taunay exists a most interesting one of 1635, in which the Carmelite monks draw up such an agreement with Jerônimo de Camargo and Antônio Bueno.

·   ·   ·

The Paulista enters the "regions and deserts of the most distant sertões." He penetrates as far as "the kingdom of Camã and parts of Peru." He cannot foresee when he will return. Sometimes six, seven, even eighteen years pass without the town having word from those who one day went off to the war of Parnaíba, like Francisco da Gama, or to the mines, like Joseph Vieira. Only after a long time does news arrive that the expeditionary has died in the "course of seven years, as affirmed and sworn to by a number of experienced witnesses who well know the risk and danger of the sertão." Or a certificate arrives from "the priest holding this curacy of the mines of Potosí and its environs in the province of the Chichas of Peru," or from another even more remote place, attesting the death of an inhabitant "of Brazil in the place of San Pablo," as happened in the case of Antônio Castanho. About others, nothing. After a certain time inheritance proceedings are begun. This occurred in the case of Antônio Nunes, "since there is no news of the people who accompanied Martim Rodrigues and all are taken for dead."

Such long trips of such uncertain duration are costly to equip. That of José Pompeu, son of Lourenço Taques, comes to twenty milréis; that of Francisco Dias da Silva, nephew of Fernão Dias Pais, to twenty-six milréis five hundred; that of Captain Antônio Pais to one hundred eight.

It is not clothes or uniform that weighs most in the traveling trunk or chest of tanned leather. The bandeirante wears almost all his attire on his person: a well-worn hat or fur cap or kerchief and head-cloth; stirrup stockings; shoes of cowhide, deerskin, sheepskin, cordovan, or soft leather; drawers and shirts of cotton; short coat and breeches of baize or coarse cloth. The hammock, the small pillow and case, the blanket, and a few towels comprise the rest of the covering and bedding—though there are exceptions. Pero Sardinha has only one hammock, one white blanket, one pair of drawers, one old shirt. In contrast, Afonso Dias requires no less than six shirts, three pairs of drawers, two pairs of cotton bombacho trousers, two face towels and as many hand towels, three doublets (one of bombazine), a sheet of two thicknesses, a quilt, a small cushion, a woolen collar, a cloak, a hat, and a hood.

Kitchen utensils and provisions amount to very little. The utensils are tin plates, copper pots, and drinking gourds. Of the persons inventoried only Estêvão Gonçalves and Afonso Dias permit themselves the luxury of taking to the sertão a table knife in the case of the first and two silver spoons in that of the second. As provisions they carry tubes or gourds of salt, and bread made from "war flour," so called . . . because it is the ammunition for soldiers' mouths. It is cooked into a compact loaf which is wrapped in leaves and thus resists humidity and extremes of weather, remaining a year or more "with its own savor." In the time of Diogo Sanches it is worth seven *vintens* the *alqueire*.

Why be laden with food when the rivers abound with fish, and the forests and plains with game, wild fruits, honey, piñons, hearts of palm, plots abandoned by the terrified Indians, and planted fields left at the stopping places of previous entradas? And if his lot denies him all this the bandeirante assuages his hunger by devouring unclean meat: snakes, toads, lizards. If he lacks drinking water he quenches his thirst with the blood of animals, the juice of fruits, the sap from leaves and roots. But in the barren sertões where even these cannot be found "people continually die of hunger."

Sometimes there appear in the baggage lancets and small boxes of alum and verdigris for sickness, as well as razors with their whetstones, and inkwells. Manuel Prêto is the only one to take along a deck of cards and two old books as a distraction. Others, more practical, pack in their "oxhide trunks" or "leather chests" a few ells of bombazine or several yards of cotton which they later sell to their companions at immoderate prices.

But the bulk of the baggage is the forged wedges, the large hewing axes, adzes, scythes, and machetes to attack the forest; picks, gold-washing pans, and the rest of the equipment for mining; fishing nets, lines, hooks. And above all else the weapons, hunting arms all of them. Some items are deceptively innocuous: needles, rows of pins, combs and scythes for barter, red caps, strings or strands of *velórios* (or brightly colored beads with coral tips), catchy trinkets which the white man uses to deceive the Indian. But there are other weapons upon which the sertanista always places value. The needs of personal and domestic defense in a society poorly policed like that of the sixteenth and seventeenth centuries, however urgent they were, were not enough to justify the arsenal found in more than one estate. Bartolomeu Cacunda has fourteen muskets; Bento Ribeiro, six shotguns and a blunderbuss; and Antônio Bicudo de Brito, a blunderbuss and a pistol of two spans. Only the predatory activities of the Paulistas can explain such quantities.

Indian weapons are listed in lesser number in the inventories, which is surprising in view of the many "mighty bowmen" in the vicinity of Piratininga. A bow and a dozen arrows belonged to Antão Pires; thirty feathered arrows with a bow and ninety tubes for *camarajuba* arrows are left by Henrique da Costa; and that is all. The reason is that since these weapons are made by the Indian archers themselves, they belong to them and are not included in the estate.

Bladed weapons are in much greater quantity: "rib of the cow" swords, "tapir hide" daggers, locally made machetes. In the attack of 1639 against the settlements of Guairá, the men of Manuel Prêto and Antônio Rapôso Tavares go armed with machetes. Almost all the blades which flash in the inventories, however, are for dress only: "black ones," that is, without points—exposed and engraved handles "with their dagger and the necessary ornament" serve only as decoration for the bigwigs as they strut about during town celebrations.

Not with swords or arrows will the Paulista be able to vanquish an enemy superior in numbers, in knowledge of the land, and in the scorn he shows for life. What assures him victory are powder and shot. Of the portable firearms the first to appear, after the hand culverin, is the arquebus. At the time of the inventories this remote ancestor of the carbine was already joining the ranks of antiques. Four or five of them are found in the estates. Shotguns are the fashion. We find them measuring four to six and a half spans, supplied with Portuguese firing mechanisms or safety bolts, and accompanied by molds for large or small shot, pouch, bag, powder horn, firing pin, and ramrods. Some are octagonal for the length of the barrel, others only at the mouth. Sometimes they are embellished with precious metal. . . .

Then flintlocks appear, with Portuguese or foreign bolts. . . . Some are decorated with brass rings. Others are silver-plated and have a silver muzzle. . . . The long firearms left by Estêvão Garcia are less opulent but of greater interest to us, for they have a "Paulista stock," and a "cartridge belt with its Paulista-style powder horn" to complement them. Carbines or carbine-type guns are mentioned in the inventories of Manuel Garcia Velho and others. Also two or three blunderbusses and a few Portuguese pistols with bronze barrels and foreign firing mechanisms.

.   .   .

Very little is mentioned in the way of armor: a helmet, a steel buckler, two shields of cloth. The band from São Vicente which attacked the reductions at Guairá used this thick cloth, or round shields. The Paulistas discover the armor called for by the environment. It is "armor of quilted cotton" or the "cotton-armored jacket," adapted from the old medieval jacket to conditions of the American setting. It is the *escupil,* already used by the Spaniards in the wars against the Indians of Mexico, Peru, and Chile—a carapace of raw leather, filled with cotton and lined with cotton twill. Like a coat of mail, it is enough to protect the body against the arrows of the enemy. Basílio de Magalhães cites a royal letter of 1684 in which Duarte Chaves, governor of Rio de Janeiro, is requested to send to the governor of Angola up to sixty jackets made "in the style used by the sertanejos of São Paulo." The price of the armored jacket is extremely high: eleven milréis.

What more is needed by the bandeirante, thus armed and accoutered, before he plunges into the unknown? He needs that indispensable element of any equipment: the chains, two or more *braças* long, with fifty or more links or rings, and five, twelve, or thirty iron neck collars. Yoked one to another at the neck by padlocked shackles, it is thus that the Indians, seized for captivity from their villages and reductions, are dragged along weeks and months on end until they reach the settlement.

. . .

"Bandeira" and "bandeirante" do not appear in the available inventories with the meaning we give them today. . . . Also, nothing indicates that the words *maloca* and *maloquero,* distinctly of new-world origin, were current in São Paulo, although Spanish Americans used them to designate expedition and expeditionary. Paulista documents of the period refer to an incursion as an entry (*entrada*), journey (*jornada*), voyage (*viagem*), company (*companhia*), discovery (*descobrimento*), and more rarely, fleet (*frota*). To identify a particular one they name its organizer or chief: entrada of Domingos Rodrigues de Paraupava, entrada of Macedo, entrada made by Belchior Carneiro, entrada in which Lázaro da Costa takes part, entrada undertaken by order of Diogo de Quadros, voyage of Diogo Fernandes, voyage made by Simeão Álvares to Caeté, journey, company, war of Nicolau Barreto. Or else the place of destination: voyage to Itaqui, entrada of the river Guaibii, voyage to the Amboupuras.

The term "war" is used when justified by the more or less official appearance and character of the enterprise: war of Jerônimo Leitão, war of Parnaíba, "war to which we now proceed with Senhor João Pereira de Sousa, captain." Those who participate in the enterprise have no special designation. "Soldiers of this camp" is a felicitous expression which appears only once or twice. As a rule, all are included in one generic term: men, people, or company.

The group, whether large or small, always adheres to the main lines of military organization. It is composed of a chief, who is the captain of the camp, one or more lieutenants, and the bulk of the troops, consisting in large part of docile Indians. If the bandeirante has no Indians of his own he hires them. The more elaborate expeditions call for other officials: the first ensign, the patrol leader, the *repartidor* whose function is to distribute the captured Indians, the camp notary, the chaplain.

It is clear that a voyage whose objective consists of the

enslavement of Indians does not require the same equipment as a colonizing bandeira. The latter is like a settlement on the march; it is a part of the colony that breaks off, taking with it all the elements of life; it is the latifúndio that multiplies by schizogenesis. Thus, when he departed to found "the town today called Vila Laguna in the plains known as Lagoa dos Patos," Captain Domingos de Brito Peixoto, "one of the most powerful men of that time," had use of "all the implements of war, powder, bullets, firearms, some fieldpieces, fighting men, provisions, armament, clothes, and all else necessary for the large body of whites, mulattoes and Negro slaves, carpenters, blacksmiths, a chaplain, and the complete retinue needed for such a conquest."

Whether it be a government official or an experienced and famous sertanista, heading a bandeira of large proportions composed of "people of quality," or whether it be a tamed Indian who, in exchange for a shotgun, leads half a dozen Indians with loaned equipment to bring back to his patron "whatever heathen can thus be acquired"—the leader of the troop must by force of circumstance gather all the powers in his hands. He is the incarnation of authority. He is a dictator. Hence he does not merely guide the bandeira toward its objective by tracing the itinerary, assuring discipline, directing military operations. He is invested with judicial functions, both civil and criminal. He even arrogates to himself the power of life or death over his companions. . . .

Of the manner in which these improvised judges dispense justice there is complimentary testimony in the inventories made in the sertão. When a bandeirante dies "of his illness" or of an arrow wound received in combat, the captain acts ex officio or upon request of a relative to order the inventory of "any and all property and weapons . . . clothing and tools, and powder and shot . . . and slaves which remained after the death and demise of" the *de cuius,* "may he rest in peace, so that the goods he had for division among his heirs may for all time be known in the town." The documents are drawn up by the camp notary or else by an *ad hoc* notary if there is no one "elected" or "deputized for this."

There are none of the complications of common process. Everything is done and reported in the most summary fashion. The situation does not call for, nor does the temper of these men tolerate, the useless verbiage of legal formulae:

imperatoria brevitas. Besides, writing material is scarce. "Because of the scarcity of paper" only the essential is mentioned. For official documents the camp notary uses whatever comes to hand: here it may be scraps of leftover paper "since there is none here"; or there, the backs of some sheets of manuscript.

It is on the ranch or in the "stockade" where he is "lodged" that, "before many men" of his camp, the captain receives from a relative or comrade of the bandeirante "dead of his illness in this sertão" the obligation to make a faithful description of the possessions. The oath is taken on a book of the Holy Gospel, "on a missal, on a prayerbook, or on a cross." At the same ceremony two assessors are named and sworn in and, when there is a widow or orphans, an attorney "of the wife left behind" and the minors. Upon receiving the will of the *de cuius* the captain has it opened and orders it probated, placed in process, and executed. Sometimes he goes further and makes the funeral arrangements, determining, for example, that the deceased be laid out "in two shirts."

This initial document bears the date of the day on which it was drawn up, and often a more or less precise mention of the site where the captain had his camp. "On January 11, in the year 1629, in this sertão of Ibiaguira, at the headwaters of the Ribeira," begins the inventory which Captain Mateus Luís Sousa ordered made of the property of the deceased Luís Lopes, "may he rest in peace." "On July 31 [1603], in this sertão and borderlands populated by the heathen Tomoninó, before the captain major of this encampment for the discovery of mines of gold, silver, and other metals, Nicolau Barreto," as the inventory of the younger Brás Gonçalves stipulates. . . .

After the goods are appraised in Christian fashion the captain puts them up for public sale and auction, "because of present danger and being in enemy land, where they can easily be carried off, thus causing the orphans to suffer a loss for having no one to protect their interest." The sale is conducted "in the presence of forty men of the company in a public place, where the captain orders all the soldiers to muster," a place that is the "plaza" or, more precisely, the "main yard of the camp." The bidders call out "what seems to them proper." Of the buyers many promise to pay the price to the heirs in two or more months, or years, the "first" ones after their return to the town "in peace and safety." In this case they offer a warrantor who also signs the most summary bill of sale.

The balance of Indians and property which finds no bidder is received by a custodian "who was elected for this purpose." He also receives the Indians who accompanied the deceased and the new ones distributed as his share, "to look after them and with God's help take them to the town." And sometimes also the legal documents delegate him to give "an account to the judges of the Town of São Paulo whenever he might be asked, or to the person who should appropriately receive such knowledge." This was a formidable responsibility in that highly uncertain environment. For this very reason the custodian insists that everything be "the responsibility and risk of the widow of the deceased, and his heirs . . . so that at no time, if something should occur . . . would they ask him for an accounting." The captain merely orders that the protest be registered, "saying that he would take no action, passing the whole matter to His Majesty's justice."

The religious prayers and other costs are paid in kind. The chaplain receives an *arrôba* of wax for the mass. The notary receives an axe, some old weapons, or some five pounds of wax. Only one of the captains claims payment for his services: Antônio Rapôso Tavares. From the few trifles left at the death of Pascual Neto, the heroic devastator of the Jesuit missions takes a pair of stockings. For those like us who are victimized by literary allusions, this petty action recalls irresistibly that leg of suckling pig which hurled Eça de Queirós's poor São Frei Gil into the eternal flames.

II

○ ○ ○

THE
SEVENTEENTH
CENTURY

4

JUSTO MANSILLA and SIMÓN MACETA

❋

Atrocities of the Paulistas

The Paulista onslaught of 1628-29 against the Spanish
Jesuit reductions of Guairá (now western Paraná, Brazil) heralded a decade or more of wholesale attacks
throughout the missions area. The Jesuit superior, Antonio Ruiz de Montoya, sent two subordinates to accompany the bandeirantes and their several thousand
Indian captives on their return to São Paulo in 1629 to
dispute the mass kidnaping with the Brazilian authorities. The following is a report to Felipe IV of Spain
by these two men: Fathers Justo Mansilla Van Suerck,
a Fleming, and Simón Maceta, an Italian. To the Jesuit
provincial they sent a similar but slightly more sober
account.

The two fathers obtained a decree against the Paulistas from the governor general in Bahia, but there was
no way to have it enforced. They returned to Guairá in
1630, where the bandeirantes continued to lay waste
most of the missions. The Jesuits soon evacuated their
settlements of Guairá and Tape, to the south, regroup-
ing them near the Rivers Alto Paraná and Uruguay.

From Jaime Cortesão, ed., *Jesuítas e bandeirantes no Guairá*
(*1549-1640*) (Rio de Janeiro, 1951), excerpts from pp. 310-38.
Translated; and printed by permission of the Biblioteca Nacional,
Rio de Janeiro.

Unable to count on help from the suspicious Spanish colonists of Paraguay, the Jesuits began to drill the Indians with muskets and even to manufacture firearms. Their defeat of the Paulistas in 1641 along the Mbororé, a tributary of the Uruguay, marked the end of Paulista raids on the reductions.

The military strength of the Paraguayan Jesuits contrasted with the situation of the Order in São Paulo. In 1640 word reached that town of a papal bull, drawn up with special reference to Brazil and Paraguay, which excommunicated those who seized, used, or trafficked in slaves. The Paulistas thereupon expelled the Jesuits in a near-unanimous act of protest. They were not permitted to return to the town until 1653, and then only on condition that they neither give asylum to escaped slaves nor publish the bull of 1639.

An account of the injuries perpetrated by certain citizens and inhabitants of the town of São Paulo de Piratininga of the captaincy of São Vicente of the state of Brazil in plundering the settlements of the Fathers of the Company of Jesus in the mission of Guairá and Plains of the Iguaçu in the jurisdiction of Paraguay with exceeding contempt for the Holy Gospel in the Year 1629.

Rendered by the Fathers Justo Mansilla and Simón Maceta of the Company of Jesus, who were in these very settlements when they were plundered by the Portuguese, and who accompanied them to São Paulo, following their parishioners, and continued to Bahia, where they pleaded for the latters' liberty and for redress in the future before the Governor General Diogo Luís de Oliveira.

For forty years the inhabitants of São Paulo have flaunted the laws of the King Our Lord with no regard for them, nor for their great offense against God, nor for the punishment which they deserve. In their raids they continually capture and carry off by force of arms the free and emancipated Indians whom they keep for their own slaves or sell. Lately their boldness has been even greater than in years past, and for two principal reasons: first, this time they have gone out in greater numbers than ever, emboldened by the little or no punishment inflicted on them for their continual and unjust entradas in the past; second, they have assaulted the reductions of the Fathers of the Company of Jesus of the Province of Paraguay and taken all the people whom we were instructing.

With regard to the first point: In the beginning of the month of August, 1628, some nine hundred Portuguese left the town of São Paulo with muskets, swords, cotton armor, bucklers, machetes, and much ammunition of shot and powder, and other arms. They were accompanied by two thousand two hundred Indians, unjustly taken captive on previous occasions, and also among them were the two judges of the same town of São Paulo, Sebastião Fernandes Camacho and Francisco de Paiva; two aldermen, Maurício de Castilho and Diogo Barbosa; the Procurator of the Town Council, Cristóvão Mendes; and the son, son-in-law, and brother of Amador Bueno, the senior judge of the town. And from the town of Santa Ana de Parnaíba which is seven leagues from São Paulo came Captain André Fernandes and the judge Pedro Álvares, his son-in-law. Thus there remained in São Paulo only 25 men who could bear arms, not counting the old men who could not go because of their age.

Dividing all these men into four companies, their captains and other officers of war hoisted their flags as if they had arisen and mutinied against your Royal Crown. The flags which they carried did not bear the arms of the King, but different insignia. Antônio Rapôso Tavares was declared captain major of the Company, and he took Bernardo de Sousa as his lieutenant and Manuel Morato as his sergeant, and for captain of his advance guard he took Antônio Pedroso and of his rear guard Salvador Pires. The captains of the other companies were Pedro Vaz de Barros, Brás Leme, and André Fernandes.

As field master of all the companies went Manuel Prêto, author of all these raids. . . .

With regard to the second point: The men of the company of Antônio Rapôso Tavares who committed these injuries which we are recording here had said many times before setting out from São Paulo that they had decided to plunder and destroy our settlements, and thus they purposely took

the route to the Plains of the Iguaçu. Here, far removed
from the towns of the Spaniards and isolated in these lonely
regions, where twelve reductions or Indian settlements have
already been built and others, for lack of priests, merely
planned, we were settling and instructing the Indians in their
own lands with infinite toil and lack of necessities, being content to carry on for the love of God and for the salvation of
those heathen. We suffered the poverty of the land in food
and dress, planting vineyards and sowing wheat so as to have
the host and wine for saying Mass.

When these bandits, then, had crossed the River Tibajiva
on the 8th of September of that same year 1628, they built
their palisade or fort of wooden stakes close by our villages.
And—to show clearly the intention they had from the beginning—Antônio Pedroso, Captain of the advance guard of
this Company, as soon as he arrived in these parts chanced
upon some seventeen Christian Indians from our settlement
of Encarnación on the Ñatingui, who had left their wives
and children in the village under the protection of the Fathers and gone to the woods to collect mate, which they
drink with warm or cold water after grinding it into powder.
Pedroso seized them and carried them all off. . . .

Thereafter, although they continued most cruelly to capture the heathen who, for lack of Fathers, had not yet been
settled in reductions, wounding, killing, and mangling many
old caciques and unbaptized children, they left us in peace
with our wards for four months; and we treated them with
friendliness, for in this way, although we could not arrest the
many evils they were committing, we at least protected our
reductions as best we could and those Indians who were
again coming to us. And when it was necessary to dispatch
some Indians of our village elsewhere we simply gave them
a note begging the Portuguese to let them pass as our own
sons; thus we treated the thief as a loyal friend, and they let
them pass. Furthermore the Fathers went now and again to
their palisade and baptized the children and the sick (for
there were many afflicted with pox) to save them from eternal captivity since they could not be saved from the temporal
one. The Portuguese themselves also sent for Father Pedro
[Mola], who was in the village of San Antonio a day's journey from their palisade, to confess a Portuguese who was
dying, although God would not allow it, depriving him of

speech and reason the whole time the Father remained with him.

This false peace lasted until a very great cacique called Tatabrana who had many vassals—and whom Simão Álvares, a citizen of São Paulo, had unjustly captured a few years previously but who, desiring his freedom, soon fled and returned to his lands—came to deliver himself with all his people to the same Father Mola. They were Christians whom we had won over, shortly before the Portuguese entered those parts, by gifts and celebrations given in their honor when they entered our villages to see us, attracted by the good word which had gone forth concerning the peace and contentment enjoyed by the Indians who lived in them with us.

Then the Portuguese, thinking that they now had some pretext to carry out their wicked intention, sent to ask the Father for Tatabrana. And as the Father replied that he could not be turned over to them since he was free and in his own lands, they advised Captain Major Antônio Rapôso Tavares requesting his approval, and then, on the 30th of January, 1629, they came to take by force not only Tatabrana but also all the others whom the Father was instructing in the village of San Antonio. Thus, as they themselves admit, they took from it four thousand Indians or burden bearers along with a crowd of others, and they destroyed the entire village burning many houses, plundering the church and the Father's house, and desecrating an image of Our Lady. With great violence they removed the Indian men and women who had taken refuge in the Father's house, and they killed an Indian at the very door of the house, as well as another ten or twelve persons in the same village. They took most of the Father's meager belongings, including a few shirts, two blankets, shoes, hats, napkins, tablecloths, spoons, knives, ten or twelve iron wedges, and six or seven chickens that he had. They killed one of three cows they found, and took other small things. . . .

What is of gravest concern in this whole affair is that the Holy Gospel is now so disesteemed and its Preachers so discredited that—with the door now completely closed to the preaching of the Gospel among all those heathen—the Indians imagine and repeat that we did not gather them to teach them the law of God, as we told them, but to deliver them by this subterfuge to the Portuguese. They also say that we tricked them by telling them so often that they were safe with us and that the Portuguese, being Christians and vassals of the same king, would not touch nor harm those who were with the Fathers, for they were then Christians and children of God. Therefore, since an action so atrocious goes unpunished and with no effective remedy, it seems to me that we shall be forced to abandon all these heathen, whom year after year we have been gathering together and instructing by order of His Holiness and His Majesty with so much labor and hardship. . . .

And so that the multitude of the infidels which was already disposed to settle with the Fathers and embrace the Holy Faith may be better appreciated: In the village of Jesús María alone, Father Concovado had almost five thousand warriors not counting their crowd of women and little ones. Besides this, the caciques of Caayu . . . saw that because of the lack of Fathers (who, in villages as densely populated as those, were almost all distributed one by one) they could not achieve their good hopes of having priests in their lands to instruct them; so they themselves with their vassals went to the village of San Antonio, just recently plundered, to be there with the Father. They had not known of the shameless action of the Portuguese there, but when they saw the village destroyed, the houses burned and so many killed, they returned to their lands and now, from what they have seen, imagine that we are traitors and deceivers, and that we have secret intelligence with these Portuguese. And therefore, as some Indians who met these people on a journey have affirmed to us, many of them are now traveling in a band looking for Fathers to kill them. . . .

What we saw along the route [to São Paulo] was the inhumanity and cruelty with which [the Portuguese] treated the Indians. For the poor creatures were overworked and sick at heart to find themselves slaves with little hope of regaining their liberty. Against their will and resistance they were leaving their lands where they had lived most contentedly and amid great plenty; and they now had to cross many rivers, swamps, lakes, and mountains, making this long march on forty consecutive days from the palisade to São Paulo, carrying their little ones on their backs, seeing them turn sick and die from hunger, cold, exertions, the maltreatment of the Portuguese, and the rigors of the journey. They ate only the little that the Portuguese sometimes gave them, stolen from their own farms and plots, or else what they themselves had to search for in the forests and woods, fatigued from the day's journey—although not all were permitted to do this for fear they would escape. Besides all this, the Portuguese loaded them with their burdens, and many caciques as well as vassals (especially those from our reductions) were taken in chains to São Paulo. All day they were scolded and at night the Portuguese kept them from sleeping, wearing them out with constant shouting and sermonizing which they themselves did or ordered their Tupi to do, or else some of the recently captured caciques. The latter were on the one hand promised, to discourage their escaping, that they would have a very good life, both temporal and spiritual, with their houses and lands in São Paulo (as if perpetual captivity could be designated a life), and, on the other hand, the Indians were threatened that if they fled they would be killed, and in fact when someone did run away they sent their Tupi after him and when he was brought back he was cruelly whipped. . . .

Two Indians whom the Portuguese released to us after persistent importunities assert that when the Portuguese left the palisade they set fire to the huts and settlements, burning with them some of the aged and infirm, and, if some did manage to escape so as not to die in the flames, the Tupi in the presence of their masters forced them to return to the fire to expire in it. In this regard we might say here that the cruelty of the Tupi was no less than that of their masters and that they no less deserve to be punished than the Portuguese. . . .

But let us return to the Portuguese and consider the wiles they employ to deceive the courts and avoid the punishment which they deserve. This does not require much effort, for they have as companions in crime not only all the people of São Paulo but also the very judges and administrator of the council of this same town. However, so that they might have a way of deceiving the higher magistrates of the state (if it can be called deceit, against persons who witness enough cases of the constant entradas, carried out with so many wrongs and cruelties, to have no illusions about such clear and open deceits) they requested I know not what sort of legal writs. Thus Pedro Vaz de Barros obtained one to pursue some who had already set out to capture Indians and to make them return. But this was only so that he and his companions might accompany them under this pretext.

André Fernandes, a great killer and flayer of Indians, carried a similar license. Judge Francisco de Paiva obtained another writ from the Holy Office of the Inquisition authorizing him to search for a heretic who he said had taken refuge in those wilds. And in this high-handed manner he accompanied Pedro Vaz de Barros as if this were the real matter at hand, and taking advantage of this trick he had it announced that all the members of this entrada carried a license from the inquisitor.

All of them are well aware, and confess it, that what they do is against the law of God and of His Royal Majesty, who has prohibited it so many times by his laws and ordinances under threat of most severe penalties.

But to excuse themselves they say that it is the custom in São Paulo to capture and sell Indians, and that King Dom Sebastião has awarded these Indians as slaves, as evident in his law which he passed at Évora on the 20th of March, 1570 (although this is very far from the truth, for he awarded as slaves only those who might be taken in a just war and by his license). And they say that now the King, because he was ill informed, declared them free men and emancipated, and that it seems that in this matter the magistrates dissemble, for the punishments set by the laws are never exacted. On the contrary, they say that all of them receive pardon from Bahia whenever they go out to capture Indians. And they said that this is also the case now, and that they had pardon for all the soldiers by paying His Majesty with one Indian of every six. However, the captains are to appear in Bahia until they obtain another more favorable decision which, as they said, they would soon receive.

. . . In past years there were governors of this state who instead of punishing the culprits, as they were obliged to do, ordered them to set aside the royal fifth, as if the captives were gold taken from His Majesty's mines. . . . In São Paulo when they returned this time we saw that each one went to make an agreement with the official of the region and to offer him some of the Indians brought as captives. And thereupon, after committing so many abominations, they were well received. For if this were not the case it would not be possible, not only for Christians or those who call themselves Christians, but even for Turks or Moors or infidels, to dare to act against the laws of their king with such liberty and audacity as do the inhabitants of São Paulo. Certainly no one could imagine such a thing if he did not see it with his own eyes, for the whole life of these bandits is merely going to and returning from the sertão, going and bringing captives with all that cruelty, death, and pillage and then selling them as if they were pigs. . . . These bandits have other pretexts, and say that they bring the Indians into the church, as if God wished any infidel to be forced or captured to become a Christian. And they readily declared that their intention was merely to bring the Indians into the church when they took them from our reductions, where some were already Christians and others were catechumens receiving our Holy Faith in order to be baptized. Another more deceitful pretext is that they bring them to perform necessary service, and that they know they do wrong bringing them in the manner they do; but they say that there is no other remedy in this land, and that after the Indians arrive they keep them in their houses and on their farms, not as slaves but as free men. The matter would be less serious if it were as they say, and if they did not go about selling them for a bottle of wine or something else for them or their wives and children to eat or wear, as is common knowledge to everyone of this state. However, the truth is that the Indians whom they have in their houses have liberty in name only, and they are used accordingly, as though they were slaves from Guinea. The situation would be quite different in this land if each were content to live according to his condition, and if all did not wish to be hidalgos supporting themselves, their wives, and children with this infamous merchandise acquired by so much theft and pillage. They also offer as a pretext for having plundered our villages this time that the Indians whom we were instructing were subjects of the Crown of Portugal, to which we reply that although the Spanish have more basis for their belief that they belong to the Crown of Castile, since they are close to the Spanish towns of Guairá and Villa Rica and for other reasons, we do not establish our arguments on this point, nor do we attempt to define the limits or boundaries of realms. We merely gather and instruct the Indians in their own lands where we find them, and if they belong now to the Crown of Spain and now to that of Portugal, we do not take them from one to the other. And, all the more, if these Indians belong to the Crown of Portugal as the Portuguese claim, why do they dare to capture them in defiance of so many and such explicit laws of His Majesty and the previous kings of Portugal . . . in which it is forbidden to capture the Indians of the state of Brazil or to carry them off by force? And these laws declare all men, Christians and infidels alike, and even those not yet gathered in reductions, to be free and emancipated, as they are by nature. . . .

What we aspire to and came to seek on such long and wearying journeys by land and sea, with such toil and hardship, is some effective remedy for the past and for what is to come. For the past, we feel that there can be no proper satisfaction unless all the captured Indians are given their freedom, and unless all or most of them are returned to their lands and the reductions. In this way they can bear witness to those of their lands that we are innocent, that we did not deliver them to the Portuguese, and that we took measures here to try and secure their freedom. And moreover they can remove the bad opinion which the infidels not yet in reductions have already formed of us of the Company, that we are traitors and deceivers, and thus we would regain the credit which we enjoyed with them and without which it seems impossible to convert them to Our Holy Faith. As for the future, let some very exemplary punishment be fixed, or in some other fashion let an order be given that extortions and enslavements such as the men of São Paulo have carried on for so many years be henceforth prevented. . . .

It is said that simply the band of Antônio Rapôso Tavares which plundered our villages carried away as many as twenty thousand souls, and it is therefore certain that if a very genuine remedy is not supplied in the briefest time, they will soon destroy everything and depopulate these populous lands as they have done in most of the state of Brazil. . . .

There were those who for five, and others . . . who for seven continuous years, and even those who for eighteen years neglected their salvation and remained in those wilds capturing Indians and living in concubinage with as many Indian women as they wished. They lived like beasts without thinking of their homes and legitimate wives or hearing Mass or confessing or taking communion in all this time. Those who went on this most recent entrada spent nine months without observing Advent, Lent, and Resurrection, or fulfilling their obligations to Our Holy Mother Church. Therefore if some remedy is not found to halt these entradas, it appears that we might as well forget all of our remaining reductions and all those numerous and countless heathen for whose conversion the King Our Lord not only sends us from Europe with so many expenses but also sustains us among the Indians with his royal alms. . . .

In this City of Salvador Bahia de Todos os Santos, October 10, 1629.

SIMÓN MACETA—JUSTO MANSILLA.

5

GASPAR DA MADRE DE DEUS

✻

A Defense of the Paulistas

Brother Gaspar da Madre de Deus (1715-1800) was a Benedictine friar who chronicled the history of the captaincy of São Vicente. Writing after the close of the bandeirante era, he claims the Paulistas to have been loyal and law-abiding, if somewhat haughty, subjects of the Portuguese king. Here he tells the incident of the "acclamation" of Amador Bueno, a Spanish-descended Paulista to whom his fellow townsmen, instigated by the Spaniards among them, offered the crown of an independent Paulista nation.

The incident conveys a sense both of Paulista separatism and of the region's internal factionalism. Although Amador Bueno refused the crown, and this episode had no further consequences, the following years saw the society torn by conflicts that centered on a vendetta between the Pires and Camargo families. Such "clan" rivalries accentuated the centrifugalism of the settlement process as seen in the proliferation of new towns on the plateau and along the Paraíba valley in the seventeenth century. They must also have influenced the dynamics of the bandeirante movement.

From Gaspar da Madre de Deus, *Memorias para a historia da Capitania de S. Vicente, hoje chamada de S. Paulo, do Estado do Brazil* (Lisbon, 1797), pp. 60-62, 127-34.

The example of the Islands of the Azores and Madeira, and the hope of being as fortunate as the Spaniards, who had discovered immense riches in the part of America which they were settling, led many good people to that town [São Vicente] since it was the first regular colony of Portuguese in the New World. Everyone had seen the very opulent and distinguished houses owned by the descendants of nobles and fidalgos whose poverty had brought them to the aforesaid islands in the first years of their settlement. And the hope of securing more certain happiness in a country where much gold was expected to be discovered had moved [these new settlers] to leave their homelands. Some quickly recognized their error and returned to Europe disillusioned, for in Brazil, where all received more free land than they needed, no one would be forced to work on the lands of another and thus obliged to pay annual rents. And therefore never, or only after several centuries, would luxurious houses come to be permanent. Experience has shown that they reasoned wisely, because in this state he who does not engage in business or who lacks slaves lives in the greatest indigence. What is more, it is not enough to own many slaves to be rich, for these are of no utility to their masters if the latter are not industrious and do not personally superintend their slaves.

The nobility of these captaincies is composed of the noble companions of the first donatary who remained here, some whom he sent at first and others who came in numbers thereafter, not only from Portugal and the Islands but also from Spain when the two crowns were united. They were attracted by the fertility of the country and by the gold mines then being discovered. This nobility remained pure, recognized, and much respected until shortly after the discovery of the general mines, principally in São Paulo and the upland towns. I have just said that in Brazil anyone is poor who does not engage in business or who has no slaves to cultivate his lands, and no one ignores the fact that in all the world wealth is customarily the support of nobility. The Paulistas of old were not without servants, for the reason that our laws and those of Spain, while we were subject to her, permitted them to enslave Indians taken prisoner in a just war and to administer them in conformance with the conditions prescribed by these laws. They therefore had a great number of Indians, as well as Negro slaves from the coast of Africa, and with these everyone cultivated much land and lived in opulence.

They were able to give many lands, Indians, and Negroes in dowry to their daughters, which allowed them to live well. In choosing husbands for their daughters, therefore, they paid more attention to the birth than to the capital of prospective sons-in-law. Generally the daughters were given in marriage to their fellow countrymen and relatives, or to outsiders of recognized nobility. When a person of this station arrived from Europe or from other Brazilian captaincies he was certain of a good marriage even if he were poor. The Paulistas of old were disinterested and generous, although excessively proud. Because of this haughtiness of spirit they sometimes begged His Majesty to send them only generals and governors of the first nobility of the Realm. Formerly they had looked down on commerce, but after laws prohibiting the capture and administration of the Indians were put into effect many of the leading men were obliged to marry their daughters to rich men who could support them. It is for this reason that many natives of the captaincy of São Paulo can demonstrate nobility and high birth from the fourth to the eighth generation of their forebears. . . .

. . . [It] is true that the inhabitants of the captaincy of São Vicente, particularly those of the highlands, sometimes forgot the laws of God and man respecting the full freedom of the Indians. But it must be confessed that the morally certain hope of pardon[1] and the experience of the concessions so often granted on this score in the interests of the State— above all its interest in discovering gold, an enterprise strongly urged upon the Paulistas by the Court—were the principal cause for their transgressing the laws and for abusing the occasional provisos whereby these laws did permit the capture or administration of Indians. It is also true, however, that if the original inhabitants of this captaincy were blameworthy in this respect until a certain time, so too were

---

[1] The first thing the governors general would do on the many occasions when they called upon the Paulistas for some important service was to give pardon in the name of the king for the crime of organizing *entradas* into the *sertão* when these were prohibited.

the Portuguese of other Brazilian colonies, particularly Maranhão and Pará, as is confirmed by some of our authors, the archives of these same colonies, and the laws promulgated at different times concerning the Indians. Yet there is one circumstance that makes a great difference in this case. The Paulistas had the misfortune (if the word is appropriate here) to become involved with the Jesuits of Paraguay and of their captaincy, and consequently to offend the whole Society [of Jesus], whose writings carried far and wide to denigrate the Paulistas before the world. But in the end time has made clear that these same Jesuits, who cried out so much in behalf of the aborigines of America, were the ones who held them in rigorous subjugation over the largest area. The Indians were freed from it in the states of Brazil and Pará by the provident laws enacted for these poor vassals' welfare by King Dom Joseph of glorious memory. Other charges made against the Paulistas by Vaissete and Charlevoix[2] are calumnies published by these said Jesuits, and also by certain Spaniards, because their cities of Jerez, Ciudad Real, and Villa Rica were destroyed by the Paulistas, who considered that they were located in Portuguese lands.

The existence of the Republic of São Paulo was a secret revealed to foreigners by some false prophet and hidden from all the Portuguese. If I had not read what Vaissete and other French authors write about the captaincy of São Paulo, I certainly would not have believed that things are being written in France in this century with such lack of judgment and that enlightened men condone such impostures. It is not only of this captaincy and the others of Brazil that these same authors speak with such falsity and exaggeration, but also of all the other peoples outside civilized Europe. The causes of all these gross errors which are flooding the Republic of Letters are the false reports which the authors follow; the desire to ridicule and disparage all that does not conform to French customs; and finally the presumption of choosing to decide in a study those things that are difficult enough to determine when seen with one's own eyes.

From its founding to the present São Paulo never recog-

---

[2] See Jean Joseph Vaissete, *Géographie historique, ecclesiastique et civile* (4 vols.; Paris, 1755), IV, 383-87, 412-13; Pierre François Xavier de Charlevoix, *The History of Paraguay* (2 vols.; London, 1769), I, 303-463. [Ed.]

nized any sovereign other than the kings of Portugal, who always held supreme dominion in the captaincy of São Vicente, even though the captaincy was subject to its donatary. Therefore its inhabitants never observed any laws but the general ones for the whole Portuguese Monarchy, as was stipulated in the grant and charter given by King Dom João III. Moreover they gave obedience to the donataries, and also to the captains major and judges appointed by them or by whoever had proper jurisdiction. These captains major and judges registered their letters patent and assumed office in the council of the capital town of the captaincy, and nothing more was necessary for them to be obeyed in the town of São Paulo and the other highland settlements which were being founded.

The governors of the state and the senior judges exercised the same authority over São Paulo that they did over the other towns of their jurisdiction. All the orders of these superiors were registered with its town council when they so provided. And if some orders which seemed just were not complied with, others were often executed which were notoriously despotic, and abusive of the powers vested in these governors and judges by the King, as is documented in these *Memórias*. The town of São Paulo was also subject to the governors of Rio de Janeiro in matters of war; to the general administrators of the mines discovered and yet to be discovered in their districts; and finally to the superintendents assigned to the Royal Treasury and the Treasury of the Dead and Missing, who were named by the King or, if not a royal appointment, by the governor general. The only local town magistrates were the lesser judges and the town senate, but even these were in conformance with the ordinances of the realm. In short, the government of São Paulo was never different from that of the other towns. In the archives one continually finds the most convincing proofs of this truth.

I have often observed that the fables published in their histories by foreigners concerning the captaincy of São Vicente are all, or mostly all, based on some fact which is distorted by the writers. To this category belongs the fabrication that the mamelucos shook off the yoke of Divine and human authority, as Charlevoix claims. It is quite natural that this fable should have its origin in one of the most notable occurrences of the past history of São Paulo, and because

I find it interesting I shall relate in substance what happened.

The news arrived in São Paulo [1641] that in the capital town of São Vicente Luís Dias Leme had acclaimed the Most Serene Lord Duke of Bragança as king under the name Dom João IV, at the order and behest of Jorge Mascarenhas, Marquis of Montalvo and Viceroy of Brazil, transmitted in private correspondence. This unexpected news dealt a heavy blow to the Spaniards, who were well established and married in the town of São Paulo, where they had flocked both from Europe and from the West Indies. They wished to maintain the plateau settlements in obedience to Spain. However, they did not dare make their intentions public, for they knew that they would be victims sacrificed to the wrath of the Paulistas if they should counsel the latter to remain under the hated Spanish yoke. Among themselves they therefore decided to use trickery, hoping to gain through cunning what they could not hope to obtain if their designs were found out.

They were certain that the captaincy of São Vicente, and almost the whole Brazilian sertão, would before many years be reunited with the Spanish Indies, either by force of arms or by artifice, if (given the communication that existed along various rivers between the plateau towns and the Provinces of the Plata and Paraguay) the Paulistas should become divided over the issue of separation from Portugal and should erect an independent government of whatever nature. With this in view, and affecting to be filled with love of the country in which they were naturalized and with zeal for the common good, the Spaniards proposed to their friends, relatives, allies, and others the means that seemed most certain to achieve their object—namely, to elect a Paulista king. As the one most worthy of the crown they named Amador Bueno da Ribeira, thus choosing a man unlikely to be rejected by his countrymen, for he united in his person the qualities of genuine nobility, and much respect and authority for the public posts, past and present, which he had held; he was also esteemed for his great wealth, his circle of relatives and friends, and the marriages of his nine sons and daughters. Two of his daughters were married to Spanish hidalgos, the two brothers Dom João Mateus Rendon and Dom Francisco Rendon de Quevedo, who had come to Brazil in 1625 in the service of the Spanish armada sent for the restoration of Bahia [from the Dutch]. But in designating Amador Bueno da Ribeira the Spaniards were catering to themselves, for since he was the son of Bartolomeu Bueno da Ribeira, a native of Seville, it was more likely that the blood of his paternal grandparents would cause him to declare himself a vassal of Spain, and less likely that his maternal ancestors, being of the noble Pires family, and his own birth in a Portuguese province would cause him to follow the legitimate party of the other provinces of Brazil, the kingdom, and the conquests.

The Spaniards used every possible argument to persuade the Paulistas and the poorly informed Europeans that, without taxing their consciences or failing in their obligation as honorable men and faithful vassals, they could refuse to recognize as sovereign a prince to whom they had not yet sworn obedience. They also played upon the vanity of their listeners by exaggerating the prerogatives of the Paulistas and principal Europeans, saying that their personal qualities and inherited nobility qualified them for other, greater empires. To relieve them of their fears they reminded them of the thousands of Indians whom they administered, as well as the slaves, who could be organized into formidable armies of many thousands of combatants. They also reminded them of São Paulo's highly defensible and advantageous position at that time. Its only access to the seaports was by the treacherous Paranapiacaba route; to turn back the assailants in defeat it would be enough to roll rocks down the mountains.

The inhabitants of São Paulo were sincere, and even though they were loyal very few of them had the necessary education to recognize the incontestable right of the Most Serene House of Bragança to the scepter, or to perceive the snares and dire misfortunes into which such machinations might cast them. Moreover, the plebs everywhere is easily moved and aroused to excesses. The Spaniards managed to seduce them and to assemble a large number of people of all classes who, unanimously acclaiming Amador Bueno da Ribeira as their king, thronged to his house in great joy and enthusiasm to congratulate him.

Amador Bueno da Ribeira was astonished to learn of this proposal; he resented the insult of those who advanced it, and with effective arguments he tried to make them realize their guilt and blind indiscretion. He reminded them of the obligation they had to conform to the vows of the entire kingdom, and the dishonor to their country if they did not rectify the error of their criminal attempt with voluntary and prompt obedience. But the displeasure of the candidate increases the obstinacy of ignorant people; they go so far as to threaten him with death if he does not grasp the scepter. In consternation the loyal vassal left his house furtively, and, carrying his sword unsheathed to defend himself if need be, he hastened toward the monastery of St. Benedict where he intended to seek refuge. Those in the crowd noticed when he left by the garden gate, and they all ran after him shouting: "Long live Amador Bueno our King!" to which he answered repeatedly in a loud voice: "Long live Dom João IV, our King and Lord, for whom I will give my life!"

Arriving at the monastery, Amador Bueno da Ribeira went in and quickly closed the doors. As the Paulistas of old greatly revered the priests, especially the regulars, no one violated the monastery, and all remained outside persisting, however, in their rash demand. The abbot, accompanied by his community, came down to the vestibule and placated the multitude with cajolery while Amador Bueno da Ribeira urgently sent for the most respected ecclesiastics and a few of the leading citizens who did not appear in the crowd. Both groups soon arrived and, all taking Bueno's part, they made the crowd understand that the kingdom belonged to the Most Serene House of Bragança and that this House would have been in peaceful possession of it since the day of the death of the Cardinal King Dom Henrique, had not the violence of the Spanish monarchs usurped its right.

Nothing more was needed for these loyal Portuguese to conduct themselves as they should. Repentant for their outbreak, all were joyful in solemnly acclaiming Dom João IV, to the sorrow of the Spaniards who, unwilling to lose the advantages that they had come to obtain in São Paulo, also took the oath of fealty to the same sovereign. Two Paulistas, Luís da Costa Cabral and Baltasar de Borba Gato, were sent to the Court to kiss the Royal Hand of his Most Faithful Majesty in the name of the senate and the inhabitants of São Paulo. And the same Ruler condescended to express thanks for this act of obedience in a letter signed by his Royal Hand dated in Lisbon on September 24, 1643.

6

JAIME CORTESÃO

❀

The Greatest Bandeira
of the
Greatest Bandeirante

One of Jaime Cortesão's main scholarly concerns was to rescue Antônio Rapôso Tavares and the bandeirantes in general from the mists of a black legend. Dismissing the more exaggerated charges of cruelty leveled against them by the Jesuits, he reminds us that at the time of the Paulista raids on Paraguay the Inquisition at Lima enjoyed the cooperation of the Jesuit Order in persecuting true Catholics "merely because they were Portuguese and rich." Cortesão relied on bold hunches and extensive research to develop his thesis that the bandeirante-Jesuit conflict produced a clash of national interests in America which hastened the restoration of Portuguese independence in 1640 and created the geopolitical interests of a new Brazilian "state." Because of its alleged service to these interests, Cortesão considered Rapôso Tavares's herculean bandeira of 1648-51 as "the greatest bandeira of the greatest bandeirante."

Excerpted from Jaime Cortesão, "A maior bandeira do maior bandeirante," *Revista de História*, XXII, 45 (Jan.-March 1961), 3-27. Translated; and printed by permission of the *Revista de História*.

Jaime Cortesão (1884-1960) was a Portuguese historian who lived in exile after 1927; in 1940 he made
his home in Rio de Janeiro. He wrote widely in Portuguese and Brazilian history and edited many collections
of documents. In his early years he published verse,
drama, and short stories. This essay is a lecture given
at the University of São Paulo which summarizes some
themes from his book, *Rapôso Tavares e a formação
territorial do Brasil* (Rio de Janeiro, 1958).

Brazilian historians have considered Antônio Rapôso Tavares to be the greatest of all bandeirantes. However, the
most ambitious of his ventures is veiled by uncertainties.

In this case when we say the greatest bandeirante we mean
it in respect to the geographic and geopolitical scope of his
expeditions. If we raise the expedition which will concern us
to the rank of the greatest exploring enterprise ever carried
out in the two Americas as one continuous exertion by a
single group of men, we are considering it also as an essentially political bandeira, of a state in formation, which in
one gigantic effort tried to establish the possible boundaries
between the two great Iberian domains in South America.

As geographic explorers, these dozens of heroes who jour-
neyed from São Paulo to Belém do Pará reflect the grandeur
of the world they invaded. But if we consider them as social
types, shaped by the age, the setting, the action, and a rare
ingredient of regional character, there were without doubt a
very few even greater bandeirantes, with perhaps Fernão
Dias Pais the greatest of the great. Moreover, Rapôso
Tavares represents a different type of expansion. An epic
figure, yet a poorly known one, who in the mid-seventeenth
century accomplished a superhuman endeavor across vast
and totally unknown distances—his personality understanda-
bly took on legendary splendor.

The myth of a vast Brazil-Isle, circumscribed by the Plata
and the Amazon, had its mythical hero. This idealized dis-
tortion received its fullest expression, as is generally known,

in the *Quadro histórico* of Machado de Oliveira.[1] According to him:

> Antônio Rapôso, leading a band of 60 men who were as audacious and adventurous as their valiant caudillo, with a retinue of a few Indians, crossed Brazil from the southeast to the northwest. Scaling the Andes he reaches Peru, penetrates that country, enters the waters of the Pacific with his naked sword held high, declaring that he has subjugated land and sea for his king. At times he is compelled to face and do battle with the Spaniards, whom he always subdues. Leaving the ancient empire of the Incas and heading toward the Amazon, he navigates that river on log rafts, following its current. He lands at Curupá, where he is generously welcomed by the inhabitants, who are astounded at the great daring of the Paulista. Rapôso Tavares's return across the sertões which lie between the two regions took years, and at the end he was so disfigured that his family and relatives failed to recognize him.

This is the legend, but a legend of political and epic character in which the hero, interpreted from a national point of view, carries Portuguese sovereignty from the Atlantic to the Pacific.

Later came the reaction, and Brazilian historians tried to discern and define the true figure through the mists of legend. To the eminent public figure and historian Washington Luís we are indebted for the first solidly documented monograph with this new emphasis, which is still today an indispensable guide and an exemplary model for applying the historico-geographic method.[2]

Relying on known documents, Washington Luís supposed that the bandeira of Rapôso Tavares left São Paulo along the Peabiru, headed for the Paraná where it joins the Paranapanema; then following the Paraná to the Paraguay

---

[1] José Joaquim Machado de Oliveira, *Quadro historico da provincia de S. Paulo até o anno de 1822* (2nd ed.; São Paulo, 1897). [Ed.]

[2] Washington Luís Pereira de Sousa, "Antonio Raposo," *Revista do Instituto Historico e Geographico de São Paulo,* IX (1905), 485-535. [Ed.]

he probably turned north to embark on the Guaporé, navigating down it and the Madeira to reach the Amazon. . . .

Among the documents which Washington Luís never saw, there stands out above all a letter by Father Antônio Vieira. Unfortunately, the only known copy is very damaged, but the original was written early in 1654 and based on the testimony of several bandeirantes who were then in Belém do Pará and with whom the great Jesuit had spoken in October, 1653. . . . Another document, disclosed by Paulo Prado . . . is a report by the secretary of the Overseas Council [of Portugal] on "the people of São Paulo" addressed to the king in 1674, or 23 years after the feat of the bandeira. This report extends its route through the Andes to Quito, whence Rapôso Tavares might have gone down the Amazon to Belém. Paulista historians hesitated and were divided over this version. . . .

Our own efforts, although in a field so fully plowed by such great pioneers, were crowned with success, at least with respect to determining the geographic extent of the expedition. We were able to discover a series of documents, some of Spanish and particularly Jesuit origin, others of Portuguese, and most of them unpublished, which permit us to complete and clarify Vieira's account and thus to trace, along general lines, the route of the bandeira. . . . Critical analysis of the whole of the available documents leads us to the conclusion that the bandeira reached the Andes but did not journey through them; and that after having visited La Plata and one or a few nearby cities it descended from this region to the Amazon basin. Thus, history approximates the legend, not only in regard to the scope of the enterprise but also, we assume, in regard to its political aspect.

Since we are forced to limit the theme of this lecture, in schematic form, to the geographic and geopolitical aspect of the bandeira, we shall simply suggest, however briefly, the geographic, economic, inter-social, historical, and political conditions which explain this undertaking.

From the geographic point of view, we must bear in mind that the basin of the Plata, unfolding in the general direction of the meridian along the axis of the Paraná-Paraguay, opens several natural route systems along the respective tributaries that extend in the direction of the parallel between the Atlantic and the Andes. In 1524 the Portuguese Aleixo Garcia had already proceeded along one of these systems from the shores of the present state of Santa Catarina to the silver-bearing region of the Andes, at that time still under Incan rule. In the mid-sixteenth century the inhabitants of São Vicente departed from those same shores and from Cananéia to follow the Pequiri and, crossing the Paraná and the Maracaju range, to go down the Jejui and the Paraguay to Asunción. . . . During the first half of the seventeenth century more than one troop of bandeirantes still used this or a similar route.

From the economic standpoint it is worth noting that São Paulo offered a striking contrast with the cities of seventeenth-century Peru. The latter, especially Lima, Potosí, La Plata (Sucre), and Cuzco, were then the great centers of commerce, wealth, and culture for all of South America. The silver and mercury mines, in full and increasing production until 1630, sustained this flourishing economy with little effort by the Spaniards. Lima, linked by its port of Callao with Panama, and by the route through Cuzco, Potosí, and Tucumán with Buenos Aires, had become the commercial and cultural metropolis of all southern America, a kind of Mecca for all foreigners (particularly Portuguese) who were avid for lucrative business or whose activities were useful only in fully prosperous and developing urban centers.

At the other extreme São Paulo was a small city of vigorous, enterprising, active people, accustomed to the severest toil and exertion, but living with no comforts and the most modest resources. Other Brazilian cities, such as Bahia, Pernambuco, and Rio de Janeiro, whose economy was based on the cultivation and processing of sugar cane, were already enjoying more prosperous conditions of life. This same source of wealth, which required the large-scale importation of Negroes from Angola and Guinea, had made Brazil the clandestine intermediary for the traffic in slave labor which was likewise so necessary to the mining industry of Peru. And, if the silver of the Andes sharply intensified commerce and accumulation of wealth in Brazil, the Negro slave coming from Brazilian ports, or from Angola by way of these ports, had become more and more the instrument indispensable for the industrial activities of the Andean plateau. If we add to the Negro slaves the sugar, the fazendas, the rich furniture, and various food products, we can conclude that Portuguese and Spanish America were, from the economic standpoint, complementary regions. . . .

This important distinction within a unitary economic system was the irresistible stimulus and attraction which led Portuguese and Portuguese-Brazilians to establish themselves in Peru. In spite of all the prohibitive laws which barred foreigners, the Portuguese being in no way an exception, the latter, thanks to the important services they could offer and to their commercial products, easily overcame the barriers of the Spanish monopoly and flocked by the thousands to Peru, whether via Porto Bello in Panama or via Buenos Aires on the Plata. Others (and this was the case of the Paulistas) because of the lack of a land barrier tried with success to cross the sertão and enter Peru; they either established themselves there or returned to their place of origin.

Merely in skimming one by one through the national histories of Brazil, Argentina, Paraguay, Peru, Ecuador, and Colombia, and the vast documentation on which the narratives rest, we become aware of the enormous importance of the clandestine Luso-Spanish exchange that transcended the imaginary boundaries of the two crowns in America, uniting interests and transmitting mutual influences and patterns of culture.

In the Peru of precious metals as in the cities of the Plata region and Tucumán the Portuguese, besides engaging in trade, contributed to the development and prosperity of Spanish America in other diverse ways. . . .

If the Portuguese flocked more to Lima because of the facilities for work and comforts of life that the metropolis offered, they nonetheless formed an equally important and very active part of the population of the mining cities, especially Potosí, La Plata, and Cuzco. The first two cities lay directly at the end of a road opened by the Guarani Indians during the Incaic period which, as we have said, was traveled by the Portuguese Aleixo Garcia before any other European.

Ambitious and tireless wayfarers of the sertões, how did the Paulistas respond to the appeal that was so seductive for so many thousands of Portuguese?

There are many documents and historical references from which one concludes that the Paulistas of that period entered Peru by two routes: the first, that of Asunción, whence one continued to Santa Fe; the other, a route leading directly across the sertão to the cities of La Plata and Potosí. The first was the normal route for those intending to remain in Peru for some time, while the second was used by those making a rapid foray to return immediately to São Paulo bringing Indians from the Sierra and large or small cargoes of silver. Although this second route was much shorter, it was infinitely more difficult and risky, owing to the obstacles presented by the inhospitable plains of the Chaco and the Indians, particularly the Paiaguá and the Guaicuru. . . .

By one or the other of these routes, certainly, many Paulistas reached Peru. Of this fact we have authentic testimony. Father Ruiz de Montoya, who as we know was from Lima, when he was sent to Madrid in 1638 as General Procurator of the Jesuit Province of Paraguay to argue before Felipe IV against the Paulista forays, referred in his report to the four scourges and dangers that resulted from these invasions. . . .

This is to say, as early as 1638 it was feared that the Paulistas, by forming a direct line from São Paulo across to Potosí, with the help of the Chiriguano Indians, might make some attempt against Spanish sovereignty in Peru. And it was already implied in the Jesuit's report that Antônio Rapôso Tavares, "the principal author of these damages," was the possible agent for the threat.

In his decree of September 16, 1639, Felipe IV turned over to the Holy Office of the Inquisition the bandeirantes accused by Montoya, and especially Antônio Rapôso Tavares, "the captain major appointed for those entradas" that "cause particular concern when they approach the provinces of Peru." Here it is also stated that in the year 1638 the Paulistas were in the province of Itatim, 80 leagues from Santa Cruz de la Sierra, which is about as many leagues from Potosí.

Having defined the problem thus, namely, in the transnational perspective, we can no longer be surprised that a bandeira commanded by this same Rapôso Tavares should have reached Peru, or rather, the Andean cities of colonial Peru.

During the first years of his reign (1640-56) two problems regarding the relation between Spanish and Portuguese America were to concern Dom João IV: the problem of the geographic extension of Brazil after the exploration of the upper Paraguay and after the voyage of Pedro Teixeira who in 1639 took possession of the Amazon basin as far as the

Japurá in the name of the Portuguese crown; and the economic and political problem resulting from the war with Spain and the interruption of Brazil's maritime trade with Buenos Aires, whence came the greater part of the silver currency which circulated in Brazilian cities.

Until the year of Pedro Teixeira's voyage the Portuguese imagined Brazil to be an island bounded by the River Plata and the Tocantins-Araguaia. These are still the boundaries of the state of Brazil on the 1640 chart of João Teixeira. But possession of the immense Amazon delta made the Portuguese realize how precarious their sovereignty over this part of the Brazilian territory would be if the Amazon valley were to fall completely into the hands of the Spaniards. This elementary observation was responsible for the expedition of Pedro Teixeira and his act of possession.

A series of unpublished documents from Portuguese archives, copies of which we possess, leads to the firm conclusion that Pedro Teixeira's expedition was essentially political in nature, for it was ordered by the governor of Maranhão, Jácome de Noronha, with the express purpose of establishing the boundaries of the State, along the upper Japurá, and founding a settlement at this point which would indicate to the Spaniards the limits of their domain. So clear is this objective that it even appears to us to be an initiative from Lisbon taken by the nationalist party that was preparing the Restoration of Portuguese independence. . . .

Once war was declared in the Peninsula between Portugal and Spain and Portuguese trade with the River Plata was forbidden by the Spanish government, there occurred the devaluation of Portuguese currency and, more important, an extreme shortage of the silver that came from Peru via Buenos Aires and via the sertão—two misfortunes having severe impact upon the economy of Brazil. Dom João IV made an effort to maintain peace in America and with it the lucrative traffic between Brazilian ports and Buenos Aires. In 1642 he sent two orders on this subject to the governor of Brazil. Spain, ever fearful of Portuguese infiltration in her colonies, especially in Peru, was violently opposed to these designs. A large number of royal orders attest that the Portuguese monarch then attempted personally and with enthusiasm to activate the search for gold and silver mines, whether in the south or in Amazônia, such was the monetary imbalance created by the intransigency of Spain and the depleted treasury of a country at war.

Salvador Correia de Sá [governor of Rio de Janeiro, 1637-43], consulted on the situation in Lisbon, where he was living toward the end of 1643, was of the opinion that the conquest of Buenos Aires should be attempted and the inhabitants of São Paulo simultaneously exhorted "to advance across the sertão upon Paraguay, because from there more help can be sent down the River to the inhabitants" of that city. . . .

About the middle of 1647 Dom João IV, who had resolved to move his court to Brazil, thus anticipating Dom João VI, was obliged to address the most serious problems of his jeopardized reign, which included the geographic formation of the State of Brazil in view of the dreamed-of mines of gold and silver, and the needs for defense or offense *vis-à-vis* the Viceroyalty of Peru.

As we have just seen, geographic and, more importantly, economic conditions on a continental scale, as well as historical and political factors, all combined to the same effect. The scheme of extending the boundaries of Brazil to the River Plata or to the Andes was in the air. Predicted by the Spanish Jesuits, it was planned by a Portuguese Jesuit. The only need was for someone to put it into practice. The direct testimony of three of the bandeirantes is convincing evidence that the great expedition of Rapôso Tavares was inspired by the factors we have just examined. The least important of his objectives, certainly, was the capture of Indians. His primary ones were the search for gold or silver mines and geographical information that would resolve the problem of boundaries with Spanish America. . . .

We are dealing with an essentially geopolitical problem of a State in formation and change, goaded by war and economic pressures. To solve this problem a man was needed who would couple the qualities of an experienced explorer of the sertão with an awareness of the geographic and political necessities of Brazil at this critical moment of expansion, along with the unselfish zeal of a citizen ready to sacrifice personal interests to those of the community.

Such a man existed. Antônio Rapôso Tavares, a Portuguese from Alemtejo, possessed that rare set of qualities. Having arrived in Brazil with his father in about 1618, already twenty years old, he was by 1648, thirty years later, the bandeirante of most prestige in the captaincy of São Vicente, whence he carried out the first grandiose efforts to extend Portuguese sovereignty to the South and West.

In 1641, when the Portuguese Restoration and the monarch Dom João IV are acclaimed in São Paulo, the signature of Rapôso Tavares appears on the act of Acclamation second only to that of the emissary who had brought the news. He deserved the honor. For in 1639-40 he had been the first organizer and commander of the one hundred fifty Paulistas who had been recruited at his own expense to help the Portuguese and Portuguese-Brazilians in the fight against the Dutch. . . .

In April of 1642 . . . he was deputized by the town councilmen of Parnaíba, receiving general rights of representation "in all the captaincy, in all Brazil, and in the Kingdom of Portugal, before Our Lord Dom João IV and wherever necessary in the said Kingdom." From then until 1648 there is no trace of his activity in Brazil. We are therefore inclined to believe that he spent some of these years in Portugal. . . .

According to Vieira, the Rapôso Tavares expedition was composed "of 200 Portuguese and more than 1,000 armed Indians, divided into two troops. The first troop was commanded by field master Antônio Rapôso Tavares, who was also in charge of the whole force, and the second by captain Antônio Pereira."

In May of 1648 the expeditionaries left São Paulo, downstream along the Tietê. . . . The main force of Rapôso Tavares headed directly to the region where Corumbá is now located, which was Albuquerque in the eighteenth century and Puerto de San Fernando in the sixteenth. This was the traditional crossing point, identified on Jesuit maps as a *paso*. Here the Portuguese Aleixo Garcia crossed in 1524 and, in 1537, Ayolas, guided by one of Garcia's Indians; both were headed for the empire of the Incas, which they reached in the Andean region of the upper Rio Grande or Guapaí. . . . Rapôso Tavares must have "wintered" here, in the Spanish Jesuits' expression, that is, spent the rainy season and ordered that crops be sown while he waited for Pereira de Azevedo's troop. . . . In April or May of 1649, when the bandeira was finally formed, it must have followed the normal route through the São José range, passing north of the marshes of Izozog, then on to the region of the Serrano Indians. . . .

Father Antônio Vieira waxes hyperbolic over the hardships suffered by this bandeira, especially from the crossing of the Paraguay to the embarkation on the Rio Grande. A month after the attack on the reduction of Mboymboy, he states in his letter: "Its perpetrators were punished by famine, plague, and war. The plague was such that not one of them escaped dire sickness; the famine was almost extreme, for roots and fruit from all the trees were all that the sick could hope for. . . . Moreover, in the midst of this weakness and helplessness they were continually attacked by savages on foot and horseback who showered them with arrows." And he called these ordeals "the worst sufferings that were ever undergone." . . .

Vieira, who so harshly censures these same bandeirantes for their offenses against the Spanish Jesuits, one of whom died in combat, does not hesitate to declare of their enterprises, in a moment of amazement, "that it was truly one of the most notable accomplished in the world before this day."

But were these bandeirantes as impious and cruel to the priests of the company as Vieira and his Spanish colleagues affirm *una voce?* Upon carefully reading the letters and accounts of the latter, one discovers that such was not the case.

It is understandable that these men, who could gamble their own lives so easily, would not be any more respectful of the lives of others. They applied to others the law of danger by which they themselves lived. Their life, so replete with fearful hardships, had not the same value that ours has for us. And Father [Bernabé de] Bonilla, in describing the attack by the troop of Antônio Pereira on Itatim in November, 1648, refers to the detention of Father Cristóbal de Arenas for a few days and confesses: "I am ashamed of the treatment given the Company in the City of Asunción [by the Spaniards] when I hear Father C. de Arenas tell of the courtesy which these enemies rendered him in word and in deed for his sustenance and comfort, with such largesse that he felt compassion for them." . . .

These men, therefore, who were guilty of blind rages and acts of violence, were also capable of courtesy, humaneness, and nobility.

In conclusion: The bandeira of Rapôso Tavares was essentially an expedition of geographic and mineral discovery, and it was related to the problem of boundaries and to the financial and political difficulties with which the Kingdom struggled after the restoration of Independence.

It was also the first expedition of geographic exploration to cover the entire continental expanse of South America between the shores of the Atlantic and the Andean cordillera, between the Tropic of Capricorn and the Equator, extending for some twenty-three degrees of latitude and twenty of longitude. It was the longest and most arduous of all the expeditions carried out in the whole of America, not only up to that time but until the beginning of the nineteenth century. If we omit the Andean journey and consider only the route by river from the Tietê to the Paraguay, thence by land to the Guapaí and then down the Madeira and the Amazon to Belém: this vast trajectory measures approximately 10,000 kilometers. If we add the Chaco excursion and the detours in the region of the Andean cities, it will certainly exceed 12,000 kilometers.

To mention only the more notable expeditions before and after that of Rapôso Tavares: Orellana's discovery of the Amazon in 1541, although epic in its daring, was limited to descending that river, always in the same latitudes. The expeditions of La Salle, the great French explorer of the Mississippi between 1679 and 1682, took place in a temperate climate and almost entirely in the direction of the meridian. Two expeditions, those of Lewis and Clark who between 1804 and 1806 explored the middle and upper Missouri and followed the Columbia to the Pacific, although outstanding for their daring and their results, took place in a continental area of thirty-three degrees of longitude but narrow in latitude, and therefore a much smaller theater.

Perhaps in conclusion the best way to define the personality of Rapôso Tavares would be to compare him to another of the great bandeirantes who were his peers.

We said at the start that Fernão Dias Pais stood forth as the prototype of the bandeirante; that is, he was the most evolved and distinguished with respect to the capacities and pagan virtues of his breed. Obedient to an Iberian concept and code of honor, he was a Quixote of the sertão who carried his obsession and sacrifice to the point of madness in his struggle with the fantastic windmill of the Emeralds. [See below, pp. 138-40.] Like the poets, philosophers, and mystics, he belongs by his will and by his actions to that rare breed who are infatuated with the Absolute. He reminds one of those terrifying Biblical patriarchs who sacrificed their sons to Jehovah; who endured, like Job, the devastating torrent of scourge and catastrophe inexorably faithful to their law; or who suffered a death agony, at once ecstatic and anguished in sight of the Promised Land.

There is something abstract and unreal about him that transcends the man himself. We know that he lived. We know his story through documents. And yet, crowned by the splendor of his deeds, he is more like one of those tutelary gods in whom peoples of rich imagination such as the ancient Greeks fused and idealized their greatest longings and virtues.

Less outstanding in his way of life and in his bandeirante character, and prototype of another kind of expansion, Rapôso Tavares yields nothing in stature to Fernão Dias. The greatest difference between them lies in the fact that the Governor of Esmeraldas lived, by his actions, turned toward the hinterland. He opened the golden doors of wealth and independence for his country. He was, in the rigorous sense of the word, a household god.

The other, Rapôso Tavares, master of the continental adventure, whose heroism also gleams of the unreal, looked toward the boundaries. In Guairá, as in Tape, Itatim, the Andes, or Amazônia, he sought to establish the ideal boundary with Spanish America—always conscious of the aim being achieved. At their initial depth he traced out the foundation of the nations of a continent. He was a boundary god, gazing into the distance, in every direction across two whole quadrants.

In exalting his heroic efforts and prowess, some Brazilian historians call Rapôso Tavares Homeric. Permit us a clarification. Homer's heroes were exposed to the horrors of the Mediterranean, an inland sea whose greatest length is not over 4,500 kilometers, and whose perils are not greater than the song of the sirens and the heavy sea between Scylla and Charybdis in the domestic Strait of Messina. If we are to compare the bandeirantes to great navigators we must then look to the discoverers who defy the stormy capes that divide the oceans. Like Vasco da Gama in the Indian Ocean or Ferdinand Magellan in the Pacific, Rapôso Tavares measured his stature against the two greatest monuments of their kind in nature: the Andes and the Amazon.

However extravagantly the word has been used and abused, we believe that Rapôso Tavares and his companions deserve by just title and right the more epic, more noble, more human, and more Brazilian epithet of Lusiads.

❋

7

The Conquest of Palmares

One famous exploit of the bandeirantes was their role in
the campaign against the "republic" of runaway Negro
slaves known as Palmares. Palmares was a *quilombo*
(fugitive community) made up of federated *mocambos*
(villages), subject to a supreme ruler, and showing African cultural influences. Located in the wild interior of
Pernambuco and Alagoas, the quilombo was formed in
about 1630. Its population increased swiftly when the
Dutch, who captured Olinda and Recife that year,
proved to be less vigilant of their slaves than the Portuguese.

The first of the documents which follow is by a Portuguese official who was the earliest to recognize the military dimensions of the challenge presented by Palmares.
Soon thereafter, several unsuccessful expeditions were
sent against the Negroes. In the second document a
later governor requests the king's permission to utilize
the military services of some Paulistas, "true sertanejos"
who were "roaming the sertões." The request was ap-
proved, and an elaborate contract was drawn up in
which the governor agreed to outfit the expedition while
the Paulistas, who had for years been colonizing in

From Ernesto Ennes, *As guerras nos Palmares* (Coleção Brasil-
iana, Vol. 127. São Paulo: Companhia Editora Nacional, 1938),
excerpted from pp. 133-34, 150-52, 204-07, 317-44, 352-55. Translated; and printed by permission of the Companhia Editora Nacional.

northeast Brazil, were promised lands in Palmares and the royal fifth of the slaves captured. The Paulistas underestimated the difficulties of the siege and failed in their first campaign of 1692. They were victorious in 1694, but only after being reinforced by troops from Alagoas and Pernambuco.

The third document is written by, and the fourth is in behalf of, the Paulista commander, Domingos Jorge Velho. Although the case has unique aspects, these reports tell much about the bandeirantes' way of life, their organization, their objectives, and their relation to various levels of Portuguese authority. The indelicate sketch of Domingos Jorge Velho in the final document suggests how he appeared to royal officials and why he had to plague them for years to fulfill their contractual obligations. In 1699 he went off to fight Indians in Maranhão, and he died four or five years later.

---

1. Letter from Governor Fernão de Sousa Coutinho dated June 1, 1671, concerning "the increase in the mocambos of insurgent Negroes present in Palmares"

Sire. For some years the Negroes from Angola who fled the rigors of captivity and the sugar mills of this captaincy have established numerous inland settlements between Palmares and the forests, where difficult access and lack of roads leave them better fortified by nature than they might be by human art. These settlements are growing daily in number and becoming so bold that their continual robberies and assaults are causing a large part of the inhabitants of this captaincy who live nearest the mocambos to leave their land. The example and permanence of the mocambos each day induces the other Negroes to flee and escape from the rigorous captivity which they suffer and to find freedom amid fertile land and the security of their own dwellings. One might fear that with these advantages they could grow to such numbers that they might move against the inhabitants of this captaincy, who are so few in relation to their slaves. To avoid this danger I intend to go to Pôrto Calvo with the entrada of this summer, which is the most suitable place from which to wage this war. From there, using bodies of men that will continually relieve each other, I will order roads opened to the above Palmares by means of which their settlements can be besieged and razed consecutively until all are destroyed and this captaincy is left free of the misfortune which so severely threatens it. For many are the obstacles confronting me in this plan, owing to the difficult terrain and the lack of roads and transportation for provisions, which throughout this State can be carried only on the backs of Negroes since there are no roads for wagons nor even for more than men traveling in single file. . . . And Your Highness may be sure that this State is in no less danger from the audacity of these Negroes than it was from the Dutch. For in their very houses and plantations the inhabitants have enemies who can overcome them if they should decide to follow the pernicious example and admonitions of those same rebels, who maintain contact with them, and who now have blacksmith shops and other workshops where they can manufacture weapons, since they already possess some fire-arms which they took from here. Also this sertão is so rich in metals and nitrate that it furnishes everything for their defense provided they have the skills, which it may be feared many fugitives do possess who are trained in all the crafts. And because irreparable harm generally results when such dangers are ignored, I decided to take measures against any which might arise from these.

May God succor me to free this captaincy of this disturbance, which for me will be the highest tribute of all the services which I hope to render Your Highness. May Our Lord protect the most lofty and powerful person of Your Highness as is the wish of us your vassals. Olinda, the first of June, 1671.

FERNÃO DE SOUSA COUTINHO

. . .

2. Request from the Governor of Pernambuco of November 7, 1685, in which he relates the new outrages and acts of tyranny committed in all those captaincies by the Negroes of Palmares

Sire. With the last fleet I sent an account to Your Majesty concerning the state in which I found the War of Palmares, in accordance with the information given me by my predecessor and what more I had gathered during the first few days of my term. Although I stood ready to give pardon in the name of Your Majesty so that [the rebels] might come and live peacefully in this captaincy, with the freedoms which Your Majesty concedes it in his royal orders, many complaints came to me from the town councils and people who surround them who dwell in these tyrannies to the effect that the latter have been killing the inhabitants, plundering their houses, and carrying off their slaves as captives. . . .

It also behooves me to tell Your Majesty that I received here a letter from some Paulistas who are roaming the sertões. It was written to my predecessor Dom João de Sousa, and in it they asked him for some letters patent for a captain major and various captains to go and conquer these heathen; as this went against Your Majesty's orders I did not dispatch the letters. Because these men are the true sertanejos and they have four hundred armed men, I have pleaded that they be used in this conquest of Palmares and that they be sent letters patent as its conquerors, and as protectors of the heathen of that district where they live, and that they be granted the . . . right of free booty. And once these Negroes are destroyed I promised that Your Majesty would bestow great honors and favors upon them, and that I would solicit them in the certainty that Your Majesty would esteem this service as a very great one. I therefore hope, sire, that these men, moved by the ambition of receiving Your Majesty's honors, will answer this call to arms. I will then be certain that the time has arrived for these rebels to meet their ruin, and I will have the pleasure of knowing that in my administration I secured many victories for Your Majesty, from whom I hope to receive approval for all these arrangements, since I wish to exercise great discretion in Your Majesty's service.

JOÃO DA CUNHA SOUTO MAIOR

. . .

3. A letter signed by Domingos Jorge Velho written from Barriga Hill, Campaign of Palmares, July 15, 1694, in which he describes the toil and sacrifices he underwent. . . .

Sire. . . . [Our] militia, sire, is unlike the Regular one which is found everywhere else. First, our troops with which we undertook the conquest of the savage heathen of this very vast sertão are not made up of people registered in Your Majesty's muster books, nor are they under obligation by wages or rations. They are groups in which some of us assemble, each one joining with the servants under arms that he possesses, and together entering the sertão of this continent—not to enslave (as some hypochondriacs would have Your Majesty believe) but to acquire the Tapuia, a fierce people who eat human flesh, so as to domesticate them to the knowledge of civilized life and human society and to association and rational dealings. In this way they will come to have that light of God and of the mysteries of the Catholic faith which is necessary for their salvation (for he who would make them angels before making them men labors in vain). And from those who are thus acquired and brought into settlements we enlarge our troops, and with them make war upon those who are obstinate and refractory to settlement. If afterwards we use them in our fields, we do them no injustice, for this is as much to support them and their children as to support us and ours. Far from enslaving them, we render them an unremunerated service by teaching them to till, plant, harvest, and work for their livelihood, something which until the whites teach them they know not how to do. Do you understand this, sire? . . .

Your Majesty's

Most humble, faithful, and loyal vassal

D.^{OS} JORGE VELHO
(signature)

.   .   .

4. Petition presented by one humbly prostrated at Your Majesty's feet in his name and in that of all the officers and soldiers of the São Paulo infantry regiment of which Domingos Jorge Velho is field master and which at present serves Your Majesty in the war of Palmares against the rebellious Negroes in the captaincies of Pernambuco

First: He begs that your royal Majesty see fit to consider that in the lower sertão of Brazil, in the captaincies of Pernambuco, a hideout for Negroes who had fled their masters was formed years ago which so many of them kept continually joining that one settlement was not enough for them all, and they founded many more in the immensity of these forests. These Negroes reached such numbers that they became a plague everywhere in the captaincies. So bold and insolent did they become that they attacked not only to steal household property from the inhabitants but also to incite and carry off their slaves, some willingly and others by force; they would kill the overseers and many times the masters and ladies, committing every form of aggression and always with cruelty. They had gained so much confidence in their forces that in a period of almost forty years the many expeditions sent with considerable authority by the governors of Pernambuco to conquer them were never successful and many were dispersed. . . . Finally the Governor of Pernambuco, João da Cunha de Souto Maior, disillusioned and knowing very well that neither a paid infantry nor a militia of the inhabitants was suited for such a war, received the news that in the upper sertão, about five hundred leagues from there, lived the said Field Master with many other men from São Paulo in his following and a great quantity of Indian warriors with whom they conquered the savages. He sent for them, directing his proposal to Domingos Jorge Velho as head of them all and the most powerful (since he alone had five or six times more followers than all the others together). . . .

Second: Without considering the great obstacles which confronted them in leaving the land where they were situated with settlements, farms, etc., and the great inconveniences of so long and continuous a march along so wild, dry, and sterile a route, which can only be understood by one who has traversed it, the said Field Master and his retinue set out in all possible haste with a thousand bowmen, two hundred with shotguns, and eighty-four white men to lead and command them. This march was made under the worst conditions of toil, hunger, thirst, and destitution that have yet been known and perhaps will ever be known in this sertão, unless the same ground were to be covered in the same space of time. Because of hunger, thirst, and suffering one hundred thirty-two persons died; sixty-three died from illness, and more than two hundred deserted because they could not bear such misery. And the greatest deprivation was always that suffered by the Field Master.

Third: Thinking that they had been summoned for a war, it was only after they had almost reached Palmares that the Field Master received an order from Governor General Matias da Cunha commanding him almost to withdraw . . . and not to continue his march but to proceed with all speed to the aid of the inhabitants of the captaincy of Rio Grande whom the wild Iandoim with other allied and rebellious peoples had placed in dire straits, attacking them to steal and to kill people and cattle. . . .

Fifth: The petitioner marched with his regiment a second time to the Palmares war, about one hundred sixty leagues along the upper reaches of the settlements with no source of provisions at their disposal. They searched for the Negroes in that part of the sertão, where they suffered great hunger both because of the general famine that existed and because of the ingratitude of the countrymen, who felt more keenly the single steer worth no more than fifteen or sixteen *tostões* that the soldiers might kill to satisfy their hunger, which knows no law, than they did the entire herds which the enemy stole from them and killed. . . .

Eighth: About one thing there is no doubt (and the oft repeated and frustrating experience of the events preceding this Palmares war during the span of thirty-eight years is ample proof), that without the aid of the regiment of the petitioners of the São Paulo Infantry the forces of the said Negroes would not have been conquered and destroyed, nor their stronghold in the Barriga range because of its almost impregnable nature. And the captaincies of the São Francisco River, Alagoas, and Pôrto Calvo would today be abandoned, and the slaves who were then with their masters would all be in this Palmares; for in making their decision the latter were waiting only for the end of that year's campaign, to see whether or not the regiment of Paulistas would be repelled. They were by then so insolent and haughty that their masters no longer dared even address them as slaves for fear they would immediately flee for this stronghold. And often before fleeing they would summon troops from Palmares to come fetch them and to loot the houses, etc. . . .

Eleventh: It is indeed true that the force and stronghold of the Negroes of Palmares located in the famous Barriga range is conquered . . . and that their king was killed (by a party of men from the regiment of the petitioner, which came upon the said King Zumbi on the twentieth of November, 1695) and the survivors scattered. Yet one should not therefore think that this war is ended. No doubt it is close to being terminated if we continue to hunt these survivors through the great depths of these forests, and if the regiment of the petitioners is kept along the frontier. If not, another stronghold will suddenly appear either here in Barriga or in any other equally suitable place. . . .

Twelfth: To extinguish completely these scattered remnants there are no men more suited than those of the petitioner's regiment (distinguished among the other troops of Paulistas for having the most valiant and warlike Indians known to inhabit the sertão: the Tabajare, the Oruase, and the Cupinharuen) because only they know how to live in the forest and track down the quilombos, which are widely scattered in these vast wilds so dense that it is most difficult to traverse them. As for settling the camp site on the frontier, it is indisputable that not only should it not be abandoned but the settlement should be preserved there and a town established. And this town can be no better populated, nor more easily and suitably, than by people from São Paulo, both those of the said regiment and others who are to come from São Paulo and wait only to be summoned for the purpose. This will yield great returns for the treasury as well as for the service of Your Majesty, and produce an abundance of foodstuffs in the captaincies of Pernambuco, for these Paulistas are much given to farming and stock raising. For the security of all the inhabitants here a protective wall will thus be erected against the wild Indians of the uplands and the runaway Negroes of the lowlands, a wall stronger and more lasting than that famous one between Tartary and China. The latter, although strongly fortified, is subject to decay from the ravages of time while the former, on the contrary, will grow with time, becoming every day stronger and more permanent.

Thirteenth: The said Field Master and all his companions with all their people were inhabiting, settling, and cultivating the lands of the River Camarões in the realm of the

Gariguê, conquered by them from the wild, resistant Indians. Thus they gathered and tamed a quantity of Tabajare, Oruase, and Cupinharuen, in whose lands the petitioner and the others were living quietly and peaceably, well supplied with those things needed for human life, and at no disadvantage save the long distance to the seaports. The latter, however, were little needed, and the deficiency was easily remedied by the custom of frugality with which people are raised in this sertão, who are unused to luxuries and to the habit of fancy clothes. Nor was it a sacrifice for them to pay the highest prices if there were things they needed from the ports, since they paid with the increases of their cattle. Under these circumstances the Field Master was summoned and requested in the name of Your Majesty by Governor João da Cunha de Souto Maior to descend with all his people to wage this war. The governor feared that the need to abandon their lands and settlements, etc., might hinder their being able or wishing to come. And he was aware that all that chain of wild forests running from the Paraíba River . . . to the Ipojuca, and from the meridian of the Haca Mountains in the plains of Unhanhu to the sertão which terminates the expanse of the said wilds, was of no utility at all, and indeed served only to provide strongholds for runaway Negroes who had rebelled against their masters. Thus as plenipotentiary of Your Majesty he promised to give them any of these lands that they needed as soon as they had conquered them. This appears in article 6 of the conditions which the governor established with the procurators of the petitioners which Your Majesty saw fit to confirm by his royal Patent of April 7, 1693, registered with the secretariat of your Overseas Council, folio 223.

Fourteenth: The Field Master and his companions, relying on the promise that as soon as they had expelled the Negroes and destroyed their mocambos they would receive lands to settle, inhabit, and cultivate, did not consider abandoning those which they already possessed, cultivated, inhabited, and settled, since they owned them having conquered them at the cost of their blood from those wild and untamed Indians. . . . They conquered the lands which had been captured, and of which they were promised any that were needed by them (and Your Majesty saw fit to confirm the promise). This was four years ago, and today they still do not know which lands they will be given to settle, inhabit, and cultivate—nor the quantity nor the location, nor the reason for the delay. . . .

Sixteenth: Your Majesty should be made aware that the petitioners are quite justified in presenting this complaint and that the whole blame has fallen on the Field Master, who according to all the others deceived them, both because he aroused them to come down to wage this war and because after destroying the forces of the Barriga mountains they wished to take leave in view of the unfair division of their booty which he made. The Field Master detained them by giving them assurance that when Your Majesty had been informed he would order that their demands be granted in accordance with their just reasons. . . . They are now frustrated in these hopes and have concluded either that the just reasons alleged to Your Majesty in their plea were not heard by Your Majesty or that they received sinister interpretation by some minister who was ill disposed toward them or less than properly zealous in his obligations and who, seduced from another side, was intervening in behalf of some ambitious person who contrary to reason and justice presumed or feigned to be injured by the promise of these lands —with the result that the minister interposed the obstacles created by the conditions set forth in the patent of March 12, 1695. He thus endowed these conditions with a supposed aura of exact compliance with laws which cannot and should not apply here, in the confidence that we were too far away to reply in time to his erroneous interpretations. . . .

It will be easy and advantageous for these people to summon their families from São Paulo to this frontier, as well as for other settlers to come and live here if the officials of Your Majesty's royal treasury order a pinnace to be loaded with salt for the port of Santos and, when the salt has been delivered as consigned, if they then order the families and other colonists to embark in it. On the return to Pernambuco this ship will enter Santo Antônio Bay where all will disembark. During the trip to Santos the ship would put in at Bahia to allow the heads of the families to take passage and accompany them on the return. . . .

Humbly prostrated at your Royal feet, the petitioner, Field Master of the said regiment, begs Your Majesty, in view of the great zeal, toil, and losses with which he has served

Your Majesty for so long, these ten or twelve years, with works and achievements known to Your Majesty, that he not find himself forcibly obliged to leave this service. For if his people abandon him he will not be able to recover and he will be reduced to abject misery and forced again to roam this sertão to conquer once more a place to live; because the lands which he left are now occupied by others, and his cattle are eaten or stolen. That this happened to Domingos Jorge Velho and his people for having cast aside all their comforts to come serve Your Majesty would remain in the perpetual memory of the people of São Paulo. And because they did thus serve may God never permit this to happen, and may Your Majesty order their just and rightful petitions to be granted as they deserve, and as the generous and royal grandeur of Your Majesty allows one to expect.

. . .

5. Opinion by the Board of Missions of October, 1697, concerning the letters from the Bishop and Governor of Pernambuco in which they relate the lack of churches and priests in the garrisons of Palmares and the Sertão of Rodelas and the offenses committed in this sertão, and the disorder in which the field master arrived from the garrison of Alagoas

The Bishop of Pernambuco in a letter of May 18 of this year says the following: The Paulistas who inhabit two camps in the region of Palmares, one with access to northern and southern Alagoas and the other at the headwaters of Pôrto Calvo, have asked me for priests who would not be under the jurisdiction of the present vicars of their districts and who would administer the sacraments to them. And for the support of these priests they request that they be assigned the tithes, which are now very scanty. Since those lands are the best in Pernambuco, when they are cultivated (as is now the case) the increment in tithes accruing to the royal treasury will be very considerable; thus I do not think it advisable to relinquish the tithes to them, lest they later claim permanent possession. At present I have furnished them with priests who administer the sacraments yet who are subordinate to the vicars. . . . Those of the camp at Pôrto Calvo are satisfied with this arrangement. The Field Master of those who inhabit Alagoas is still insistent. Not only does he want a priest who is not under the jurisdiction of the vicars, but he also wants to be the one to name him. Indeed, he presented me with a clergyman who, in addition to having led a dissolute life—and this must be the only reason for his having been chosen—could not tell the difference between attrition and contrition when examined. However, the Field Master very freely indicates that I should be disposed to select him. This man [Domingos Jorge Velho] is one of the worst savages I have encountered. When he met with me he brought along an interpreter, for he cannot even speak correctly. He is no different from the most barbaric Tapuia, to say nothing of calling him a Christian. And although he was recently married, seven Indian concubines attend him; from this one can infer all his other habits. Until now, ever since he first had use of reason (if indeed he ever possessed it; for if so, he has lost it and I venture that he will not easily regain it), he has roamed the forests hunting Indian men and women, the latter to satisfy his depraved appetites and the former to work in the fields which he possesses. I have provided these men with priests, and although I have done this in the manner described, it would be helpful and indeed quite necessary for the cultivation and settlement of those lands (which will certainly produce an increase for the royal treasury) to erect two churches on the two sites for which Your Majesty should lend the necessary help; and under no circumstances should the tithes be turned over to them, a point which deserves special attention because highly dangerous consequences are involved. . . .

The opinion was that the contents of these two letters[1] are the particular concern of the Overseas Council and the Board of Conscience, both with respect to the maintenance and settlement of the Paulistas in the region of Palmares and the security of their lands and villages and with respect to the curacies which should be erected there and in the Sertão of Rodelas. The tithes and ecclesiastical revenues which the Paulistas request should be assigned by Your Majesty's treasury to the priests of both places. And insofar as it behooves

---

[1] That of the bishop, just cited, and that of the governor, the summary of which has been omitted. [Ed.]

this board to bring before Your Majesty the case of Palmares, it is necessary, as experience has proven, that the Paulistas occupy this place; and the Field Master should recognize the jurisdiction of the Bishop and amend his inveterate errors. For he should be warned that otherwise not only will Your Majesty cease to employ him in your service but that you will order proceedings against him with the severity which his faults deserve. With respect to the Sertão of Rodelas and its settlements, the remedy should be both spiritual and temporal: spiritual in behalf of the priests and missionaries, temporal for the correction and punishment of offenses. Your Majesty shall command what is most fitting to his royal service. Lisbon, October 29, 1697.

> FRANCISCO DA CRUZ
> SEBASTIÃO DE MAGALHÃES
> ROQUE MONTEIRO PAIM
> FRANCISCO SARMENTO

III

∗ ∗ ∗

THE
EIGHTEENTH
CENTURY

8

ANTONIL

✳

The Opulence of Brazil

André João Antonil was the pseudonym of an Italian Jesuit, Giovanni Antonio Andreoni (1649-1716), who studied civil law at Perugia and was received into the Society of Jesus in 1667. In 1681 Andreoni came to Brazil as a protégé of the celebrated Father Antônio Vieira and lived there until his death. He remained mostly in Bahia, where he served twice as rector of the local college and in 1705-1709 as provincial of the Brazilian Province of the Society. C. R. Boxer feels that his *Cultura e opulência do Brasil por suas drogas e minas,* written in good, terse Portuguese, "is generally acknowledged to be the best book on the economic and social conditions of Brazil during the first half of the eighteenth century." This selection from the *Culture and Wealth of Brazil* describes the immediate effects of the Paulistas' discovery of gold. The book was published at Lisbon in 1711 but was promptly suppressed as being too informative for foreigners. It was not reprinted until 1837, and the identity of Antonil was revealed by Capistrano de Abreu only in 1886.

From André João Antonil, *Cultura e opulência do Brasil* (Salvador, 1950), excerpted from pp. 211-35, 285-87. Translated; and printed by permission of Aguiar & Souza Ltda., Livraria Progresso Editora.

Concerning the gold mines discovered in Brazil

Reports always persisted that there were mines of iron, gold, and silver in Brazil. But there was also always a good deal of negligence in their discovery and utilization. This may be because the inhabitants, content with the fruits which the surface of the land gives in abundance and with the fish which are caught in the large, handsome rivers, never attempted to alter the natural course of these rivers to examine their beds, or to penetrate the depths of the earth as many other nations were influenced to do by insatiable ambition. Or it may be that their bent for catching Indians in the forests turned them from this less demanding and more useful activity. . . .

Concerning the gold mines called "general" and their discoverers

A few years ago, when Artur de Sá was governor of Rio de Janeiro, the discovery of the general mines of Cataguases began. They say that the first discoverer was a mulatto who had been at the mines of Paranaguá and Curitiba. He had gone to the sertão with some Paulistas to fetch Indians, and on reaching Mount Tripuí he went down to the stream, today known as Ouro Prêto, with a wooden bowl to get water. After scraping it along the river bank he saw that it contained some nuggets the color of steel which he could not identify. Neither could his companions recognize or evaluate what he had so easily picked up. They simply supposed that it was some metal which was poorly formed and therefore unrecognizable. When they arrived at Taubaté, however, they did not fail to ask what kind of metal this might be. And without further examination they sold some of the nuggets to Miguel de Sousa at half a *pataca* for each *oitava*, without their knowing what they were selling or the buyer what he was buying. They finally decided to send a few nuggets to the governor of Rio de Janeiro, Artur de Sá; and when they were examined they turned out to be the purest gold.

Half a league from the Ouro Prêto washing another mine was found which is called that of the Ribeiro de Antônio

Dias; and another half league from there, the mine of Ribeiro do Padre João de Faria; and near this, a little more than a league away, the mines of Ribeiro de Bueno and Bento Rodrigues. And a moderate three-day march by daylight from there was the mine of the Ribeirão de Nossa Senhora do Carmo, discovered by João Lopes de Lima, and still another called Ribeiro Ibupiranga. And all these mines took the names of their discoverers, who were all Paulistas.

There is also a stopping place on the way to these general mines, eleven or twelve days distant from the first ones if one makes good time until three o'clock each afternoon. This place takes its name from the River das Mortes, so called because some men died there while swimming across it, and others killed each other by gunshot while fighting over the allocation of wild Indians which they had brought from the sertão. And gold is found in this river, as well as in the streams that flow from it and those that flow into it. This stopping place serves for lodging those who are going to Minas Gerais, and here they supply themselves with necessities because those who are now settled here have farms and sell livestock.

I do not mention the mine of the Serra de Itatiaia (which means white gold, which is gold not yet well formed), which is a moderate eight-day journey by daylight from the Ouro Prêto washing. For the Paulistas show no interest in this mine as they have others of completely formed gold and much greater output. And they say that these general mines are at the latitude of the captaincies of Espírito Santo.

·   ·   ·

Concerning the yield of the washings and the different qualities of gold taken from them

. . . There was a year during which more than 100 *arrôbas* of gold were taken from all these mines, or washings, excluding that which was and still is taken surreptitiously from other washings which the discoverers did not report. . . . And if the King's fifths reached seventeen or twenty arrôbas even though so much untaxed gold is concealed, it is easy to see that the gold taken out each year exceeds one hundred arrôbas without any exaggeration, and that during these past ten years more than one thousand arrôbas were taken out. . . . Only the fifths owed His Majesty have been diminishing conspicuously, whether because the gold dust was diverted to other regions, or because it did not reach the royal smelting house, or because some, using a more despicable ruse, stamped the gold with false seals. Yet even so, His Majesty did not fail to realize a large profit through the mint at Rio de Janeiro; for by buying the gold at twelve *tostões* per oitava and in two years minting three million in national and provincial gold coin, he made a profit of six hundred thousand *cruzados* in advance.

Concerning the people who go to the mines and take gold from the streams

The insatiable thirst for gold impelled so many to leave their lands and take to such arduous roads as those leading to the mines that it would be difficult to calculate the number of persons who are now there. However, those who have stayed there for a long period during these last years and have visited all the mines say that more than thirty thousand souls are employed, some in prospecting, others in directing the prospecting of the gold washings, and others in doing business, selling and buying the essentials not only for life but also for pleasure, with greater activity than in the seaports.

Every year great numbers of Portuguese and foreigners arrive with the fleets to go to the mines. From the cities, towns, coastal regions, and sertões of Brazil go whites, mulattoes, and blacks, and many Indians whom the Paulistas make use of. There is a mixture of people of every condition: men and women; young and old; poor and rich; nobles and plebeians; laymen, clerics, and religious of various orders, many of whom have neither convent nor house in Brazil.

With regard to temporal power, there have so far been no restraints or even a moderately well-ordered government. Only a few laws are kept, pertaining to the claims and the allotment of the washings. Beyond this there are no ministers or justices who handle or might have authority to handle punishment of crimes, which are not rare, particularly homicide and theft. With regard to spiritual matters, since the prelates have hitherto been uncertain about the question of jurisdiction, the representatives of one or another group, whether local priests or visitors, have found themselves quite perplexed; and they have caused no little perplexity to others, who in the end do not know to which pastor these new flocks belong. And when the right to appoint priests is determined, few of them will be feared and respected in those parishes which move from place to place like the children of Israel in the desert.

The King's superintendent of mines was the Crown Judge José Vaz Pinto, who after a final two-year term returned once more to Rio de Janeiro with a handsome capital. And I suppose that through him the King must have been kept fully informed on what is happening in the mines, and that he has indicated the disorders and the remedy for them when such is possible. Also present at the mines are a crown procurator and a crown representative (*guarda-mor*) on a stipend. Until now there have been smelting houses in Taubaté, in the town of São Paulo, in Parati, and in Rio de Janeiro; and in each of these houses are a superintendent, a notary, and a founder who casts the gold into bars on which he stamps the royal seal, signifying the fifth that was paid to the King on that gold.

If there were mints and smelting houses in Bahia and Rio de Janeiro (since these are the two poles which eventually attract all the gold) His Majesty would make a much greater profit than what he has till now. And he would make a much greater one still if the mints, well equipped with the necessary apparatus, always had money on hand to buy the gold which the miners bring in and are delighted to sell without delay.

We have just learned that His Majesty is sending a governor and ministers of justice to the mines and ordering a regiment of soldiers levied so that everything will proceed with more control and order.

Concerning the allotments or distribution of the mines

To avoid the confusion, tumult, and deaths that would arise from the discovery of the gold washings the following method of allotment was agreed upon. The discoverer has the first claim as discoverer and a second as a miner. Next follows the King's share and then that of his representative.

The rest are distributed by lot. Those known as whole claims are thirty square braças, and such are those of the King, the discoverer, and the royal representative. The others which are drawn by lot have an area proportionate to the number of slaves brought for prospecting, with two square braças allowed for each slave or Indian so used. Thus a man with fifteen slaves receives a whole claim of thirty square braças. To be admitted to the distribution by lot one must submit a petition to the superintendent of these allotments, who receives an oitava of gold for filing the petition, as does his notary. And it sometimes happens that five hundred petitions are presented, which means that the superintendent and the clerk take in one thousand oitavas. And if, because some claims fail to produce, all the miners do not extract from them an amount equal to what they paid, they therefore look for other claims as soon as new washings are discovered. The King's claim is sold straightway to the highest bidder. Anyone can sell or exchange his claim, and this has given and continues to give rise to many different arrangements, for one miner may extract much gold from a few braças while others extract little from many braças. There was one man who sold a claim for more than a thousand oitavas from which the buyer extracted seven arrôbas of gold. This goes to prove that whether or not gold is found in a claim is simply a turn of good or bad fortune.

Concerning the abundance of provisions and all the necessaries found today at the mines and the slight attention paid to the extraordinarily high prices

Since the land that gives gold is completely barren of everything needed to sustain human life, as are most of the routes leading to the mines, one cannot imagine what the miners suffered at the beginning for lack of provisions. More than a few were found dead clutching an ear of corn as their only sustenance. However, as soon as the abundance of the gold extracted became apparent, and the largess with which everything sent there was paid for, lodging places were built and soon merchants began to send to the mines the best that arrived by ship from Portugal and other parts: not only provisions but also luxuries and elaborate clothes, as well as a thousand trinkets from France which also

found their way there. In this regard all parts of Brazil began
to send everything the soil produces, with profits not merely
large but excessive. And as there is no currency but gold dust
at the mines, the least that could be given for anything would
be oitavas. Shortly, the cattle herds from Paranaguá, those
from River das Velhas, and those from the plains of Bahia
were sent to Minas Gerais, along with everything else which
the settlers imagined might fill a desire, including every kind
of product, natural and manufactured, foreign and domestic. . . .[1]

And these high prices so prevalent at the mines were the
reason why the prices of all things rose so much elsewhere,
as is felt in the ports of the cities and towns of Brazil; and
why many sugar mills were divested of their necessary
slaves; and why the inhabitants suffer a great scarcity of provisions, which are almost all taken to be sold where they will
yield greater profit.

Concerning the harms done to Brazil by the greed which followed the discovery of gold in the mines

There is nothing so good that it cannot occasion many evils
through the fault of him who fails to make good use of it.
And even against things sacred the greatest sacrileges are
committed. Is it any wonder then that gold—being such a
handsome and precious metal, so useful for human commerce and so worthy of being made into the vases and ornaments of the Temples for Divine Worship—be transformed
by the insatiable greed of men into a continual instrument
and cause of many harms? The fame of mines so abundant
in Brazil attracted men of every rank and from all places,
some with means and others vagabonds. Those of means,
who came by much of their wealth through prospecting, be-
have as a result with hauteur and arrogance; they always
travel accompanied by bands of musketeers who need little
pretext to commit any violence and to take great and thun-
derous revenge without any fear of the law. Gold induced
these men to gamble unrestrainedly and to spend enormous

---

[1] Here Antonil gives a list of commodity prices in Minas Gerais
for the year 1703. A translation of it appears in C. R. Boxer, *The
Golden Age of Brazil, 1695-1750* (Berkeley and Los Angeles,
1962), pp. 330-32. [Ed.]

sums on frivolities without blinking—to buy, for example, a Negro trumpeter for a thousand cruzados, or a mulatto woman of easy virtue for double that price to compound with her continual and scandalous sins. The vagabonds, who go to the mines to extract gold not from the washings but from the tubes in which the gold washers collect it and save it, were guilty of the most shocking treacheries and the cruelest killings. These crimes went unpunished because at the mines human justice did not yet have a tribunal or the respect that it enjoys in other places where there are qualified ministers reinforced by numerous and reliable prisons. Only now that the governor and ministers are going there can some relief be expected. Even the bishops and prelates of several regions profoundly regret that no heed whatever is paid to their censures which would return to their dioceses and convents the goodly number of clerics and religious who roam about there in defiance or as fugitives. The fact also that the very best provisions that could be desired go to the mines caused such a sharp increase in the prices of everything sold that the owners of sugar mills and the planters find themselves in very bad straits. For lack of Negroes they can no longer produce sugar or tobacco as they so abundantly did in times past when theirs were the true mines of Brazil and Portugal. And the worst is that the larger part of the gold extracted from the mines is sent as dust or in coins to foreign kingdoms, while the smaller part remains in Portugal and the cities of Brazil, except for that spent on necklaces, earrings, and other baubles, which are seen worn today by mulatto and Negro women of easy life much more than by ladies. No prudent person can fail to admit that God has allowed the discovery of so much gold in the mines in order to punish Brazil with it, just as in the wars that are now so plentiful He is using iron to punish the Europeans.

9

PERCY ALVIN MARTIN

❊

Minas Gerais and California

Percy Alvin Martin (1879-1942), a historian of Brazil and of Latin America, was one of the first scholars to cultivate the serious teaching and study of Brazilian history and civilization in the United States. Educated at Stanford and Harvard, he spent most of his professional career at Stanford, where he was named professor of history in 1923.

In the years since Martin's study of Minas Gerais and California appeared further research has sharpened our knowledge of the Brazilian gold rush in many details. The essay remains, however, a succinct and comprehensive account of this important event and of the conflict between the prospecting bandeirantes and the "outsiders," or *emboabas,* who swarmed to vie for their claims. It is enhanced for the American reader by the comparison with the California rush.

. . . [To] the student of American history in the continental sense, nothing could be more interesting than a

From Percy Alvin Martin, "Minas Geraes and California: A Comparison of Certain Phases of Their Historical and Social Evolution," *Annaes* (Congresso Internacional de Historia da America) (9 vols.; Rio de Janeiro, 1925-30), I, excerpted from pp. 250-70. Minor orthographical changes and corrections have been made.

comparative study of the way in which the peoples and the governments of Portuguese America and the United States have reacted to great social crisis or dislocations brought about by similar causes. Such a crisis or break in the development of both countries is to be found in the discovery of gold; in the case of Brazil in what is now the state of Minas Gerais at the end of the seventeenth and beginning of the eighteenth centuries; in the case of California in 1848 and the years immediately following. In the present paper an attempt will be made to suggest the broad outlines of such a comparative study. The basis of comparison will be the changes wrought in Brazil by the opening of the gold regions, and as occasion offers, reference will be made to the points of contact or differences presented by California a century and a half later.

. . .

During the period of Portugal's union with Spain, "the sixty years' captivity," Felipe III in 1603 caused to be drawn up in Madrid an elaborate and minute *Código mineiro* against the impending discovery of precious metals. . . .

For a long period the mining code remained unused and all but forgotten. The crown officials, however, lost no occasion to keep alive popular interest in the elusive gold fields. Thus, for example, a royal decree of August 19, 1670, commanded the Captain General of Pernambuco to aid by all means in his power the endeavors of the gold seekers; another dated March 18, 1694, and addressed to the Governor General of Bahia, offered as a reward for the discovery of gold, silver, or precious stones a diploma of nobility and admission to one of the orders of knighthood.

If the crown could reward it could also punish. We learn, for instance, that [quite early in] the seventeenth century an adventurer named Marcos de Azeredo, with a single companion, penetrated into the present state of Minas Gerais, probably by the valley of the River Doce. They brought back to civilization a number of emeralds and samples of silver ore. On their steadfast refusal to reveal the source of their treasures they were thrown into prison at Bahia by order of the governor and remained incarcerated for the rest of their lives.

By all odds the most important and spectacular of these

early exploring expeditions was that of Fernão Dias Pais, who was also one of the most daring and successful of the bandeirantes. To him more than to any one else was due the first authentic knowledge of that vast interior plateau which because of its mineral wealth is to this day known as Minas Gerais, or "General Mines." Fernão Dias was a wealthy Paulista, a veteran in years but young in spirit, who had become inured to hardships and privations in many a bandeira in quest of Indian slaves. In 1672 at the age of [approximately sixty-four] he determined at his own expense and on his own initiative to equip a great expedition in search of precious metals and jewels. The governor general of Bahia conferred upon him the title and prerogatives of a *capitão-mor* [captain major] with the commission "to seek out and discover emerald mines." [It was in the year 1674 that] he set out at the head of a large company into the wilderness; from time to time halts were made and crops were planted whose yield should furnish subsistence on the return journey. At length, after enduring terrific hardships, with the loss of many of its members, the expedition reached the wild tangle of mountains lying between the headwaters of the River Doce and the River São Francisco. Here in a locality called Sumidouro, Fernão Dias made his headquarters for four long years.

Reckoning little of the sufferings and privations among his companions, obsessed with the determination not to return unless laden with emeralds, the veteran chief penetrated far into a region even to this day but little known. Legend had it that in this remote wilderness precious stones were to be found in great heaps. Nothing daunted the intrepid explorer. Rebellion among his followers he put down with an iron hand; his own son, as one of the leading conspirators, was executed. At length his persistent efforts were rewarded; on the shores of a mysterious lake, whose poisonous miasmas decimated the ranks of his companions, he discovered the coveted emeralds. The location was christened Vapabuçu or "Great Lake," a name soon changed into Lagoa Encantada, as all subsequent efforts to discover this lake proved fruitless. Though his goal was attained. Fernão Dias was fated never to profit from his discoveries. Worn out with fatigues and hardships, he died on the shores of the River das Velhas. He was at least spared the deception of learning that the

stones in whose search he had laid down his life were but the
semiprecious though beautiful tourmalines.

To whom belongs the honor of having first discovered gold
deposits in Minas Gerais is still a matter of debate. Following the tragic death of Fernão Dias Pais [in 1861] a large
number of expeditions set out into what is now the state of
Minas Gerais in quest of gold. One under Manuel de Borba
Gato, the son-in-law of the ill-starred "emerald hunter," discovered extensive gold washings on the site of the present city
of Sabará. But his find availed him nothing. Some time previously he had come into collision with a royal functionary,
one Rodrigo de Castelo Branco, formerly *intendente* of the
gold washings of São Paulo, but now like Borba Gato, in
search of gold deposits in the mountains of Minas. In the
clash, Castelo Branco was killed and his [presumed] murderer
dared not return to civilization. For twenty years he and his
companions lived in exile in the wilderness about the upper
waters of the São Francisco River. Finally through the media-
tion of his family, the governor of São Paulo promised him
full pardon if he would reveal the location of the gold washings and deposits he had discovered during his long exile.

Even before this happy intelligence was conveyed to the
world, a Paulista from Taubaté, Antônio Rodrigues de Arzão, had explored in 1693 the valley of the River Doce which
he descended to Vitória in the captaincy of Espírito Santo.
On his return to São Paulo he brought with him a number of
gold nuggets. Finally, in 1694 Rodrigues's brother-in-law,
Bartolomeu Bueno de Siqueira, at the head of a large exploring party, discovered near the site of the future Vila
Rica, the capital of Minas, unmistakable traces of gold. So
convinced was the governor of São Paulo that the great con-
summation had at last been attained that he commissioned
a certain Carlos Pedroso, who had submitted to him samples of the gold discovered at Vila Rica, to erect at Taubaté
a smelter and to collect on behalf of the crown the royal
fifth of all the precious metal discovered.

Far different were the circumstances under which gold
was discovered in California a century and a half later.
The finding of the precious metal came not as the culmina-
tion of a search extending through generations but purely as a
result of accident. In January 1848, less than two years after

California had passed from the control of Mexico to that of the United States, a certain James Wilson Marshall, a retainer of the Swiss *hacendado* John A. Sutter, chanced upon particles of gold while building a saw mill on a branch of the American River, near Sacramento, at present the capital of California.

However the precious metal may have been discovered, the immediate effects were not dissimilar in Brazil and California. As the news rapidly spread through the length of populated sections of Brazil and across the Atlantic to distant Portugal it aroused the wildest excitement and most extravagant hopes. In vain did the government take measures to check the stream of humanity which began to pour into the promised land. . . . A kind of wild intoxication or vertigo took possession of all; there were no perils or obstacles which they hesitated to affront.

Fazendas were abandoned; shops in the cities were deserted; crews in the harbors left their ships; even government officials, infected with the contagion, neglected their duties. For instance, the governor of Rio de Janeiro, Artur de Sá e Meneses, so far forgot his dignity as to abandon his post and join the rush to the mines.

Somewhat similar scenes were enacted in California in the spring and early summer of 1848. By the middle of June the town of San Francisco had been virtually abandoned by its inhabitants. As early as May 27, barely six months after Marshall's discovery, the editor of the *Star* complained that "stores are closed and places of business vacated, a large number of houses tenantless, various kinds of mechanical labor suspended or given up entirely, and nowhere the pleasant hum of industry salutes the ear . . . but as if a curse had arrested our onward course of enterprise, everything wears a desolate and sombre look; everywhere all is dull, monotonous, dead." . . . And while the military governor, unlike Sá e Meneses, remained at his post, he was forced to cook his own dinners.

In contrast with the stagnation with which the formerly densely settled regions of Brazil and California were afflicted was the teeming activity of the mountain slopes and river valleys. In remote regions of Minas, whose solitude had hitherto remained unbroken save for the occasional passage of a bandeira in quest of slaves or gold, villages and towns sprang up as if by magic. From these primitive mining camps arose the opulent cities of Mariana, Vila Rica de Ouro Prêto, São João d'El Rei. California likewise saw the emergence of an immense number of thriving communities. Few of these, however, attained to lasting importance, owing chiefly to the fact that they were remote from the rich agricultural lands of the state.

As has already been suggested, the stampede of the gold workings in Minas adversely affected other sections of Brazil. For a time the plantation system, on which the economic progress of the colony had hitherto depended, was threatened with ruin. Especially was this true of the sugar-growing areas of Bahia and Pernambuco. Many of the wealthy fazendeiros, together with their slaves, abandoned their homes and set out for Minas. The plantation owners who resisted the lure of gold mines and remained at home found labor all but unobtainable. Speculators bought up the Negroes at fantastic prices and shipped them to Minas in such numbers that the government forbade under penalty of confiscation the transfer of plantation Negroes to the mines. New sources of labor supply were cut off, as the slave dealers, owing to the high prices which their wares commanded, shipped all the Negroes to Rio as the nearest point to the gold washings. Largely as a result of this violent economic dislocation within a few years Brazil lost her virtual monopoly of supplying sugar to Western Europe and was destined never to regain it. With a quick appraisal of their new opportunities the French and English in the West Indies began to invade Brazil's most profitable markets.[1]

As has happened the world over when the lure of gold draws men into strange and unknown parts, lawlessness, turbulence, and disorder became rampant throughout Minas. During the height of the gold rush, deeds of violence were frequent and for the most part went unpunished, for among the hordes of goldseekers were many criminals who feared neither God nor man. As the overwhelming majority of the population was recruited from among the Brazilians and Portuguese, national jealousies and racial animosities did not assume the proportions which they did later in the gold

---

[1] It should be noted that the Brazilian sugar industry had begun to suffer from West Indian competition and from a decline in the world price years before the gold strikes in Minas Gerais. [Ed.]

fields of California and South Africa. Yet the first rush had hardly spent itself before there developed a sharp line of cleavage between the Paulistas on the one hand and the remaining Brazilians and Portuguese on the other. Within a few years this rivalry was destined to involve Minas in bloody and cruel civil war.

We have already seen that the gold washings of Minas were discovered by adventurers and explorers from São Paulo, chiefly the redoubtable and intrepid Paulistas. These same men constituted the first settlers of those regions which they regarded from the political point of view as dependent on the captaincy of São Paulo. It was quite logical therefore that the Paulistas should look upon themselves as the proprietors of the gold fields and should regard with growing animosity the swarm of adventurers from other provinces who invaded the gold workings. With even less favor did they view the stream of immigrants from Portugal and the Azores and Madeira Islands. All of these intruders were given the blanket designation of *forasteiros* (foreigners) or dubbed with the opprobrious epithet of *emboabas*.[2] For a time the lot of these "outsiders" was very hard; as defenseless interlopers they were treated by the Paulistas with scorn and even with violence. As long as they were in the minority they could only suffer these indignities in silence. But gradually the influx of new gold seekers from distant provinces or from across the sea upset the balance; with the increase in numbers the courage of the forasteiros steadily grew; for purposes of common defense they stood shoulder to shoulder and soon began to retaliate in kind on every attack of the Paulistas. Pitched battles were waged for the possession of a particular gold washing; murders were followed by vendettas; large sections of the country became a prey to anarchy. The memory of these sanguinary encounters is preserved in a number of place names. The *Rio das Mortes* (the "River of Death") and *Capão da Traição* (the "Hedge of Treason") are still pointed out in the vicinity of São João d'El Rei.

As time went on the whole gold district was separated into two hostile camps. When a series of outrages caused the rumor to be bruited about that the Paulistas were planning a

---

[2] The term *emboaba* probably meant "bird with feathered legs" and was scornfully applied to Europeans who used protective leggings against the Brazilian bush. [Ed.]

general massacre of the Emboabas, the latter, thoroughly alarmed, chose for their chief one Manuel Nunes Viana, a Portuguese, "in order," in the words of Rocha Pita,[3] "that he might curb the insolence of the Paulistas and compel them to live in obedience to the laws." Gradually the whole country drifted into a state bordering on civil war. . . .

When the news of the civil war in Minas, culminating in the massacre of the Paulistas, reached Rio de Janeiro, the governor general, Dom Fernando Martins Mascarenhas, determined to set out at once for the disaffected region without waiting for authority from Lisbon. With four companies of troops he repaired in [March-April of 1709] to the River das Mortes, near the scene of the massacre. The scattered Paulistas flocked to his standards, protesting their unswerving allegiance to the Portuguese crown and inveighing against the Emboabas and their leaders as traitors and assassins. Their representation naturally inclined the governor to side with the Paulistas and he forthwith promised them his full protection. The Emboabas meanwhile became thoroughly alarmed. Rumor had it that the governor had come to Minas for the express purpose of meting out punishment; that he had even brought with him handcuffs and fetters for those culprits who should fall into his power. With destruction staring them in the face the only course apparently left open to the Emboabas was to defy the governor and to expel him from Minas. . . . Dom Fernando, who apparently was not cast in heroic mold, made a virtue of necessity and returned to the coast, leaving Viana in virtually undisputed possession of Minas. . . .

Meanwhile Dom Fernando Mascarenhas was succeeded in Rio by Antônio de Albuquerque Coelho de Carvalho, former governor of Maranhão. The new executive was at once invited to come to Minas by Viana and the other leaders of the Emboabas who hoped by a voluntary tender of obedience to disarm resentment and possibly to anticipate punishment.

Antônio de Albuquerque, like his predecessor, was a man of tact and discernment. Accompanied only by an escort of honor, he appeared in Minas in 1709. At a meeting with Viana held in the little town of Caeté the leader of the Emboa-

---

[3] The *História da América Portuguesa* of Sebastião da Rocha Pita was first published at Lisbon in 1730. [Ed.]

bas relinquished all his authority, and asked permission of the governor to retire to his fazenda on the São Francisco River. His followers were equally emphatic in their protestations of loyalty and obedience. The governor, on his part, issued a general pardon to those who had taken up arms against the Paulistas; he officially confirmed all the appointments of Viana and apparently brought to the mining regions the first real peace they had enjoyed for nearly a decade.

The calm which settled down upon the erstwhile turbulent mining camps was but the lull which precedes the storm. The Paulistas had been entirely ignored in the new dispensation introduced into Minas by Governor Albuquerque. Their resentment is easy to understand. It was they who at the cost of countless perils had discovered and opened up the mines; and now their rights and possessions were being shamelessly filched from them by a horde of hated foreigners. If we are to believe Rocha Pita it was the women of São Paulo who felt the disgrace with the greatest poignancy. The crestfallen Paulistas who had been expelled from the gold-workings were received by their wives and mothers with stinging reproaches. Not only had they abandoned their mining claims, but what was worse, they had left the massacre of their brothers unavenged. It is probable, however, that the Paulistas needed no additional incentive to right their real or fancied wrongs. An army was quickly organized and under the command of a tried and tested captain, Amador Bueno, set out for Minas in 1709. On the way it fell in with Governor Albuquerque who had just left the mining districts with the intention of allaying the ferment in São Paulo. Expostulations on the part of the governor fell upon deaf ears; the Paulistas were in no mood to be deterred from their purpose by blandishments or arguments. Hearing that a plan was on foot to make him prisoner, Albuquerque hastily left for Rio, at the same time despatching couriers to the Emboabas to apprise them of their danger.

The warning came none too soon. The Emboabas had apparently not considered the possibility of an invasion and were quite unprepared to cope with this new and unexpected peril. The first clash came at the River das Mortes. Here the Emboabas felt the full fury of the Paulistas who were burning to avenge their fallen comrades. For a time fortune favored the Paulistas, but with the arrival of large reinforcements for the Emboabas, the tide of battle suddenly changed. Realizing that a continuation of the struggle would invite destruction, the Paulistas abandoned the field and in good order retired to São Paulo. With their defeat at the "River of Death" all hope of the domination of the mining districts by the Paulistas vanished.

While the Paulistas were still smarting under their defeat, Governor Albuquerque energetically set about to make further invasions from the south impossible. A considerable body of regular troops were assigned as patrols to protect the gold districts from further incursions. And in the same year as the Battle of River das Mortes, 1709, a royal order was issued at Lisbon entirely separating São Paulo and the mining districts from the captaincy of Rio de Janeiro. A new captaincy, that of São Paulo-Minas, was created, and as the first captain general was appointed Antônio de Albuquerque, who derived his authority direct from the Portuguese crown.

Save on two occasions, the revolt of 1720 and the great conspiracy headed by Tiradentes in 1789, the mining regions of Brazil were, during the remainder of the colonial epoch, under royal control. The administration of the first captain general of São Paulo-Minas Gerais was from the outset signalized by a vigorous assertion of royal authority. The most obvious and pressing need was to make certain the loyalty and tranquility of the turbulent population of the mining camps. To this end a number of important decrees were issued. A royal ordinance of July 24, 1711, expressly provided that in the organization of the local militia of the mining districts no Paulistas might serve as officers, though exception might be made in the case of those whose loyalty and obedience were beyond question. A systematic effort was made to remove the more lawless elements and to prevent undesirables from entering the captaincy. An interesting commentary on the role played by the clergy in these troublous times was the injunction laid on Albuquerque to lend every aid to the Archbishop of Bahia and the Bishop of Rio to expel from the mining regions all members of the clergy who were there without authorization or who meddled in affairs in which they were not concerned. Foreigners, monks, traders, tavern-keepers, and their like were particularly singled out for expulsion. A variety of regulations were designed to check evils of brawling, drunkenness, and gambling; dice and games of chance were absolutely forbidden. The number of dram-shops was rigidly restricted, and in order to check deeds of violence the use of certain kinds of weapons was entirely prohibited while other kinds were restricted to certain classes of the population.

Although many of these regulations were more honored in the breach than in the observance they doubtless contributed to the gradual decline in the lawlessness and turbulence so characteristic of the first days of the gold rush. The bitter enmity between the Paulistas and the Emboabas gradually yielded to the softening effects of time and to the more equitable administration of justice. While the Paulistas never regained their one-time preponderance they suffered no great discrimination save in the matter of local militia. They were freely permitted to return to the gold workings, and the mining claims from which they had been illegally ousted were restored to them. The old party designations and shibboleths were gradually dropped; within a few years, notably after Minas had become a separate captaincy [in 1720], all of the inhabitants, irrespective of their origin, were known as *mineiros*.

Although California, even at the height of the gold rush, offered no spectacle of armed conflict comparable to the pitched battles between the Paulistas and the Emboabas, on several occasions national jealousies and racial prejudices threatened to precipitate hostilities in the mining regions. Like the Paulistas the men from the United States regarded the members of other nations and races who poured into the country to share in the golden harvest as intruders. Yet they did not have the justification of the Paulistas as they themselves were newcomers into the mining region. Particularly was their antipathy visited upon the Spanish Americans, notably the Mexicans, Chileans, and Peruvians whose experience and tact had frequently won for them some of the choicest claims. . . .

Possibly the most striking differences between the mining industry as it existed in Minas and California were to be found in the methods of regulation. From one point of view these regulations but reflect the deep cleavage between the absolutism as practiced in Portugal in the eighteenth century, and the democracy of the nineteenth century as it had evolved in the United States. It was thoroughly in keeping with the policy of the Portuguese crown, particularly after the advent to power of the Marquis of Pombal, the great minister of King José I, that the mining industry should be subjected to a complicated and harassing system of regulation whose chief purpose was the increase of the royal revenues. These regulations were put into effect as rapidly as royal authority could be enforced in the mining districts. The eternal bone of contention was naturally the payment of the royal fifth or quinto. As early as the mining law of Felipe III of Spain, elaborated, as we have seen, in [1603 and] 1618, provision was made for the payment to the crown of twenty per cent of all the gold and silver extracted by the miners. . . .

At length even the government was convinced that the quinto system was unsuccessful. In 1733 the authorities determined to grapple with the problem from an entirely different angle. For the quinto was substituted a capitation or poll tax. . . . From almost every point of view the new system was vicious. It was entirely lacking in equity since it fell with equal weight on the finder of a bonanza or a luckless gambler. Nor was it in the long run of any benefit to the royal treasury. To be sure, it stimulated the miners to feverish activity since they were naturally anxious to secure the maximum output in the minimum time. It also freed them from the harassing surveillance of the government officials. On the other hand the capitation system directly made for the rapid and superficial exploitation of the workings. As the miners had no proprietary interest in their claims, and haste was the all important consideration, they contented themselves with the rapid extraction of gold from the richer workings and entirely neglected the others. Thus many mines and workings which were abandoned as exhausted might have long remained productive had the government followed the method later adopted in California and Australia of granting the miners full ownership and control of their claims. Finally it should be noted that the imposition of the poll tax greatly aggravated the lot of the slaves, whose hard condition had already led to the threat of a race war.

In the case of California the government adopted a policy in many respects the exact antithesis of that followed by the Portuguese crown in Brazil. . . . Until the land was opened to actual settlers, when ownership in fee simple embraced the soil and everything beneath, the miner might freely file his claim to any locality not already preëmpted. The size of and title to such claims were determined by rules adopted by the communities themselves. Disputes and controversies were comparatively rare and the testimony is overwhelming that this system, so consonant with the spirit of frontier democracy, was successful.

It does not fall within the scope of this paper to discuss the life and activities of the inhabitants of Minas and California during the flush times of the mining era. . . . Yet the main facts as regards Minas are clear enough. Despite the disabilities under which the miners labored and the faults of an unintelligent and oft times corrupt administration of the mining districts, from 1735 to 1751 Minas Gerais attained a prosperity and opulence never again reached during the colonial period. The population rose to a quarter of a million of which a full third were engaged in mining. The new captaincy soon became known as the wealthiest and most flourishing portion of Brazil; the crude mining camps grew into substantial cities; Vila Rica de Ouro Prêto, the Potosí of Brazil, could boast of 20,000 inhabitants. Its narrow streets, so steep that no wheeled vehicle could traverse them, swarmed with a gay, dissolute, luxury-loving populace. The wealth and extravagance of its citizens are attested by the palaces, stately churches, and imposing public buildings which invest the present moribund city with such a romantic charm, and which still bear "an incomparable perfume of things gone by."

Although the prosperity of Minas Gerais caused a steady stream of gold to flow into the ever depleted Portuguese treasury, the great minister of King José I, the Marquis of Pombal, was convinced that the revenues of the government could be still further augmented by the restoration of the quinto. This was done in 1751 at the time when the yield of gold reached its maximum. The hopes of Pombal were not realized. Hardly had the half century mark been passed before a sharp decline in production set in. . . . By the end of the century the mining camps were all but deserted; the English traveler Mawe who visited these regions in 1809 declares that Vila Rica de Ouro Prêto "scarcely retains a shadow of its former splendor."

It is a striking coincidence that the population of California in 1852, when the mining industry was at its height, was approximately that of Minas Gerais just a century earlier. According to the census report the number of inhabitants of the state totaled 225,000 of whom some 100,000 were miners.

Comparative estimates regarding the yield of the gold mines in Brazil and California are unsatisfactory and misleading. Not only are exact data difficult to obtain but changes in the purchasing power of money in the century which intervened between the halcyon days of mining in Brazil and California rob comparisons of much of their value. . . .

On the basis of the most reliable estimates it would seem safe to assume that the total yield of the gold mines of Brazil from the time of their discovery up to the end of the colonial period was between a quarter and a third of a billion dollars. Approximately three-fourths of the amount came from the captaincy of Minas Gerais. . . .

In the case of California data on the yield of the gold mines are more reliable. . . . For many years the output continued to fluctuate between fifty and sixty millions. The total value of the gold produced during the first nine years was $456,000,000, an amount equal to or exceeding the total yield of the gold produced during the [colonial period in Brazil].

Despite the different conditions under which the gold deposits were discovered and exploited in Minas and California the consequences both national and local reveal points of similarity. Both in Brazil and California the lure of gold—and in Brazil the additional incentive arising from the lure of diamonds—led to a great influx of population. This immigration in the case of Brazil came not only from the motherland but also from various sections of the colony. Of the various elements perhaps the immigrants from São Paulo were the most important. The stubborn, independent, and self-assertive Paulistas added an all important ingredient to the progressive nationalization and assimilation which in time was to produce a purely Brazilian type. In the crucible of the frontier, to use a phrase of Professor Turner, the immigrants were "Brazilianized," liberated, and formed into a new race, Portuguese in neither nationality nor character. It is significant in this connection that the very names of the new mining settlements were mainly of local origin and seldom

Portuguese. Cases in point are Sabará, Pindamonhangaba, Caeté, Pitangui. Minas Gerais as we now know it—a domain truly imperial in extent, and the most populous state in Brazil [more recently overtaken by São Paulo]—was prior to the gold rush an almost unbroken wilderness, save as it was traversed by the bandeirantes in quest of slaves. The decline of the mining industry led to an appreciation of the real wealth of the state as revealed in its agricultural and pastoral resources. Even during the gold excitement men were driven by shortage of food to cultivation and cattle raising. The spirit of enterprise, daring, and self-reliance, so characteristic of the heroic days of the captaincy, though temporarily dimmed, suffered no permanent eclipse. It is in no sense fortuitous that the first movement towards independence, the heroic but ill-starred conspiracy of Tiradentes, had its origin in the "Rich City of Black Gold." In the events leading up to the separation of Brazil from Portugal, Minas played an honorable part. In the trying days when Brazilian unity was at stake Minas with her central location, her relatively large population, and her keen sense of loyalty might be said to have served as a keystone of the arch which united north and south. And in our own days the spirit of progress allied with practical patience and laborious perseverance has placed Minas in an enviable position among the twenty states of the Brazilian Republic. . . .

It is quite impossible in a few words to indicate all of the larger and more remote consequences of the discovery of gold in California. As was the case in Minas the space of a few years witnessed an increase in population which under normal conditions might have spread over several decades. As regards the effect of the gold discovery on the social evolution of California conditions *mutatis mutandis* were not so dissimilar to those existing in Minas. The immigrants, in so far as they came from different parts of the United States, were subjected to a process of assimilation which deeply affected California life. The unhappy sectional quarrels which had prevailed at home were softened and forgotten. The intimate union of men from the North and the South, from the Atlantic coast and the Mississippi valley tended to accentuate American characteristics as distinguished from local characteristics. In the case of both Minas and California there was evolved a type which is national in its fullest sense.

10

SÉRGIO BUARQUE
DE HOLANDA

❀

The Monsoons

The historian Sérgio Buarque de Holanda, born in São
Paulo in 1902, has been concerned more with backlands
than with coastal Brazil and more with his country's
Indo-European than with its Afro-European colonial
culture. His studies contain a wealth of detail on aboriginal artifacts, crafts, and lore, and on the tactics
and "Edenic vision" of the pathfinder. This reading
deals with the "monsoons," the riverborne prospecting
expeditions which succeeded the bandeiras, and with the
process of settlement in the Cuiabá-Mato Grosso region.
It is interesting that the convoys of pirogues described
here bear many resemblances to the "brigades" of canoes
which the North West Company dispatched along the
rivers of Canada in the late eighteenth century.

Formerly director of the Paulista Museum, Buarque
de Holanda holds the chair of History of Brazilian Civilization at the University of São Paulo. His works include *Monções* (Rio de Janeiro, 1945), a book-length
study of the monsoons, as well as those cited in the
Introduction.

From Sérgio Buarque de Holanda, ed., *História geral da civilização brasileira* (2 vols. in 4; São Paulo, 1960-64), I (Part 1),
307-21. Translated; and printed by permission of Difusão Européia do Livro Ltda.

From the history of the bandeiras, taken in the strict sense, one may omit without great loss the chapter of the monsoons. These make their appearance when the bandeiras are already in decline. Monsoons utilize different techniques, are guided by their own methods, and are activated, to a certain extent, by a new breed of men.

In a broader, perhaps somewhat arbitrary sense, however —one which seeks to combine under one heading the various movements tending to expand our frontiers and make use of our territory—the monsoons deserve a definite place, and a place neither small nor irrelevant.

The monsoons represent in fact one of the clear expressions of that expansionist force which seems to have been a constant in Paulista history; it had previously revealed itself in the bandeiras and was later to drive the cattle herders along the southern routes. Viewing them as a whole, today's historian would perhaps identify these phenomena as a single constellation.

One may properly indicate, nonetheless, a special affinity between the bandeiras and the monsoons, and even an uncertain moment of transition, a kind of shadow zone where they meet and merge. The discovery of the Coxipó-Mirim mines, which marks the starting point for the history of the monsoons, preceded by several years one of the greatest bandeirante undertakings, perhaps the last great one—the journey of the second Anhangüera [Bartolomeu Bueno da Silva, the younger] to the Goiases. For that matter another bandeirante enterprise with equal claims is the expedition of Pascoal Moreira Cabral. It is precisely because of this expedition, as well as that of Fernando Dias Falcão, that the monsoons are entwined with the history of the bandeiras and become in a certain sense their prolongation.

It has already been observed that the first monsoons of Cuiabá must have recruited the same rough people who had composed the bandeiras of the seventeenth century. As long as these river journeys lasted, the situation apparently did not change. . . .

This surface commotion, however, should not conceal from us the deep transformation that was gradually being wrought in the mentality of these new sertanistas. One cannot but realize that the long river journeys had a disciplinary and somewhat dampening effect on the traditionally adventurous spirit of these men. The very confinement within the pirogues of the monsoons was itself a way of organizing unruliness, of inducing good harmony or, at least, the ephemeral concurrence of conflicting ambitions. The absence of the unlimited spaces which invite movement, the unending spectacle of riverside forests that block the horizon from view, the forced abdication of private desires when the lives of all are in the hands of a few or of one alone, all this would have powerfully influenced the adventurers seeking the distant sertão. If the image of this band clustered at the stern of a boat appears in some way disorderly, it is the disorder not of passions in tumult but of methodical and submissive ambitions.

The use of different means of locomotion but also, more important, the pattern of attitudes and behavior determined by each of these means will help us to grasp more clearly the essential distinction between the early bandeira and the so-called monsoons of settlement. For the former the rivers were actually obstacles to travel, and boats, generally simple bark canoes or crude rafts, were merely an occasional recourse of the sertanista, available where foot travel became impossible. For the monsoons, on the other hand, water transport was the rule and travel by foot, horse, or wagon . . . the exception.

It was not by chance that in São Paulo the technique of river transport reached its phase of greatest development principally in the eighteenth century, with the decadence of the bandeiras. Although the Tietê had come to serve as an inland route long before this, the truth is that its course became generally used, and made more easily navigable by new contrivances, only when a system of regular communications with the heart of the continent became necessary.

As a result, those who participate in the commerce with Cuiabá and Mato Grosso have more systematic ambitions without renouncing the mobile existence of the bandeirante. The rhythm that governs all their activity is no longer that of simple individual energy, wholly free to expand. They must submit their very lives to new boundaries and new pressures. To those divine and natural limits which were in fact the only ones that many of the sertanistas of old understood there now accrue with increasing strength the tyrannies of law and justice, the norms of social and political life, and the frequently capricious demands of those in power. What remains as an element common to both groups is perhaps serene courage, an apparent indifference to threats, to dangers, and often to the greatest catastrophes.

Parallels between the monsoons of the Orient and those of Brazil

How and in what period did this new phase of Paulista sertanismo with its own distinct features begin to emerge? The very word "monsoon," apparently of Arabic origin and in general use among Portuguese sailors during the great maritime discoveries in the Orient, was probably unknown in São Paulo in the sense later given to it until the second decade of the eighteenth century. In its original meaning in Portuguese it must have designated the alternating winds which determined the sailing seasons.

Here enters an important distinction, since sail navigation was unknown to the Paulistas on our riverways. It is true that even in Portugal the term had eventually come to designate simply the seasons suitable for voyages, the periods of favorable winds. . . . Generally speaking, however, it was simply the season of the rains, and not of the winds as in Arabia and India, that determined the schedule for us.

We have yet to point out [another] comparison, relating to the duration of the voyages. The trip from São Paulo, or rather Pôrto Feliz, to Cuiabá, took no less than five months, exactly the usual time for voyages from Lisbon to India, and incidentally much more than that necessary to sail from Rio de Janeiro to the mouth of the Tagus.

Like the distant Orient, our Cuiabá was for a long time a place of legendary riches, riches to be acquired through audacity and heroism and not base labor, as judged by the notions of the age. In both cases these riches exercised an enormous power of attraction over men, resulting in the progressive abandonment of all other useful activities. In the day of a Sá de Miranda [Portuguese dramatist, d. 1558] the smell of cinnamon could depopulate the kingdom, and the incense of India could pervert the ancient, austere customs of the Portuguese people. Here, the gold of the sertão ruined São Paulo and reduced it to misery, so much so that its sons had to endure the loss of their very autonomy, to become wholly subordinated to the government of Rio de Janeiro for a period of more than fifteen years.

Discovery of the mines and decadence of São Paulo

The more certain although more arduous rewards of farming were quickly abandoned for those of the shining metal of the mines, which, according to the old chronicles, was so accessible that it could be extracted from the ground as cream is skimmed from milk. Those who remained anchored to their homes engaged in less lucrative tasks were not sufficient to support the population of the captaincy by their agriculture, so that some went to the mines seeking wealth and others some relief that would allow them better to sustain this earthly life. Of few could it be said, as in the elegy by Camoëns, that:

> One lives with his trees content,
> His restful slumber quite unbroken
> By the enormous greed for gleaming gold.

The havoc to which these mines—wealth-producing, to be sure, but only superficially so—were to condemn the other branches of activity in the colony, and principally this captaincy, had such effects that even at the end of the eighteenth century Bishop José da Cunha de Azeredo Coutinho, in the curious *Report on the Boundary Division between Portugal and Castile in America,* of which a manuscript exists in the National Library of Rio de Janeiro, proposes that the mines be abandoned, even if in favor of the Spaniard. For in this way, he claimed, the Portuguese would come to be their real and effective owners. Returning to the thesis developed in his well known *Discourses on the Present State of the Mines of Brazil,* he asserts: "It is a proven fact, demonstrable by experience, that the Nation which trades directly with a gold-producing Nation is always the richer of the two." It should be added that when the prelate-economist wrote this tract neither the mines of Australia nor those of California or of South Africa had yet been discovered or exploited.

Let us disregard, however, what is specious, artificial, and purely theoretical in the complaints of Azeredo Coutinho, inspired in part by the doctrine of the French physiocrats, his contemporaries, and let us focus on the impression of disenchantment which the riches of our western sertão, already in decadence, were creating. At the time of their discovery this pessimistic note might certainly have existed among some dissatisfied or melancholy souls, but it was in no way a general rule. Rather, the general rule is expressed in the excitement which was kindled, according to a chronicler of the time, by the news of the discovery. In his words: "Many people [flocked there] leaving houses, plantations, wives, and children, casting themselves upon these sertões as if this were the hidden Paradise where God placed our first ancestors."

Countless exaggerations concerning the new mines and the fame of Cuiabá spread like wildfire, continues Barbosa de Sá, a witness or near-witness of the events: "Word echoed to the ends of the earth, passing the Boundaries of Brazil and Portugal and thence to foreign Realms." It was said that hunters used pellets of gold instead of lead in their muskets and that hearthstones of gold were used for kettles. Such was the abundance of the precious metal that if one pulled up clumps of wild grass their roots came to view covered with gold.

But it was not this wealth that had first driven the sertanistas to the remote sertão. During most of the seventeenth century the lands west of the Paraná River were looked on as great reserves of tamed or wild Indians, whom the Paulistas went to capture for their farms. . . .

As far as is known, however, the first Paulista to reach the banks of the River Cuiabá was Antônio Pires de Campos, who was still searching not for the precious metal but for the Coxiponó Indians who lived in these parts. The second was Pascoal Moreira Cabral, who while also hunting Indians chanced upon some gold nuggets embedded along the banks of the River Coxipó-Mirim. From this site he ascended to the Forquilha, where he captured some Indians who carried bits of gold in their labrets and other ornaments.

He then decided to assemble his companions and pitch camp at the site where the chapel of St. Gonçalo was later erected. The labor of prospecting for gold began immediately. As they had not come prepared to mine, the expeditionaries had to improvise instruments. Thus eating plates were used as gold-washing pans and musket barrels as picks. Some dug the earth with their hands and might occasionally by this method collect as much as two hundred oitavas of gold in a short time.

While engaged in this activity they received the help of the Antunes brothers from Sorocaba, whose forces joined those of the discoverers. Later when, lacking arms, powder, and shot, they were suddenly attacked by hostile Indians, they received unexpected and opportune help from another bandeira, that of Fernando Dias Falcão. It would seem that this help was decisive, for the bandeira was composed of one hundred thirty fighting men and was in every way equipped for mining and for fighting Indians.

The first successful results of an enterprise which would considerably expand the Portuguese domain in America can be attributed to the spirit of initiative, the experience, and the substantial resources of Fernando Dias Falcão, as much as to Pascoal Moreira Cabral. Upon returning to São Paulo, perhaps in company with Antônio Antunes Maciel, the fearless man from Parnaíba sets about organizing at his own expense a new expedition which in 1719 is already en route to the River Coxipó, with the skills necessary for exploiting the new-found riches. With him went blacksmiths, carpenters, tailors, everything in fact that was needed to establish the camp. Besides the heavy outlay to which he had to pledge himself to purchase and transport a great amount of equipment (six arrôbas of gunpowder alone), he loaned large sums to many companions. . . .

On his return to the camp Dias Falcão was elected leader of the miners, while Pascoal Moreira retained the post of military commander for which he had been previously chosen. Though relegated to a secondary position, the discoverer did not fail to recognize Falcão's great merits when later he alleged that the latter knew how to act "in a Catholic manner," looking after the inhabitants and keeping the people united. It is easy to judge the prosperity soon achieved by the settlement when we consider that back in São Paulo in about 1723 the leader of the miners of Cuiabá was able to pay twelve pounds and eighty-four oitavas of gold as a royal fifth to the king's treasury.

The mines of Senhor Bom Jesus do Cuiabá

This prosperity was heightened when by a stroke of luck the adventurers discovered the extremely rich alluvial deposits of a site near that of the Coxipó-Mirim, precisely where the city of Cuiabá stands today. . . . News of these fabulous riches, which apparently surpassed anything yet seen in Brazil, spread quickly despite the precautions taken by the discoverers. The result was the almost complete abandonment of the old encampment of Coxipó-Mirim. Everybody flocked in tumult to the "workings of [Miguel] Sutil."

Soon the thick vegetation that covered these rich lands had been cleared away, and after a month of frenzied labor the mines of Senhor Bom Jesus do Cuiabá, as they were later called after the church that was built there, had yielded more than four hundred arrôbas of ore from diggings generally not much exceeding a depth of half a meter. When the news reached São Paulo it caused the almost immediate exodus of its able-bodied population. During the first years of production the persons, Paulistas and emboabas, who arrived at the Cuiabá encampment numbered in the hundreds and thousands.

Under these conditions it was difficult to attempt to establish any political order and economic control, in spite of the efforts of Pascoal Moreira, who tried to set up a kind of rural senate in which he himself, as the military commander, along with a notary, a bailiff, and twelve elected functionaries served with the title of deputy. At the same time it was decided to collect the royal tribute on the basis of gold-washing pans, or rather, the number of slaves or workers who used them. This was to adopt the scheme that had been employed in Minas Gerais before the introduction of a flat assessment by Dom Brás Baltasar da Silveira. It was the system that had been commended by the new governor of São Paulo, Rodrigo César de Meneses, as being the most useful for the crown and the least severe for the people.

In spite of all these efforts these people were victims of their own passions, divided into turbulent factions and often at the mercy of the whims of caudillos such as the terrible brothers Lourenço and João Leme da Silva. Little else could be expected, given the remoteness of the encampment and the difficulties of communication with São Paulo.

Itineraries and river convoys

The itinerary of the first river voyages varied, since they were undertaken without plan and at no fixed season. The canoes used to proceed down the Tietê to its mouth, follow what is today the Paraná, and then take one of its right-bank tributaries, generally the Pardo. In the latter case they next went up the Anhanduí-Guaçu to the watershed of the Paraguay River, which they eventually reached along one of its eastern tributaries. Heading up the Paraguay, they came to the São Lourenço and finally the Cuiabá, which took them to the new promised land.

It was in about 1720 and thanks to the efforts of the Leme brothers that the advantages were perceived which would derive from altering this itinerary so that the pirogues would ascend the rapids of the Pardo, above the bar of the Anhanduí-Guaçu, as far as the Sanguexuga. It is precisely here that the watershed of the Paraná and Paraguay is narrowest, about two and a half leagues wide. . . .

There were obvious conveniences in a short portage here for the pirogues, both for more efficient transportation and for more effective defense against hostile Indians. Once the site was chosen, however, it was necessary to plant crops and provide cattle for supplying the expeditions. This is what was done soon after 1725 when the plantation of Camapoã was established at the portage.

Another measure more and more required for purposes of defense was the formation of large convoys to replace the generally isolated units used in the early days. Because the season most favorable for these trips was relatively short, and large sums of money were usually tied up in them, only one convoy embarked each year as a rule. For their better protection, private canoes were allowed to sail with the official vessels, which were well fitted out and armed for war.

Other measures learned through time and experience had to do mainly with the protection of the merchandise and foodstuffs transported as well as of the travelers. Lack of such protection caused severe losses in the early days. For example, a convoy which left São Paulo in 1720 lost all of its passengers and crew. Those who came after found rotten food along the route and, in the canoes, the dead bodies of the travelers. The whole year of 1720 passed without a living soul arriving at the Coxipó settlement, although numerous persons had embarked on the Tietê with that destination. . . .

Vessels, crews, and merchandise

. . . [The] technique of river navigation adopted by the monsoons was virtually a continuation of Indian methods. One can say that the manufacture of the canoes, the materials used for their construction, and the very methods of navigation reveal no European influence at all. Dugout canoes hollowed from a single trunk were generally employed. It is natural that these should have been preferred for their strength and durability to the simple bark canoes, also of Indian origin and used by many of the old-time bandeirantes. . . .

One gathers from old accounts that the normal size of these canoes was twelve to thirteen meters in length by a meter and a half in width. The relation of width to length is thus approximately one to ten, giving the long, slim silhouette which to contemporaries suggested similarity to a cotton-weaving shuttle. It should be added that both stern and bow were extremely pointed, which reinforced the comparison.

During the journeys the central area was reserved for cargo. In the open spaces at the bow, which did not exceed two or three meters, went six oarsmen with the pilot and the bowman. Where there were rapids an extra guide or pilot was carried, or sometimes two who worked alternately. In methods of navigation as in construction technique the indigenous tradition clearly prevailed—for example, the practice of the oarsmen to stand as they rowed. Before the coming of the white man this was the custom not only in Brazil but throughout the American continent.

The bowman seems to have been the most important crew member, for he carried the keys to the salt-meat chest and the liquor supply. He was in complete charge of the bow, where he set the beat for the oarsmen by striking his heel on the deck. Navigational experience had so sharpened his powers of observation that from the slightest movement of the water he could often detect where it was deep or shallow and where there were channels or rocks. Frequently he knew from memory all the conditions which could affect navigation along this route of more than one hundred rapids. It is therefore not surprising that he enjoyed great prestige and, as a chronicler of the day noted, could show off with "all the swagger of an indulged and respected commoner." At certain places the crew was forced to travel by land, dragging the pirogues or hoisting them with ropes, which consumed much time and effort. At medium or small rapids the vessels were not taken from the river, although cargo and passengers had to be removed.

The combined total of passengers and crew never exceeded twenty-five or thirty. . . .

It is known that the larger craft could carry up to three and four hundred arrôbas of merchandise, not counting the food consumed en route, which was generally replenished at the Camapoã fazenda. Boatmen and passengers were both content with a daily ration of slightly more than one hundred grams of bacon, a liter of flour (either corn or manioc), and half a liter of beans. These products, particularly the beans, which were the *panem nostrum quotidianum* of the boatmen, in effect comprised, according to one of them, the basis of their entire diet. . . .

The merchandise transported included everything to meet the immediate necessities and also the comforts of life—from the salt, destined for the kitchens of the wealthy and poor alike, to the silk fabrics for celebrations or solemnities. For the only export from Cuiabá was gold, and little else was produced there: "Gold that the land is now weary of yielding . . . ," as Luís D'Alincourt, an engineering sergeant major, commented a century after the first monsoons.

The commercial fleets, which sometimes included as many as three or four hundred canoes, carried enough food to guarantee the inhabitants of Cuiabá against famine, and later those of Vila Bela and other settlements born of Cuiabá's expansion as the early ore deposits were depleted. The crops and animals which they themselves raised served merely to insure that mining operations would not slacken, placing their source of wealth in jeopardy of fatal collapse.

The settlement process

Some of the bases for a subsistence economy were laid only gradually and, in some cases, not without strong resistance from the authorities. The first settlers of the Cuiabá encampment led a life comparable to that of the Indian hunters and gatherers, an existence conceivable only in wide, free spaces and compatible only with a nomadic, uncertain way of life. By its nature, however, the activity of mining required a striking of roots and a sedentariness ordinarily achieved by the concentration and reproduction of the irreducible means of subsistence within a relatively limited locale.

A few vague references by old chroniclers help us to accompany various stages of this settlement process, which were frequently disturbed by serious crises. Thus we know that the first corn crop harvested in Cuiabá in 1723 was not sufficient for the inhabitants. Hunting and to a lesser degree fishing therefore became compulsory for anyone wishing to survive. Planting of corn, done in conformance to bandeirante traditions, was followed after subsequent monsoons by cultivation of beans, squash, and possibly manioc. In 1728 sugar cane was brought in by a settler—surreptitiously, because its cultivation in the area of the diggings had been prohibited by the authorities. One reason for this restriction was that the cane tended to draw off slaves from their work in the mines. The other apparently more plausible one was the mischief that might result from the consumption of aguardente by the miners.

But the imbalance created by the intrusion of more or less stable and domestic types of activity in a sertão still unprepared to receive them was not to be corrected merely by cultivation of the soil. This measure had to be complemented by the introduction of livestock. The first animals, pigs and chickens, came with the monsoon of 1723. Only later would the ox and horse be brought in. It is reported that toward the end of 1727 the first cows arrived in pirogues, four or six small heifers which had reproduced by 1730. One can imagine what the task was to transport this cattle both overland and in pirogues along innumerable rapids from Araritaguaba, now Pôrto Feliz, all the way to the mines. The worst is that apparently the animals could not keep on breeding for long, owing perhaps to a lack of salt, so that a new shipment of animals had to be made in 1739.

Although so limited in their resources and so remote from the rest of the world, the inhabitants of Cuiabá were nonetheless able to create a stable and lasting center of settlement. They were even able to transform this center into the fulcrum of a new system of colonization, which by 1734 reached the Amazon basin along the banks of the Guaporé with the discovery of the Mato Grosso mines by the Pais de Barros brothers.

In what sense can one say that this surprising colonizing movement of our Far West was fruitful for the present and even the future civilization of Brazil? . . .

The Paulista colonization of Cuiabá and Mato Grosso repeats on a smaller scale the Portuguese colonization of Brazil. São Paulo gave what it could, which certainly was not much, since it lacked in manpower and material resources what it possessed to surfeit in energy. The central lands which were finally annexed to Portuguese America through the efforts of its sons had to make do with a kind of reflex existence based, in turn, on what might be called a purely "extroverted" economy. Human labor was totally mobilized for the search for gold. In this, the effort of which the monsoons were a conspicuous part can be roughly likened to a monstrous and disorderly capitalist enterprise—"capitalist" in the broadest sense and, naturally, a less rigorous one than the word properly admits. All gestures, all actions are determined in this case by love of money, and they aim toward a precise, formulated objective. So absorbing, in turn, is this objective that it relegates to a lower plane whatever does not immediately serve it.

Thus, in the system of communication adopted, the only real advances, gradually introduced, were at the initiative of the private individuals who ventured on the journeys, and they were born of direct experience with no outside help or stimulus. The testimony of a passenger written in 1727 gives an idea of what these river trips involved: "I left Sorocaba with fourteen Negroes and three canoes of mine; I lost two along the way and arrived with one and with seven hundred oitavas I had borrowed, having also laid out for supplies en route. Of the Negroes, I sold six of mine that I had bought on credit in Sorocaba and four of the eight my uncle had given me, and all ten went for payment of debts. Of those that remained, three died and I had only one left, and the same happened to all who went to Cuiabá. Finally, of the twenty-three canoes in which we left Sorocaba, only fourteen arrived at Cuiabá; nine were lost, and the same happened to the other convoys, and it happens every year on this trip."

We might add that this would continue to happen with little change until the first decades of the last century, when the river journeys to Cuiabá became more and more infrequent. We know that the last trips occurred around 1838, a year when an epidemic of typhoid fever raged along the banks of the Tietê, leaving few survivors among the remaining boatmen and pilots of Pôrto Feliz. During the period of more than a century, from 1719 to 1822, the mines of present-day Mato Grosso had yielded, according to the necessarily uncertain estimates of Calógeras, a little more than 5,000 arrôbas of gold.

Could such wealth compensate for all that the monsoons exacted of the settlers of Central Brazil? Whatever the answer, there is no doubt that they made an inestimable contribution to the national unity of Brazil. The opening of regular communications between Mato Grosso and Pará, which created one more trade route for those sertões, is in large measure attributable to the experience of the rivermen, pilots, and bowmen of the pirogues of the monsoons. Actually, this route constitutes a prolongation toward the far north of the old river route which extends from the south, from the Paulista plateau.

The historic function of this route, more than a thousand leagues long, traversing almost the entire country, is more important than that of any other lines of natural circulation in our territory, not excluding the São Francisco itself, a river called by many the "river of national unity."

Another permanent result is that the monsoons admirably corroborated the work initiated by the bandeiras, assuring us full and tranquil possession of an area of millions of square kilometers. It is significant that this aspect did not pass unperceived at the time the voyages were made. Writing toward the close of the eighteenth century, the Paulista geographer and explorer Francisco José de Lacerda e Almeida noted that, although there perhaps existed a more convenient route, which might advantageously replace the arduous ascent of the River Pardo, he did not dare recommend abandonment of the latter by the commercial monsoons. The fact is that, while they did not populate the plains of Vacaria and other lands between the Paraná and the Paraguay, conditions made it advisable for them to continue frequenting these parts by the usual route, lest they be left open to the greed of the Spaniard.

IV

● ● ●

THE
BANDEIRAS
IN
HISTORICAL
PERSPECTIVE

11

MARIO GÓNGORA

✺

Some Comparative Points of View

The Chilean historian Mario Góngora has done important work on the institutional history of Spanish America, notably in his study of the state in the law of the Spanish Indies, *El estado en el derecho indiano* (Santiago, 1951). In the book from which this reading comes he analyzes the bands (*bandas*) or mounted foray parties (*cabalgadas*) of the Spanish conquerors in northern South America. He suggests a parallel between them and the bandeiras, and common antecedents for both in medieval Iberian history. This is one of the few systematic attempts to establish a comparative historical context for the bandeiras, although other historians, such as Torquato de Sousa Soares in his *Presores—bandeirantes* (Coimbra, 1953), have tried to identify their specifically Portuguese origins.

Mario Góngora is director of the Center of Colonial History, University of Chile.

From Mario Góngora, *Los grupos de conquistadores en Tierra Firme (1509-1530)* (Santiago, 1962), excerpted from pp. 91-105. Translated; and printed by permission of the Centro de Historia Colonial, Universidad de Chile.

The Cabalgada in the Iberian Frontier Wars

One finds the image of medieval Iberian history as an advancing frontier repeatedly set forth, sometimes in the traditional military version, other times as a settlement frontier in an interpretation having something in common with the famous thesis of North American historiography.

The "cabalgada," the institution of particular interest in this study, is typical of the frontier war. Like the *algara* (mounted raiding party) which it greatly resembles, it may be affiliated with the Arab raid. The relationship between Hispanic and Arab military units has been demonstrated in a few cases. The cabalgada appears in systematic legislated form in the Fuero (Code) of Cuenca and the Second Partida [of the Code of the *Siete Partidas*]—that is, in the mid-thirteenth century—which, as one would expect, undoubtedly codify the standing custom. The Spanish versions of the Fuero of Cuenca and the Fuero Viejo of the Cabalgadas complete this regulation. While the word "host" (*hueste*), aside from its generic meaning, is applied specifically to an army of considerable masses, often commanded by the king, the Partidas speak of "cabalgada" when "a few companies set forth without a host moving rapidly to strike at some point or to inflict damage on their enemies, or when they separate from the host after the latter is in movement with this same objective." The algara and the *corredura* are used for riding about the land to pillage what they can. Hence we are speaking of the forms of light warfare carried on by companies or parties. . . . The cabalgada is sent out by the local magistrates or by the chiefs. Its members share the authority and the profits.

One obtains a true picture of frontier warfare and the cabalgadas from the chronicles. Those of the fifteenth century are of particular interest to us because they describe the wars on the frontier of Granada, an area which was pacified only in 1500, as they immediately precede the conquests in the Indies in which so many Andalusians participated.

These wars took place on the plain of Granada and in the large surrounding mountain ranges, from Tarifa to the kingdom of Murcia, constantly endangering all of Andalusia. The chronicle narrates countless episodes of the cabalgadas: sieges of forts, ambuscades, destructions of crops, pursuit of trails, assaults, etc. But there is also the frontier life in times of truce, marked by other relations that are especially studied by J. de M. Carriazo: pledges, ransom of captives negotiated by special officials (*alfaqueques*), etc. The booty, also called "cabalgada," consists mainly of cattle, captives, clothes, or other movable goods carried by the rearguard pack animals. A good part of the captives were ransomed, in accordance with the amount of their wealth. Others fell definitively into slavery. . . .

The Castilian, Leonese, and Aragonese frontier produced specialized warriors, as is normal in long-lasting wars. On one hand are the high-ranking Military Orders, first formed as small fraternities of soldier-monks living on the frontier, a tendency common to both Islam and European Christianity. Later these fraternities took on a corporative and aristocratic character, although this did not occur in the Indies and therefore does not concern us. On the other hand, there was a class of warriors of lesser rank, eager above all for booty, experienced in small local warfare, who were fully acquainted with the environment and the enemy's forms of combat, and whose establishment within the limits of a city had been inherited since the resettlement of Andalusia in the thirteenth century. . . .

Too strict a comparison between the peninsular frontier wars and those in the Indies cannot be drawn. The settings are too different with respect both to physical environment and to the opposing enemy. A genetic relation rather than a parallel is involved. On the peninsular and, more recently, on the Andalusian frontier there had evolved various kinds of war and of social situation which were experienced by men of the generation just preceding that which took part in the emigration to the Indies.

The Andalusian-Berber-Canary Island Area and the Caribbean Area

From the end of the fourteenth to the end of the sixteenth century there developed a chain of relations through maritime trade, privateering, and slaving at the western end of the Mediterranean and in the waters of the Atlantic to Cape Bojador. The participants were Andalusians, Portuguese, Canary Islanders, inhabitants of Castilian and Portuguese garrisons in Africa, and Berber corsairs. Beyond Bojador, the Portuguese had gained recognition of their supremacy by [the Treaty of] Alcáçovas (1479) and [the Convention of] Sintra (1509). Here began another cycle of European expansion: in Guinea, land of ransom and trading posts, closed except occasionally to Spanish forays and commerce, which in the fifteenth century had also appeared in the area.

If we turn our attention exclusively to the first of these areas we are struck by the analogy to the world of the islands and mainland outposts of the Caribbean, as it developed in the first four decades of the sixteenth century. In both zones we find rich lands with already long-established colonial populations, dependent on slave labor, self-supplying in foods, breeding-grounds for conquistadors who confront enslaveable men and lands which produce or traffic in gold. In both cases the captives are obtained through sudden assaults by small flotillas or else through the presence of coastal forts, garrisons, or cities from which cabalgadas set forth into the aboriginal interior.

The relations are essentially of this nature in Africa. . . . Andalusia and the Canary Islands have specialized in assaults and the brief coastal entrada. Toward 1494 an anonymous author writes that the knights of Jerez, the men of Puerto de Santa María, Cádiz, San Lúcar, the duchy of Medina Sidonia, Gibraltar, Cartagena, and Lorca have for years been accustomed to sweeping the land, falling upon the *aduares*—the circular villages of tents of the Moroccan Moors—and capturing Moslem ships. The chiefs of these places had an intimate knowledge of the fortified points, the landing places, the watchtowers, and the stratagems employed. These men, he adds, cost the king no money, for they are always available to go on a cabalgada and to seize male and female Moors. He says that officials of the guard and knights have been able to go forth for several days almost without expense, in numbers up to 50 horsemen and 700 soldiers, returning laden with booty. . . .

The Canary Islands, another classic theater for slave-raiding cabalgadas from the fourteenth century until the conquests of Alonso de Lugo, are in turn a starting point for cabalgadas in the Atlantic Berber region, and sometimes in Guinea. . . . The slaves captured by the Canary Islanders serve to augment the manpower for their sugar mills. Those who fall into the hands of Andalusians and Portuguese are used principally in Iberian territory proper. However, the number of captives ransomed for money in Africa, as along the Granada frontier earlier, seems to have been considerable. The alfaqueques who negotiated these transactions would of course be particularly concerned with the case of prisoners having higher economic standing, while the poorer ones easily fell into slavery. In any case the medieval practice of ransom applied by the Europeans to the Moriscos differs greatly from their behavior with respect to the Indians of America. Aside from a few exceptional instances revealed in the chronicles, there is no doubt that the captives taken by the American entradas fell almost in their entirety into perpetual servitude, either as legal slaves or as allotted servants.

But the brief assault expedition is only one of the forms of action. The other, namely, the conquest or founding of outposts or frontier towns for the security of coastal navigation or for penetration into a hinterland, is more complex. The objective of these establishments forms part, in each case, of a broad political history which is not relevant to examine here: the history of Portuguese expansion and of Spanish domination in Africa which, be it said, ended in the abandonment or loss of almost all the outposts for lack of sufficient internal dynamism. All that concerns us here is to point out that precisely because it was a "limited occupation," which in both cases sought to evade the immense problems of deep penetration and a striking of roots in Africa, the cabalgadas played an important role. In the Spanish garrisons of Melilla, Orán, Bujía, Mers-el-Kebir, Peñón de Argel, the cabalgada is a remedy for the soldiers' poverty and overdue wages: a *coup de main*. In the stronghold and town of Arzila, which we know well thanks to the Annals of Bernardo Rodrigues written in 1560, ten years after the fall of the fort and town, the cabalgada is the preferred occupation of the population. In practically every chapter of the Annals a cabalgada is described, starting with the first decade of the sixteenth century. This population is composed of front-line horsemen, men of the king's household who receive payment and fight in these towns equipped as knights, soldiers, inhab-

itants, merchants, artisans, adventurers, prospectors, contra-
bandists, etc. The booty, in addition to the Moriscos, consists
of cattle and camels. Sometimes gold from the Sudan is
obtained as ransom. The export of captives, wax, and hides
serves to provoke a lively exchange with Algarve and Andalusia, two regions rich in cereals—a commercial system well
described by Robert Ricard.

Military technique is the same as that of the Peninsula.
Renegade Moriscos usually serve as guides, but the cabalgada
is composed only of Spaniards and Portuguese.

Some who have been in Berber lands, generally Canary
Islanders, participate in the war of the Indies, and the chroni-
clers emphasize their prowess. Such is the case of Agustín
Delgado, lieutenant of Jerónimo de Ortel, who took part,
Pedro de Aguado tells us, in the Canary entradas in Africa.
The Canary Islands population recruited for Santa Marta
and Cartagena must have appreciably increased the number
of those soldiers habituated to capturing slaves.

The analogy of the Andalusian-Canary-Berber situation to
the complex of relationships existing between Tierra Firme
and the islands of the Caribbean is quite evident. In both
areas there are attacks or plundering assaults on the native
population; provisions are paid for by traffic in slaves; and
there is the interminable series of cabalgadas. But the fundamental difference is that in America the choice was always
made to proceed as quickly as possible toward complete
domination. And as the cities of Tierra Firme become increasingly involved with the interior through territorial
control, the more they become in a sense independent of the
islands. Panama acquires more stability than Darién as it
becomes established on the encomienda system; at the same
time the cabalgadas become less frequent, and are now directed only toward lands not yet appropriated or explored.
In the case of Mexico, from the founding of Veracruz and
the march to the interior Cortés already seems to wish to assert himself in full control of the world which he is conquering. And here the analogy with Africa ceases.

In spite of the undeniable similarities, the difference is
evident in the contrasting pattern of forces obtaining between the protagonists: the rich and ancient lands on one
hand; the cities or strongholds of the conquistadors on the

other; in short, the indigenous world and the wealth of its territories.

Cabalgadas and Paulista bandeiras

Although the whole history of Brazil abounds in the process of territorial expansion, we can for purposes of comparison limit ourselves to the Paulista bandeira and leave aside the Pernambucan, Bahian, and Amazonian expansion which, although likewise related to the search for metals and to enslavement, fails to exhibit the bandeirante character in its purity.

Not all that Brazilian historiography labels "bandeiras" is of interest for our purpose. According to the classifications of [Basílio de] Magalhães and Taunay, this general phenomenon includes the expansion of cattle raising toward the São Francisco River and the sertão of Pernambuco; the great emigrant wave which advances toward Minas Gerais, Cuiabá, Goiás, and other mining regions discovered after the 1690's; and the colonizing expeditions to Laguna and the southern territories. The bandeira which lends itself to comparison with the Spanish cabalgada is specifically the slaving bandeira, which also has prospecting for minerals in view but does not result in new settlement; instead it returns to São Paulo with its booty of Indians. It is, in other words, the depopulating bandeira.

The best definition given in historiography for this type of band is that of Rocha Pombo: small assault groups which were detached from a body of troops or from a garrison for a swift operation. It is synonymous, that is, with the algara or cabalgada of medieval Castilian legislation. Thus in medieval Portugal it was a small group of about thirty members; but in São Paulo it assumed a very different composition.

It would be beside the point to refer here to the politico-territorial significance of bandeirante expansion, so much emphasized in studies by Brazilians from Capistrano de Abreu to Jaime Cortesão. We are more interested in the internal structure, the best analysis of which we owe to Alcântara Machado, based on the wills and inventories of the sertanistas.

This expansionist movement, epitomized in the bandeirante expeditions, develops not from the coast but from the inland plateau which is abruptly elevated above the São Vicente littoral. Its base is a city of insignificant wealth, inhabited by small or medium owners of ranches and farms (*roças*) of wheat, millet, cotton, and sugar cane, a far cry from the rich sugar plantations of the coast. . . .

The entrada into the sertão is, in the words of a 1681 document, a "remedy," "the normal business of this land." The city specializes in bandeirismo. . . . It acquires a marked military aspect and is independent of the bureaucracy. The Paulista bands in the sertão of the Northeast deal autonomously with the governors in negotiating their support for the authorities to put down the rebellions of the Palmares Negroes and of the Indians of coastal Bahia. Their caudillo, Domingos Jorge Velho, will make clear in 1694 that his troops are not registered in the king's muster books but are "groups in which some of us assemble, each one joining with the servants under arms that he possesses, and together entering the sertão of this continent." [See p. 118 above.]

The Indian and mestizo factors are of utmost importance. The Tupi who go along as military auxiliaries, recruited from the "administered" Indians (the "servants under arms" in the document just cited) and the Jesuit settlements, comprise the bulk of the force. The number of Portuguese or Brazilians generally varies from a minimum of 12 to 200 or 400 in the large bandeiras; there are always several hundred Indians, as many as 1,500. . . .

If we wish to establish what the Paulista bandeira before 1690 had in common with the cabalgadas and Spanish conquests, we would point out the spirit of a military band with its sense of independence, the slave-hunting trait, the search for metals and precious stones, the appeal to all classes of the city to share in the booty, and the financing through partnership contracts, which by no means implied resistance to accepting official aid when available.

But the differences between both types of enterprise are also great. With respect to armament, Brazil does not witness the predominance of the cavalry over the foot soldiers, with all that this implies for methods of war and for social mentality. The infantry, in spite of possessing firearms, is closer to the mass of allied, burden-bearing Indians, and like them it often uses the bow and arrow. The Negro does not have the great significance as an auxiliary that he had in the Spanish conquests. But above all there is the disparity in the time factor.

The Spanish conquests last, all in all, but a few years. Francisco Pizarro, who arrived in 1502 and died in 1541, at about the age of sixty, managed to take part in the whole sequence of events which unfolded in Santo Domingo, Tierra Firme, and Peru. The entire history of the conquests in Tierra Firme runs its course in twenty years; that of the central heartland of Mexico, in four or five. In São Paulo, on the other hand, the bandeiras determine the history of a city for about one hundred forty years before the new wave of mineral discoveries depopulates and exhausts it for another period. During that century and a half each generation educates the next for its role in the sertão. Youths of fourteen years set out; the caudillos take their brothers, fathers-in-law, brothers-in-law, etc. Paulista endogamy is so pronounced that it molds a population of initially very mixed origins— Portuguese from all the provinces and islands, Spaniards from Seville, Extremadura, and Castile, a handful of Flemings, etc.—into a group which over the generations becomes very homogeneous. Crossbreeding penetrates this society broadly, showing preference for the bandeiras and arising from them. Reciprocal interaction with the Indians could not be matched on this scale during the period of the Spanish conquests, and crossbreeding is a phenomenon which produces its effects after the conquests. São Paulo is like a prolonged, endemic conquest, established as a frontier way of life that is even more accentuated for being removed from the sea. Something of this process doubtless took hold in the Caribbean with the "islanders"; and the cabalgadas in Tierra Firme or Venezuela, lasting for twenty or for fifteen years, are a foretaste of what would occur in Brazil. The similarity in form between cabalgada and bandeira is in our opinion quite strong, although there are notable differences of degree.

Conclusion

The peninsular wars and later the Canary and African conquests reveal the formation of frontier warrior types and the practice of almost continuous cabalgadas, which the

Spanish and Portuguese transplanted to the new lands of conquest in America. Among the warriors one observes a distinction between Military Orders and loose bands which are differentiated by their measure of social and spiritual discipline; but in Africa and America the action of the Orders has already ceased, after their conversion in the fifteenth century into oligarchic institutions with neither corporate life nor functions to perform. The conquests fall into the hands of spontaneous bands of a type similar to the *adalides* (chiefs) with their *almogávares* (trained raiders).

What is peculiar to this type of combatant is not precisely the zeal for booty, since this is common to all ancient, medieval, and modern armies until the early eighteenth century— a constant that was conditioned by, among other things, a phase in the development of the Rights of War. In the internal wars among Christians it was even normal to take prisoners with the intention of ransom. What is peculiar to these frontiers is slavery. In the war against the Moslem, slavery and ransom are still alternatives, but such is no longer the case for Canary Islanders and American aborigines. The peninsular cabalgadas and, even more, the African and American ones are therefore an institution characteristic of war between peoples of different cultures who do not effectively recognize a common juridical system.

The duration of these slave-catching conquests and the vitality of the bands are a function of the limited or total occupation of the territory and of the conditions prevailing there to sustain a superimposed seignorial stratum which could eliminate the bands and raids. This stage was never reached in the Berber lands, where the Europeans remained faithful to a policy of limited occupation, alliances, and protectorates. In America the transition occurred at different moments, depending on the location and wealth of the territory and the type of indigenous population. São Paulo is an unparalleled example of prolonged duration of the bands.

We may ask ourselves if the phenomena described are peculiar to Iberian expansion or whether they form part of processes more vast. In the frame of this study we can merely formulate the question. In the German Northeast, the Teutonic and Brothers-of-the-Sword Orders—whose "warrior mission" is so similar to the official Spanish position as it is formulated in the *Requerimiento* [manifesto of the faith proclaimed to the Indians]—achieve domination over village peoples not by uprooting them but by subjecting them to a manorial system. The Cossacks, another large-scale example of frontier warriors conquering new territorial domains, have a different way of life: fugitive villagers, they limit themselves to booty from the caravans and later, in western Siberia, to tributes in furs. The clearest analogy to the Iberians is perhaps found in Islam. Besides the monasteries of soldier-monks, we find there voluntary combatants in the holy war, canonical sharing of booty, technique of the *razzia,* and enslavement of enemies. Whether these analogies between Moslem and Iberian represent a genetic relationship or a parallelism explainable by a larger factor is something which we can elucidate no further.

The comparisons established, which should in no way be considered exhaustive, point to one conclusion. The setting in which the bands of conquerors and the whole way of life bound up with their existence generally appear is essentially characterized by location on the frontier between peoples belonging to different cultures who do not recognize a shared juridical community. The incentive of the slave trade works to the same end, increasing the intensity of these conquests. The duration of the frontier of wars of enslavement varies widely, from a few decades to one or more centuries.

AFONSO D'E. TAUNAY

❋

Effects of the Bandeiras

Afonso d'Escragnolle Taunay (1876-1958) was the dean of bandeirante historians and one of Brazil's most prolific writers. His works include an 11-volume history of the bandeiras and a 15-volume history of coffee in Brazil. Though born in Santa Catarina and educated in Rio de Janeiro, Taunay spent most of his life in São Paulo, where he became director of the Paulista Museum in 1917. He was a disciple of Capistrano de Abreu, who encouraged him to devote himself to the Paulista bandeiras.

José Honório Rodrigues has emphasized two central aspects of Taunay's historiography. First, he was a revisionist who re-examined the broad panoramas, "correcting, refining, adding, and bringing up to date." Second, he wrote about collective, popular movements rather than elites and commanding personalities. "His vision centers on the economic and social foundations." Taunay's books are rambling and unpolished. The sheer flow of narrative leaves little room for analysis and interpretation. Yet his extraordinary energies as a re-

First part from Afonso d'E. Taunay, "O epos bandeirante e São Paulo vila e cidade" in *Ensaios paulistas* (São Paulo, 1958), pp. 644-46. Second part from Afonso d'E. Taunay, *História das bandeiras paulistas* (2 vols.; São Paulo, 1954), II, 273-74, 317-20. Translated; and printed by permission of Edições Melhoramentos, São Paulo.

searcher made him by the time of his death "the *bâtonnier* of Brazilian historians." (*The Hispanic American Historical Review,* XXXVIII, 3 [Aug. 1958], 389-93.)

---

1. *The bandeirantes and the town of São Paulo*

The heroic period of the bandeirante movement was to last less than a century and a half. The final great feat occurred in 1725 with the return of [the second] Anhangüera from Goiás, where the last of the great figures of the entradas, Bartolomeu Pais de Abreu, had brought him to take refuge. Thereafter the continual presence of the captain-general governors impeded the carrying out of sorties into the forests. Rodrigo César de Meneses [governor of São Paulo] appeared to make this official by going to Cuiabá and organizing the expedition which discovered the Goiás placer deposits. . . . The great era of the individual bandeiras ended during the long reign of Dom João V [1706-50].

From São Paulo and its environs the thrust of reconnaissance had radiated to the four quadrants. To the north it covered the greatest distances from its center of origin, for it delivered spearheads into the lands of modern Peru and Ecuador; it ascended the River Negro and identified the mouth of the Araguaia; it established dominion over the modern territories of Goiás, Piauí, Ceará, and Maranhão; it assisted the crown in defending the northeast against Indian resistance and the revolt of the Africans.

To the west the bandeirante movement covered the vast area of Mato Grosso by herculean river navigation; it crossed the Paraguay River to reach the territories of Peru and Paraguay; and it established river communication between the central lands and Amazônia, along the Madeira and the Tapajós, the Araguaia and the Tocantins.

To the east the movement took the form of maritime exploits in the Dutch and Northeast campaigns. To the south it caused the withdrawal of the Spaniards from the lands of Paraná and occasioned the progressive advance of settlement along the littoral of our three states of the far south, toward the plains of Uruguay. It cooperated to sustain Colônia do

Sacramento, so dear to the Portuguese policy of continental expansion. . . .

Practically speaking, however, no direct benefits accrued to São Paulo, town and city, from the backland sagas of its sons.

During the seventeenth century, the great phase of the bandeiras, the town developed very modestly, never coming near to attaining the dimensions of the coastal cities. Its economy made only the slightest progress. It continued to be a nucleus of small farmers and stockraisers of limited re-sources, in sharp contrast to the other principal centers of Brazil.

The penetration of the sertões was frequently motivated more to satisfy a sportive instinct than to answer an economic necessity. Do the chroniclers not tell us that many, many of the wanderers in the sertão spent years and years immersed in the forests, possessed by the craving to roam unknown lands?

> Through regions never used nor yet explored,
> Slashing forests and digging up the mountains,
> Fording rivers that inspired the greatest awe
> In rafts and floats, canoes or across bridges,
> Suffering now from heat and now from cold,
> On peaks and plains, ranges, valleys, rivers. . . .

So wrote the mysterious author of the earliest bandeirante saga at the end of the seventeenth century, the enigmatic Diogo Grasson Tinoco—an epic still today almost wholly unrecovered. The bandeirantes might spend years and years in the sertão, sometimes five, ten, or fifteen, "living like beasts without thinking of their homes and legitimate wives," as Father Mansilla reported to Felipe IV [see Document 4]. The frenzy of the sport of roaming the forests seemed to seize them, just as others are enthralled by the death-defying risks of alpinism.

Apparently the discovery of the extremely rich gold beds of the Espinhaço range had an immediate effect on the town of São Paulo. Several of those greatly fortuned by the first strikes of the metal returned to their land of birth, but São Paulo suffered a great decrease in its population with the outpouring of those who later hastened to the region of the deposits in Minas Gerais. This exodus was twice accentuated by the gold rushes of Cuiabá and Goiás.

What remained to São Paulo, ennobled [in 1711] by the illusory honor of the title of "city"? What was left to it from the immense effort of its sons, the "leather breeches" of the sixteenth, seventeenth, and eighteenth centuries? In 1765 the [governor of São Paulo] Morgado de Mateus credited it with a smaller population than had the governor of Rio de Janeiro in 1690.

Had the home of the bandeirantes enjoyed any material profit? Not a bit! . . . The century-old church was falling in ruins and it had become necessary to reconstruct it. In 1745, when the arrival of the first bishop of the newly created diocese of São Paulo was announced, the pitiful church of the Santa Casa da Misericórdia had to be elevated to the dignity of provisional cathedral. So lacking in resources was the city that for decades after the creation of the captaincy the captain-general governors lived in rented houses. Only after Pombal's confiscation of the property of the Jesuits [1759] could they install themselves in the big house of the former College of the Company. The monastery churches were of the crudest construction, as was the military barracks erected toward the end of the eighteenth century. The last decade of that century was to see the city's first public fountain worthy of mention. The private buildings flanking the wretchedly paved streets showed the same poverty. All in all, not a single structure of architectural and artistic note had yet been erected in the capital city of the bandeiras, whose exertions produced no wealthy Carthaginian metropolis, nor even a city embellished as a result of the great mining activities. . . .

Thanks to the clear and accurate image that becomes constantly more apparent with the progress of historical studies, Washington Luís could eloquently characterize this glorious depression caused by exhaustion of energies. Speaking of the government and era of Rodrigo César de Meneses, he observed that beginning with the rule of this satrap the Paulistas cease to exist; there is merely the captaincy of São Paulo, and even this is so decadent that some years later it will be dismembered and end up as a direct dependency of the captaincy of Rio de Janeiro. To his capital, however, capital of the pioneers of the sertão, one may apply the conclusion which the eminent historian draws for the whole Paulista region: "It was going to come to an end, but like the phoenix, which withdraws into its own ashes to be reborn strong and vigorous."

2. National and international effects

Euclides da Cunha wrote that "the heroic tradition of the entradas constitutes the only original aspect of our history." This opinion of the illustrious author of *Os Sertões*[1] is not precisely true. Brazil must share this originality with two of the largest territorial empires of the globe today, Russia and the United States.

During the reign of Ivan the Terrible (1533-84) the Russians, under the famous Cossack Ermak, undertook the easy occupation of Siberia in 1578. Some sixty years later they reached the shores of the Pacific Ocean. By 1689 the Treaty of Nerchinsk had established the Amur as the Sino-Muscovite border. In 1720 the immense Siberian region, with an area comparable to that of the South American continent, formed a single political unit. In those unrivaled expanses, however, nothing had seriously opposed the conquest. A few sparse tribes lived there, lost in the solitude of the steppes. In 1875, three centuries after Ermak's invasion, the whole of Siberia contained barely five million souls, while Brazil, with only about one-third the area, had a population of ten million.

Geographically, the obstacles impeding this penetration were certainly far less imposing than those to be overcome in the conquest of Brazil. If the Siberian plateaus are swept by blasts of extreme cold from the pole, the Brazilian hinterland confronted its pathfinders with burning temperatures. And the healthfulness of Brazil is less than that of the Asiatic north. Its warmth favors scourges from the unbearable parasitic attack of countless legions of hematophagous insects and arachnids which cause endless despair to the strongest will—not to mention the invisible attack of agents transmitting microorganisms that produce frightful ills. Furthermore, the resistance of the primitive Siberians to the Muscovite advance was incomparably weaker than that of the Indian peoples of Brazil in bandeirante times.

---

[1] Translated by Samuel Putnam as *Rebellion in the Backlands* (Chicago, 1957). [Ed.]

In the United States, as we know, the inland penetrations took place two centuries later than the Brazilian ones. In 1783 its territory occupied the coastal fringe of New England [*sic*]. By 1802 it still did not include lands west of the Mississippi. The exploration of the Rocky Mountains took place only in the early nineteenth century, while Brazil's western boundary had already been defined by the Treaty of Madrid in 1750 and the era of the bandeirantes had closed. The inland expansion of the North Americans was to get under way decades later. This march of the white man would encounter the resistance of fierce, exceedingly fierce, Indian nations; but it would be supported by a more effective instrument of conquest, an extraordinary superiority in arms, which were incomparably more efficient than those of the Brazilian forerunners, as measured by the advance of the rifle over the shotgun, the revolver over the pistol.

The feat achieved by the Paulista bandeirantes, which gauged in spatial terms covered an area of several million square kilometers, was left for Auguste de Saint-Hilaire to make known to the world in 1830. He coined expressions to give a clear and exact impression of the astonishment which had come over him: "After one learns the details of the interminable marches of the early Paulistas, one is thunderstruck and inclined to believe that these men belonged to a race of giants." This feeling of admiration was to be reinforced when he declared after contemplating the colossal journey of the monsoons to Cuiabá that the Europeans, accustomed to navigating their puny rivers, could in no way appreciate what such an enterprise represented.

It is indeed this last phase of the bandeirante movement which finds no parallel in any other comparable episode in the annals of any nation of the world. The prodigious feat of river navigation from Araritaguaba to Cuiabá . . . truly exhibits the great mark of originality which Euclides da Cunha attributes to the whole movement of inland penetration. . . .

The epoch of pathfinding and slave-hunting in itself contributed little to the marking out of Brazilian territory by boundaries established through implantation of permanent advance posts. This was to be expected, for the nature of the operations of the bandeiras implied the practice of nomadism. Indeed, what actually remained from the whole seventeenth-century bandeirante movement as a sedimentary process of settlement? Perhaps barely half a dozen outposts in the sertão.

In the immense region explored only an occasional camp-site appeared, such as the stockade of Batatais or Pascoal Moreira's base of operations at Mbotetéu. Of the trading posts of Fernão Dias what would survive? Miniscule present-day hamlets like Sumidouro and São Pedro do Paraopeba. The same happened to the efforts of Domingos Jorge Velho and Apuçá [Francisco Dias de Siqueira] in the distant reaches of Piauí and Maranhão. As perhaps a unique example of survival we have the very modest Morrinhos of Matias Cardoso. In the vast extent of the lands roamed by the seventeenth-century bandeiras almost no vestige remains of civilizing settlement.

The push toward the far south, which resulted in the colonization of Santa Catarina, obeyed above all the mandates of the crown such as that which was the immediate cause of the founding of Laguna, the bridgehead for Colônia do Sacramento and the territory of Rio Grande do Sul, still to be annexed to the Portuguese realm.

Gold was the real motivation for the definitive possession of the central lands. Had the camp settlements of Bom Jesus do Cuiabá and of Guaporé not existed, Alexandre de Gusmão[2] would have had a weak basis for invoking *uti possidetis* in favor of setting the boundary of Brazil two thousand kilometers west of the Tordesillas line. In the seventeenth century the founding of Paranaguá, Curitiba, and São Francisco do Sul had already resulted from the search for gold.

This search was to give extraordinary impetus to settlement in the following century, whether in the regions nearest the littoral or in the remote areas. Thus in the earliest years of the 1700's we witness the appearance of the principal mining centers of Vila Rica (Ouro Prêto), Ribeirão do Carmo (Mariana), Rio das Mortes (São João d'El Rei), Vila Real (Sabará), Vila do Príncipe (Cêrro do Frio), Vila da Rainha (Caeté), Pitangui, etc. A wide network of secondary villages was to grow up around these dominant nuclei, and the exploitation of auriferous lands caused a remarkable in-

---

[2] Gusmão, a Brazilian-born diplomat and private secretary to João V, was the Portuguese negotiator for the Treaty of Madrid of 1750. [Ed.]

crease in the first great current of immigration that poured into Brazil, the African.

A quarter of a century later another zone was also filling up with mining camps, although on a smaller scale. This was Goiás, with Vila Boa, Meia Ponte, and villages and hamlets which at times received a dense influx of population, only to become mere heaps of ruins around abandoned workings. A few years before the colonization of Goiás started, that of Cuiabá had gotten under way. But this had been more limited owing to its enormous distance from the coast and to the tremendous difficulties of access by the interminable river journey. Here the principal settlement nucleus was Cuiabá, to be followed a few years later by that of Mato Grosso. The other centers were all insignificant, and it was a miracle that the larger ones managed to survive amid so many hostile circumstances threatening their existence.

The main impact of the events of the gold-mining epoch was produced, as was to be expected, on Rio de Janeiro, where the production of Minas Gerais drained off to induce very substantial commercial development. So advantageous was the economic situation created in Rio that, in the third quarter of the eighteenth century, it was to dictate the transfer of the Brazilian capital [from Salvador, Bahia] to the southern shore of Guanabara Bay. . . .

The infusion of great streams of Brazilian gold into European markets exerted a very strong influence on the economy of the Western world. During the eighteenth century this had already been noticed by authorities as important as Montesquieu in his *Spirit of the Laws* (1748) and Adam Smith in his famous *Inquiry into the Nature and Causes of the Wealth of Nations* (1776). In 1728 the first of these great authors had called public attention to the abundance of Brazilian gold circulating in civilized Europe as exercising beneficial influence on the economy of the northern part of the continent. Adam Smith emphasized how much the plentiful Brazilian metal had increased Anglo-Portuguese commercial exchange. He went so far as to admit that in his time almost all the gold coined in England came from the Brazilian deposits.

Certainly the first consequence of our gold appearing on the world scene turned out to be the famous treaty of May 16, 1703, which perpetuates the name of its negotiator, John Methuen. This is the treaty which attracted and still attracts so many reproaches from the Portuguese historians, for whom the agreement enfeoffed or even fettered the trade of their kingdom to the heavy British yoke—to the extent that an illustrious Portuguese publicist was moved to remark, pungently and bitterly: "With respect to the gold of Brazil, Portugal assumed the role of the mouth and England that of the stomach."

Another famous and, so to speak, modern authority, Werner Sombart, considered that without the discovery of the gold deposits of Brazil the development of modern economic man would have been delayed. It was the Brazilian metal which enabled Great Britain to build up the large reserves which assured her predominance in world commerce, as long-lasting as it was remarkable, through the progress and improvement of her industries. Owing to the enormous profits of such expansion, this instrument of conquest would bring her the concomitant accrual of capital which was for so long to make London the real seat of the great universal bank that came to the aid of governments suffering from undermined and precarious finances—and to the aid of every sort of candidate for a loan, whether adventurous or not. Observing what had happened to the Count of Oeiras [the Marquis of Pombal] in his captaincy, the Morgado de Mateus recalled in the third quarter of the eighteenth century that His Most Loyal [Portuguese] Majesty traded the rich gold of his mines for the cheap cloth produced by the factories of His Britannic Majesty.

Although the gold-mining phase left in Brazil no enterprises of great consequence for the future, it immensely expanded the possibilities for receiving the agents of civilization, promoting a heavy movement of European and especially African immigration, and intensifying the process of settlement. This led to the creation of numerous cities and towns of our own time, which tended to take root while other settlements dating from the first impetus of the mining boom later stagnated and many disappeared. The scattering of settlement centers resulted in the opening of extended lines of communication, carved out in many directions and subject to the attraction of demographic nuclei which were spread over vast areas. This in turn was responsible for the progress of cattle raising and for commercial and social exchange between the country's northern and southern captaincies, which strengthened the weak bond of the sentiment of national unity.

The transfer of the capital of the colony would serve to formalize the predominance of the southern over the northern region. And since Rio de Janeiro, with its geographically tributary hinterland, was to constitute the leading center of commerce, the mining movement would create in the city the opportunities for capital formation. Half a century later this capital would be the great lever for the coffee boom of the province of Rio de Janeiro, which was subsequently to culminate in the magnificent expansion of coffee planting along the whole Paraíba valley, in the northern Paulista zone, and in the virgin lands of Minas Gerais alongside the western highlands of São Paulo.

As another original contribution of the mining area we can point out the extent to which the exploitation of gold brought to flower in the heart of the mining country an interesting cultural movement, which left a copious literary and artistic record, above all valuable for outstanding achievements in plastic arts and architecture. What is still more unusual, this whole phenomenon burst forth and developed in a land area surrounded by zones of wild forest like those separating the towns of Minas Gerais from the lowlands of Rio de Janeiro and the Guanabara coastal region.

The mining era had less influence on the definitive marking out of the limits of Brazilian territory. Before it began Colônia do Sacramento already existed, and the settlers of Laguna led by the Brito Peixoto family were advancing toward the south. Pedro Teixeira had already set Brazilian territorial markers four thousand kilometers from the mouth of the Amazon. To the west, thanks to Pascoal Moreira and his townsmen from Sorocaba, Portuguese markers had already been planted before 1690 on the left bank of the Paraguay, "barring the way to the lions of Hesperia," in the verse of Evaristo da Veiga. In any case the discovery of the Cuiabá deposits and the maintenance of the mining camp of Bom Jesus, a formidable task of perseverance and spirit of sacrifice, were the fruit of the second great gold-mining cycle and a consequence of the establishment of a base at Mbotetéu.

The discovery of the placer deposits at Guaporé would round out the conquest and serve as a natural consolidation of the western boundary line of Mato Grosso.

Paraphrasing Brasílio Machado's well-known image of Portugal, "cramped by Spain and expanded by the Ocean," we may conclude that São Paulo was cramped by the coastal mountain range but expanded by the sertão, the remedy during two centuries for its intrepid "leather breeches."

13

CASSIANO RICARDO

❁

Westward March

Cassiano Ricardo—poet, essayist, historian, and journalist—was born in São Paulo state in 1894. In the
1920's he was associated with nativist and nationalist
currents of the "modernist" renovation of the arts in
Brazil. *Westward March,* subtitled "The Influence of
the Bandeira on the Social and Political Development
of Brazil," was published in 1942; it has appeared in
three editions and in Spanish translation. In somewhat
the vein of a Brazilian Carl Sandburg, Ricardo celebrates
the bandeirante movement as a source of democratic
energy, cultural nationalism, and a protean will-to-do
for the whole of Brazilian history. This lyricism is not
without sociological insight, and Ricardo has perhaps
done more than any other writer to vitalize the bandeirante legend for modern Brazilians. The selection is
the preface to the second edition, which summarizes
his main interpretations. His view of the bandeirante
legacy should be contrasted with that of Clodomir
Vianna Moog in *Bandeirantes and Pioneers* (New York,
1964), a fellow Brazilian who shares little of his euphoria.

From Cassiano Ricardo, *Marcha para Oeste* (2nd ed.; 2 vols.;
Rio de Janeiro, 1942), I, 19-33. Translated; and printed by permission of the author.

I

How, sociologically, was the idea of a strong and disciplinary government born in Brazil?

Which was the social group that gave birth to our democracy?

Whence came the rhythm of Brazilian civilization in its march toward the West?

II

In the first edition of *Marcha para Oeste* I tried to find out which social group gave birth to democracy in Brazil. In this connection I referred to the various groups which—each with respect to its geographic location—were the points of origin for the colony's three societies:

a) The agrarian society of the coast, "with its absorbent monoculture: a minority of whites and near-whites, patriarchal and polygamous, from the height of the 'big houses' of stone and lime dominating not only the slaves bred in swarms in the slave quarters, but also the sharecroppers, the *agregados,* living in houses of rammed earth and straw—vassals of the 'big houses' in the full sense of the term." These "big houses" (all this is from Gilberto Freyre) "represent enormous feudal power."

b) The pastoral society, "with possibilities of democratic life," (Freyre) in which that curious democracy of leather was tried out of which Capistrano de Abreu speaks; having a "horror of any neighbors" (Henrique Handelmann), however, and displaced to the sertões: the Northeast of the cowpunchers and ranches.

c) The bandeirante society to the south, with its "intramontane" location, interbred with Indians, separated from the other social groups by distance and by the coastal range, and dedicated to the objective counseled by Martim Afonso when he settled on the coast of São Vicente: exploration for gold and silver, which an anonymous castaway and the Indians, who were already his friends, had said to exist, a sight to behold in the ravines beyond that ridge of mountains. One had only to climb straight up the mountains, leap over their cliffs, and return in no time with four hundred burden-bearers laden with gleaming metal. At least this is how the donatário saw it in his anxiety to seek out the riches of the fable.

III

There are some who point out the degree to which the corporativism of Portugal is suited to the nature of Lusitanian civilization. Which were the two most privileged occupations? Naval carpenters and minters. "Connect this fact with the two great possibilities for Portugal, the discoveries and the mines, and you will understand the political realism behind it." (Severino Sombra) Meanwhile, once he had crossed the Atlantic the Portuguese conqueror had to "return to feudalism in his aristocratic methods of colonization." This is what happened in the Northeast, as is seen in the studies of the sociologists who identified the social landscape of the "big house" and the regime created there with the profound separation between masters and slaves and with the introduction of the latifundiary monoculture of sugar cane. This could not have occurred on the [Paulista] plateau (the difference was already beginning in this minor detail), where there was no rich earth for large cane-fields nor stone for the construction of "big houses."

In the Northeast, the ties to landed property, to the latifúndio, explain the feudal seignior of the region who commands his own rural militias; in the South, the lack of such ties between the plateau dweller and the idea of landed property would explain the "bandeira." Precisely because of the shortage of stone for "big houses" and because of the disengagement arising from lack of commitment to landed and latifundiary property, the man of the plateau can be a bandeirante and, at any moment, leave the goods he possesses to put on his high boots and plunge into the wilderness after legends and gleaming stones.

On one hand, headed inland and marching Westward, the bandeira. On the other, in league with European capitalism, the "big house."

The result is that, initially, these two social groups take contrary directions. One reverts to feudalism, as we said; the other moves toward fresh formulae for life and the economy.

IV

The mere confrontation of the three societies allows us to see, when we examine the representative types of each one, that the farmer, the cattleman, the planter, the sugar-mill owner, the landed proprietor may have something in common, but they cannot be confused with the "social type" of the bandeirante, which is unique and original. And just as the Jesuit, for example, without prejudice to his mission (note the case of [José de] Anchieta), took up a number of occupations, including that of commerce, the bandeirante can be involved with subsistence agriculture or cattle raising without these accessory activities distorting his character. If, however, he takes up one of them on a full-time basis, he ceases being the "social type" of the bandeirante. Such is the case of bandeirantes who became permanent farmers or became cattle raisers.

The sugar-mill owner and the bandeirante were truly two opposing social types. The proof is that not one mill owner ever became a bandeirante, nor did the opposite ever occur. At the same time the cattleman and the bandeirante did have their points of contact, although they occupied zones of influence clearly characterized by the respective economic processes.

Only the miner continues, in some degree, being a bandeirante. The bandeirante himself has this attitude when, as in Cuiabá, he includes among the several functions of the superintendent that of "sending forth bandeiras for gold as well as against the barbaric enemies." Thus, gold mining is the objective of the bandeira, and even at the mines new bandeiras are organized to make new discoveries.

In the hunt for Indians, the bandeirante is the agent of the farmer, "furnishing manpower for cultivating the land grants and small plots, as well as bows and arrows to defend the colonist."

V

In an ethnic sense, the bandeira is born with "the first generation of mamelucos." Democratization through race mixture is therefore its point of origin, a mixture resulting from the mating of the white men with the maidens of the Guaianase nation. But the plateau dwellers were not only Portuguese. We will encounter there a goodly number of Flemings, English, Italians, French, and principally Spaniards, to say nothing of those of the "Hebrew nation" and Africans imported from Angola in 1590 by Afonso Sardinha.

It is the Indian, the Spaniard, the Portuguese, and the Negro who, in descending order, contribute most to the ethno-cultural explanation of the bandeira.

Besides this we know, in light of extensive documentation, that *polyculture* and *small property* characterized the organization of plateau life.

From the very beginning André Fernandes made numerous large donations from his enormous grant of land. Using officially published documents, an astute researcher into our past [Alfredo Ellis Júnior] was successful in locating about 136 plantations of various sizes for the middle of the seventeenth century, from more or less one square league to two hundred square braças—that is, from the average large plantation of 1,500 alqueires of land (these were rare and, when they existed, were soon split up by inheritance) to miserable little plots (which were the most numerous) only slightly larger than the lands of Portuguese country houses. . . . Today it is well known what there was in Piratininga in the way of polyculture. While sugar, as Gilberto Freyre says, "sterilized the land of the Northeast for attempts at mixed farming," this system was intensively used on the small farms of all sizes which I just mentioned, and it marked the first phase of the social life of the plateau. Moreover, as early as 1583 Fernão Cardim noticed "those fields full of cows which are a delight to see," alongside that world of grapes, that man who gathered twelve thousand quinces, those fields of wheat, corn, beans, and manioc which evoked from him such admiration.[1] While the boundaries of the sugar plantations separated more than they brought together, the economic and agricultural life of the plateau brought together much more than it separated. Cattle raising, in small herds, completed this democratic pattern.

And we see the River Tietê collaborating, in its turn, to

[1] See "A Treatise of Brasil" in Samuel Purchas, *Hakluytus Posthumus or Purchas his Pilgrimes* (20 vols.; Glasgow, 1905-07), XVI, 500-02. [Ed.]

democratize customs and to channel in the same psychological direction all the desires of a population infected by fascination with the unknown.

VI

There is no preoccupation with class and position. Families drink from the same glass. The settlers raise cattle in common. Equal treatment for all. Life in constant danger generates a clear feeling of social solidarity for which the acts of the town council are the best evidence. Persons of noble origin modestly perform manual tasks. New Christians [i.e., converts] and old ones are on a plane of equality with the other inhabitants in their requests for protection of farms and herds. When a certain tax collector (Jorge Neto Falcão) executes the order of the magistrate, he decides to extend the assessment "to all he encountered, be they new Christians or old." [2] Poor but intelligent bandeirantes married Indians to Negro women, producing the *cafusos* (sambos) of the plateau described by Spix and Martius, who are startled at "the excessive length of their hair."

The population of the plateau and its environs was conspicuous for its industriousness.

And politically? Politically, a rudimentary democracy was practiced, highlighted by its electoral process for choosing local officials. The will of the people prevailed; it even made itself felt upon the most important resolutions of government, which amounted to real plebiscitarian decisions.[3]

---

[2] In one session of the town council when a nomination is being made for treasurer of the orphans' possessions, an old Christian is mentioned for that function. But the explanation is that a representative of His Majesty was present (which was extremely rare). The people of the plateau, so given to social camaraderie, were never concerned with the distinction.

[3] In 1713 the Overseas Council felt it necessary to punish a very serious offense which the Paulistas had committed against a royal official because "otherwise Your Majesty will be king and lord of São Paulo in name only, and only as long as the Paulistas see fit." If it is not too bold, "Your Majesty might lose hope of being king of the Paulistas."

VII

Once the group is on the march, its specific composition becomes clear: division of labor as a function of color; hierarchical disposition, in the same group, of the colors which the colony takes pride in maintaining separate from one another in the villages, in the slave quarters—and even in its regiments, each of which is composed of persons of one race; utilization of all human elements, even those which the latifúndio casts as debris at the fringe of its social area.

With the same psychological incentive established for all, one man ceases, in some measure, being the slave of another, for everyone marches together. The "commander" or "bandeira chief" replaces the feudal lord. The "Indian on the move" replaces the enslaved Indian. The obedience of the Negro and the advantage he takes of the hours of pause redress his slavery. Composed of all the races, each bandeira exhibits three clearly defined psychological moments in its moral structure: command, obedience, movement. Command is the moment of the mameluco; movement is that of the Indian; pause is that of the African. The contribution of the white and mameluco is in the thinking which leads the bandeira and governs the action. The Indian contribution is in the long marches, in the warrior impetus, in the hours of "psychological anxiety." The Negro contribution is during respites, in the settlements around the discoveries, in the labor at the mines, in the organization of plantings to supply the troops: in short, during the hours of "psychological relief," so congenial to the sedentary African.

Concerning this aspect of the bandeira I have written: "Even the 'inferior' mestizos, whom the poet of Aryanism describes as 'averse to Aryanization,' unconsciously make an enormous contribution to the creation of that social and biological democracy."

Bandits, ruffians, longshanks, mestizos, sambos, mulattoes.

All the anonymous crowd which makes up the retinue of the bandeira plays a providential role for which their defects are often strong points. There occurs not merely the individualism that creates wealth and heroes. There is also social solidarity, much broader than that of the family and caused by the unitary economic objective, by the increment of associative spirit which the entradas kindle, by the collective awareness to external danger, and by the suffering which equalizes all men in the heart of the sertão. Economically, we find hierarchy on a basis of individual effort, categorization according to land ownership, a spirit of initiative enriched by cooperation, proportional distribution of prisoners during the so-called Indian-hunting cycle, community prospecting during the gold-washing cycle, and a certain individualist dispersion around the discoveries compensated by extreme social concentration. Socially, there is no preconception about color, creed, or origin; biologically, there is correction of social prejudices through intensive interbreeding with Indians, and even of the latter with Negroes.

The bandeirante is not domineering, as many think. He is the protector, the creator of strong autocratic government; he is the guarantor of tranquility in certain zones of turbulence, as in the cattle regions. When some ethnic or economic enclave develops, it is the bandeira which combats it, "democratizing it." While the sugar aristocracy "is meshed with European capitalism," the group from the plateau moves in the opposite direction in its westward march. Democracy could not have been born in the zones of cattle or of sugar mills. If the latter is feudal, the former precludes small holdings and thins out the population; both work against democracy. While the bandeira is born in a democratic setting, its mobility is explained only by small holdings and small farming—this activity in addition to settling the country and creating its living substance of democracy; correcting red and black ethnic enclaves, such as those of the Tapuia and of the Negro quilombos of Palmares; bringing the colors into fraternity and hierarchy as a single human and social group, with a single direction.

If the society of the North shouts for help before "the savage who consumes human flesh," it is the bandeira that comes to its aid; if the Jesuit wishes to found his theocratic Guarani empire (which so impressed Voltaire and Montesquieu) it is the bandeira that puts an end to this idea by destroying his reductions to the South and West; if the Dutch enemy establishes himself in the Northeast it is the bandeira that comes to help the Brazilian of this region expel the in-

truder; if pirates prey along the coast it is the bandeira
that will drive them out. If a disaster such as that of
Mbororé occurs it is because the bandeira is fighting the
blond pirate in the north and, at the same time, the obstinate Spaniard in the south.

Whites, Negroes, and many Indians whom the Paulistas
make use of set forth.

Poor and rich, men and women, old and young, lay and
religious set forth.

But the bandeira group is not the only point of radiation
for colonial society. If it gave birth to democracy in a sociological sense, and if this democracy later became generalized, we should observe the extent to which the democratic
group contributed to such an occurrence, owing to the external mobility through which it obtains: an anti-totalitarian
geography, anatomically federalist and democratic; enough
space for our joy of living in freedom, in primary social
groups; hierarchical absorption of the Negro and the Indian
displaced from tribal communism into the social area where
the bandeira operates; crumbling of ethnic enclaves when
these impede biological and social democracy; defeudaliza-
tion of plantations by the gold rushes; settlement that begins
with the ranch and farm along the routes to the mines; immediate fragmentation of the land grants flanking these
routes into small parcels (small particularly in comparison
with the latifúndios of the sugar and cattle zones)—and this
last for three purposes: to hasten settlement; through small
holdings to keep farmers from becoming powerful satraps
and bosses; and by subsistence farming to assure abundant
provisions, available to the poorest person. Consider furthermore the greater division of labor in the gold region;
the decentralization of government, since each bandeira
chief not only exercises majestic prerogatives but also prac-
tices a living experiment in self-government; easy employ-
ment for thousands of Negroes, Indians, and mestizos, who
are devoted to prospecting for gold which they collect for
themselves as well as for their masters; greater social level-
ing, as in the case of a certain judge (to cite an example off-
hand) who is most solemnly scolded once while His Majesty's
fifths are being shipped because he feels that taking up an
oar is beneath his dignity—and this at the same time that

smuggling is "democratizing" the highways in the fight against monopoly. Every open road meant certain smuggling in the economic dialectic of the colony.

It is a man of the plebs, Manuel Correia from Itapetininga, who discovers the gold of Araés with a simple tin saucer. The associative spirit of the bandeira is powerful, for no one can go on a bandeira alone. The entire population of the colony collects around the discoveries. The miner may be a man of few possessions. In the sertão division of labor is much greater than it is in the social organization in the Northeast. At the right moment the African enters the bandeira as a stabilizing factor. Thousands of free Negroes and mulattoes who earn their living by washing gold in the rivers and streams have fled from the plantation, despite energetic measures by colonial authorities to prevent such escapes. Mulatto women dripping with jewels shock the gentle Antonil. More and more manumissions occur in the mining zone. Without knowing it, the slave works for the advent of the industrial revolution, which is to replace slave labor with free. Keeping profits secret against the greed of the satraps is a recognized right. Democratic jewels like tourmaline and beryl challenge the metropolitan aristocracy of the diamond.

The "baroque" was democratizing the "classic." . . .

VIII

Let it not be said that the Jesuit came closer to the Indian, as in the reductions of Guairá, because he maintained him in a life of out-and-out communist promiscuity. The bandeirante preserved his gregarious spirit as well. It is true that with hierarchical ordering of the colors and the consequent specialization of functions the bandeira modified Indian communism; but "social hierarchy" does not destroy the gregarious spirit "which Iberia inherited from Rome and we inherited from Iberia." Without this, the bandeira could not have been realized. Moreover, the bandeirante all but became an Indian in his "return to primitivism." The bandeira glorifies the aborigine in his traditional nomadism. Far from enslaving him and segregating him in sedentary agriculture, it utilizes his biological and psychological capacity in its mobility. In this connection it would be interesting to investigate to what degree the bandeirante gave himself up to tribal collectivism. We know that Borba Gato was the chief of a tribe, and that the economics of the bandeira, in its "return to primitivism," reverted to barter *in natura*. On this point I have already had occasion to suggest the hypothesis of the *cultural mobility* which led the bandeirante to be as much an Indian as possible (more so than the Portuguese ever became a Negro), which brought me to the conclusion that in his encounters and dialogues with primitivism he never lost his concept of social hierarchy. He did not regress to the point of losing grasp of his culture of origin, giving way to the tribal communism within him. However, the dissolvent influence of the Indian on the bandeirante must have been enormous. It begins with the latter's lack of attachment to landed property, an attitude toward which the savage, for whom all possessions were common, must have contributed greatly. Even in a sense of social "destratification," from the natural infatuation with the blissful advantages of life in common, the Indian male or female must have caused many a bandeirante to forget prejudices of every order and succumb to the sheer joy of the "cosmic spectacle."

IX

The bandeira is born in the Republic of Piratininga and develops directly toward the Brazilian society whose formation it so strongly influences. It is born on the plateau and it goes on to conquer the physical foundation for our destiny as a people and a nation.

In space, it was the bandeira which sketched the green-physical image of Brazil. In time, it survived for us in the blood and in the psychic "modulus" which is today the moral portrait of our human group. In both its first and second phases, in short, the bandeira left a sharp imprint of originality (a) on the geography of the modern world and (b) on the social and political life of America. These are the two important effects.

For me, then, the bandeira is not merely the most Brazilian historical episode. Besides having traced the geographic profile of Brazil it is a social and political phenomenon which helps to clarify many of our present institutions. To explain further: The bandeira has been studied externally, in its handsome heroic apparel. The study I am attempting in this unpretentious essay of historical criticism and social psychology deals also with the bandeira from within, caught off guard in its psychological behavior, in the little daily, anonymous dramas which go to compose the vast and immortal drama. An essay of this nature gains through reflection what it loses in richness of color. The bandeira, thus understood, gain in the explanation of its obscure points what it loses in spectacular grandeur.

Many times the leaders will cease to dominate the scene because my intent is to study the people, those obscure masses who performed the great anonymous march.

The bandeira depends on two fundamental conditions: the People and the Sertão. I offer three typical instances—that of the "people who could not live without the sertão," that of the bandeirante who took Sertão as his surname (out of his love for his wilderness), and that of the sertanista who signs one of the municipal acts using the surname People, so certain was he that he spoke for the popular masses.

Contrary to custom, no longer it is merely the group on the march, battling against the constant enemy, in search of yellow nuggets, crossing mountain ranges and cascading rivers—as our imagination paints it and as we receive it from the historians for whom, in the last analysis, everything boils down to a question of itineraries and dates. No. Within each grouping there is a typical and original society. All the acts of civil life are performed, some in writing and others imperfectly, for later completion by the sertão and by His Majesty. Wills are drawn up, criminals are punished, commercial transactions and acquisition of property are effected. Masses, celebrations, dances, games are held. Even powerful dramas are put on. One finds everything, from the individual creating wealth and heroic beauty to the State, in embryo and alive.

There is no doubt that the bandeira represents a quest for individual wealth, but this quest can be carried out only through the association of individuals and families within the same group. Moreover, when the mines are discovered and personal interests multiply, it is these interests of the private order which make felt the need for public power. Each vein of gold means a population clustering around a new strike. Bandeirante "imperialism" presupposes, above all, the political unity of the "group on the march," and this political unity imposes its social, extra-familiar unity. Whether in its organization, in the camps it lays out, or in the transportation of peoples from the coast, the bandeira is an "anti-private and anti-dissociative" political organization.

In spite of the supremacy of the rural over the urban environment—particularly for provisioning the bandeira—this organization comes only from the city. It is a group which "de-ruralizes" itself to organize, its ultimate objective being "de-ruralization" through mining.

The custom of seeing the bandeira chief only as a hero leads us to forget still other aspects of his person, among them: the governor invested with all powers; the executive chief who issues all orders; the legislator who decrees the laws of the sertão; the judge who settles the quarrels and complaints arising among the members of the troop and who thus provides all the formalities of civil life. The group which he leads is a society full of human sentiments. Wrangling is not unknown to this society, and neither are moments of intense collective solidarity. Without an authority to enforce the law, punish criminals, distribute justice, recognize new rights and execute wills, how could this society endure? The most serious aspect of the matter, however, is the amount of military power which the generalissimo of the bandeira exercises, whether on his own or by royal delegation. He is not merely the troop commander, the generalissimo: he is the public power itself, the dictator, the Chief of State.

Yet how could this group, beyond the radius of colonial government, achieve its objective without a chief to lead it militarily, in the Roman manner? This must occur so that the State in miniature, which any bandeira on the march reproduces, may preserve its way of life and its unbreakable unity. In our social and political genesis, then, the troop commander represents the creator of a strong, courageously American government.

Finally (and here is the chance to correct another error) the bandeirante is not, as many suppose, a caudillo in his exercise of military power. The social type of the caudillo arises from the conflict between pastoral individualism and urban gregariousness. At least this is the explanation given us by the South American sociology which specializes in the subject. Now the bandeirante, who differs from the shepherd or cattle raiser, occupations which for him are merely subsidiary, reconciles individualism (spirit of initiative) with gregariousness (bandeira) to constitute an urban type who feels the need of grouping together to achieve his economic objective.

Therefore the confusion which is made between clan chieftain, territorial caudillo, and bandeirante has not the slightest reason to occur.

X

I alluded to the "old devil setting fire to the water of the rivers." [See above p. 62n.]

Continuing with this subject, and with the legend which surrounds it—the bandeirante offers occasion for a psychosocial study of the greatest interest. First, the bandeira is a product of the myths of gold and green stones. Through its contact with the Tupi, it received from him and transmitted to us most of the myths which dwell today in the popular imagination. Second, the bandeira not only creates myths but also corrects already existing ones, such as those which the civilized world had invented concerning the Indian, who was the monster of the fable (pessimistic phase) and the "noble savage" of romantic ideology (rose-tinted optimistic phase). Third, the bandeira transcends the domain of history and mingles with the mythological. To explain its heroes, does not a learned man like Saint-Hilaire find himself obliged to classify them as a "race of giants?" To his way of thinking only giants . . . could have conquered a continent on foot. Fourth, today's "mechanical" world, unsentimental and anti-human, heightens in us the tendency to place the bandeira in the mythological world. It thus acquires a new force in our collective dynamism. What is "ephemeral" in historical fact becomes eternal in legend, perhaps because the myth is an "image" which in history acquires the power of a symbol. . . . Fifth, so great is the force of the mythological that even the bandeirante defended himself against it when he said to the king concerning the journeys on foot from the plateau to Peru: "We will go to Peru by land . . . and this is no fable." And even today, the chief of the Nation himself [President Getúlio Vargas], when he speaks of a new Westward march, is careful to say that "it has nothing to do with an image." More than a mere image, "it is an urgent and necessary reality to cross over the plateau and pick up again the trail of the pioneers who planted the territorial boundary markers in the heart of the Continent, in a vigorous and epic thrust."

Sixth, on studying the bandeira from within rather than in its heroic projection, I had a vague fear of becoming disenchanted in the light of the documents. The more intimate contact with the "leather breeches" whose signatures I kept seeing in acts, records, and testaments does not, however, diminish the aura of mystery. Nor does it weaken the predilection which all of us have for the mystical aspect of their feats. On the contrary, our amazement only grows.

—Well then, so these people really existed?

And I was thinking that it might be a fable.

XI

The contribution of the Spanish element to the bandeira cannot be overemphasized. . . . The "love for the fabulous," the quixotism of the Anhangüera in the fire episode, and the acclamation of Amador Bueno reveal the Spanish aspect of certain phases of bandeirante conquest and independence. The drama of the Conquest, a specific phenomenon of southern Brazil, which expanded our borders and bequeathed us our present geographic contour, would be incomprehensible "if we did not distinguish it from the Portuguese effort as an undertaking"—here I follow Sérgio Buarque de Holanda—"which finds in itself its own explanation." The official order was to scratch along the coast like crabs, in the picturesque phrase of Frei Vicente do Salvador. The charters of the captaincies made the same stipulation, that no one should slip inland to the sertão. It was the Brazilian of the plateau who, independently and at his own risk, disobeyed the order of the crown and tore up—devil take it—the famous Treaty of Tordesillas. The work of geographic expansion, then, is an achievement exclusively ours, since "the crown took cognizance of the conquest only after it was completed." The verb *banderizar* is

Spanish (as Carvalho Franco, one of our foremost modern historians, teaches us), and the custom of going out on bandeiras is Indian (as our master, Capistrano de Abreu, made us see). In a recent study of the acclamation of Amador Bueno I even attempted to show that one of the psychosocial and ethno-cultural reasons for the "bandeira" is the contribution of the Spanish element which ascended the plateau via the Tietê or the Paraguay (or as a result of those maritime expeditions in search of the Plata River which broke up, nearly always, in the vicinity of São Vicente and Santa Catarina), where they settled and mixed with the Paulistas. If we but recall an André de Zúñega, a Martim Tenorio de Aguilar, a Jaques Félix, a Bartolomeu Bueno de Ribeira, the three Anhangüeras (all descendants of Spaniards), and also Juseppe Camargo and his descendants, outstanding "leather breeches" who led their bandeiras to the far reaches of the south, we will see that the Spanish element, in combination with the indigenous, explains a large part of the bandeirante phenomenon, and we will gain an exact sense of how far this historic expansion is from being exclusively Portuguese.

XII

In saying "Westward march" rather than "march to the West" my intention is not as subtle as it may seem. "Westward march" merely indicates direction, without yet specifying the region which would be conquered by the bandeirante. "Westward" merely means "headed west." Any displacement from the coast to the interior would be westward, that is, toward the setting sun and not yet toward the region of Brazil where, now that the boundaries are established, lie the areas adjacent to those countries bathed by the Pacific.

Colonization was achieved by leaps, and it could not have been otherwise. In such a case, comparisons are not dangerous only insofar as they prove the originality of our process of extending society into the interior of the country. Had the bandeirantes allowed themselves the luxury of comparisons, however, and had they wished to adopt the Greek, Saxon, and German processes of colonization, our destiny would have been another and, at this moment, we would be lamenting their preoccupation with such comparisons, which were then not only dangerous but deadly. Our social expansion had to occur by leaps, in the anxiety to seize positions and mark the land with rapid signs of possession and conquest—in this fantastic game of blindman's buff played by a small population over the vast distances.

Yet no matter how important these nuclei of settlement became, social continuity was to emanate less from its points of geo-physical intersection than—even had there not been the leaps—from the geo-economic determinants that were diversifying, or homogenizing, the new human landscape.

I do not wish to suggest—and this qualification goes without saying—that the bandeira marched only Westward. Its radiation toward the North, for example, was no less important. And what is most interesting is that many expeditions proceeded east from the dividing line [of Tordesillas]; and in this category we find those that helped to subdue and settle the Northeast itself, which constitutes one of the most interesting chapters of the bandeira in its relations with the other social groups of the colony. In large measure the Amazon owes its definitive integration into Brazilian territory to the bandeirante who conquered and settled the north of Mato Grosso. Frequently the bandeirante entered by way of the "back door" (or "by the rearguard of the sugar mills," as Roberto Simonsen would say) to clear the way for the advance of the groups which had left from the coast in other regions of the country, or to make the Amazonian circuit as Antônio Rapôso Tavares did on his magnificent excursion via the waters of the river-ocean. In any case, the long-term thrust of the march to the interior, whether from the North, the Northeast, or the South, was always Westward, in the opposite direction to the Jesuit-Spanish penetration, which of necessity radiated out in search of the eastern ocean. And the total effect of all the marches was the conquest of the central body of the country, west of the line drawn by the two crowns.

The groups which left the plateau, then, took diverse and divergent routes: some toward the South, others toward the Center and the North. But the steady thrust of penetration, product of initial and parallel efforts, had to be to the

West. West, in the Brazilian case, as the antithesis to the coast. Even when bandeiras are born on the coast, they are born in "opposition to the coast."

These arguments presumably explain the title of this essay, and the larger meaning which I have tried to give it at this moment of Brazilian civilization.

XIII

Some observers point out that the migrations of ancient times always occurred from east to west. The same would have to be true of the search for lands "situated to the West" at the time of the overseas discoveries. And this law, says Tristão de Araripe, had also to be valid for the colonization of America.

In Brazil, however, the phenomenon occurs in a completely original manner. Among the many forms and manners of the "Westward march" are the entradas, the Jesuit missions, agro-pastoral expansion, the expeditions sent to repel invaders, the migrations of people from the coast, and the bandeiras, although these last have a wider radius of action and a characteristic organization.

Entradas, migrations, and bandeiras occasionally coincide, but they never lose their identity. In a schema presented to Paulo Prado, Capistrano de Abreu did attempt to extend the designation "bandeiras" to the entradas that left from other points of the Brazilian coast. He speaks of Bahian bandeiras connecting the São Francisco to the Tocantins, of Pernambucan bandeiras between the Capibaribe and the Ibiapaba range, of short-distance bandeiras from Maranhão connecting the Itapicuru to the Paraíba and São Francisco, and of Amazonian bandeiras which, by way of the Madeira, joined with those of São Paulo to reach the Javari and occupy Guiana. The merit of the admirable expeditions which had other origins is certainly indisputable. As a matter of method for designating the groups which accomplished the Westward march, however, I prefer to call only the group from the Piratininga plateau a "bandeira"—without forgetting the characteristics which make it a phenomenon "peculiar to the South," in the words of Rocha Pombo. But the habit of referring to the bandeira as synonymous with historical penetration in general is coupled with another one, still prevalent, which is to identify the bandeira with the geographic area it conquered, limiting its effects to that area. Now viewed historically and with an eye to its genesis, the bandeira is not a phenomenon that occurred throughout the country. But in a social sense, on the contrary, the bandeira was not limited to the already immense geographic area it had conquered; it had impact on all of Brazil through its relations with the other groups of colonial society.

Over a long period bandeirismo under mandate supplies the sugar plantations of the Northeast with thousands of Indian workers. At this point it collaborates toward the prosperity of the very group established in the "big house." How much and in what proportion did the bandeirante contribute to the splendor of the sugar industry? This is a question which Gilberto Freyre could answer. In any case the acts of the São Paulo town council reply, at least at the beginning of the seventeenth century, by crying out against the traffic in Indians with the Northeast which "left the whole plateau desolate, except for the trees and fields."

XIV

We cannot, then, restrict the bandeira to social, geographic, and temporal confines, for it is above all a marvelous case of unintended consequences and coexisting purposes. It begins by opening routes in all directions without perceiving that it is heading in one single direction, that of the future Brazil. It reaches its first objective, the Indian; but it transcends this objective to reveal to the world the "human reality of the Indian," which had hitherto been deformed or unknown. It reaches its final economic objective, which is gold, but transcends it by contributing to the industrial revolution and the notion of *homo economicus*. It proceeds to another objective, that of settlement, only to give grounds for the *uti possidetis,* applied for the first time in international law. It halts at the boundary, but it has repercussions in all the South American countries, along whose borders it collaborates to mold the continent and produce the greatest geographic revolution of the modern world. It drives out the Jesuit and thus contributes toward the complete expulsion of the Company of Jesus. It sends gold to the mother country, but enriches England. Therefore one cannot say that the bandeira will do this or that, for its objectives are overlapping or entangled. Nor did the bandeira make use only of the Indian and the mameluco for its conquests. Economically, it begins with the Indian and ends with the conquest of gold; ethnically, it begins with the Indian and ends up as African; geographically, it begins with the plateau (with its enduring and special traits) and ends at the frontiers, South and West, and West and North. Temporally, it moves in three registers: the time from the beginning of the expansionist phenomenon to its close; the time which each bandeira spends on its journey; the time of duration for its effects—and these will always be at the social, psychic, and economic core of our life. It is a force which always renews itself in search of new objectives, in addition to the quest for traditional objectives, since the Brazilian has not yet thoroughly accomplished the conquest of the land.

Even had the bandeira concluded its historical "cycle of behavior" (the conquest of the land)—which is not the case —it would not have completed its social "cycle of behavior."

XV

Therefore I am not limiting this essay to the first three centuries. I leave behind the social area which the bandeira occupied historically because its effects are as contemporary as they are numerous. If it has a limit in space, it does not have one in time. Today, for example, the march of the economic frontier is deliberate, and marked by production statistics rather than by shouts of discovery. Man now lives wedded to the land, while the historic bandeirante went to conquer his bride through adventures in the virgin forest, dreaming of green stones and battling fabulous monsters. Once the march for the country was completed, the bandeira flowed back in search of nationhood. The bandeirante, then, is no longer merely the author of our geography. Every Brazilian has a heavy dose of wanderer's blood. An anonymous bandeirante moves in the blood of each one of us toward three new frontiers: the economic, the spiritual, and the sentimental. Indeed the word "frontier" in Brazil is inseparable from "bandeirante." Each stage of civilization leads to its own frontier. Each cultural horizon has its bandeira on the march. And parallel bandeiras will extend the moving frontiers which will one day combine in a single geographic, economic, spiritual, and sentimental frontier. Geographic frontier, economic frontier, and spiritual frontier will coincide, like three waves along a single stretch of beach.

Even so, there will be new bandeiras. This is not mere indulgence in a commonplace. But because bandeirante is synonymous with the pioneer which the original Brazil created to take his place alongside all peoples on the march.

And time, for a bandeirante people, is a kind of frontier in permanent mobilization.

XVI

Still today we speak of "Westward march."
The "rhythm of Brazilian civilization" is precisely that.

Glossary

Alqueire. Dry measure: 13 liters. Area: 24,200 sq. meters. (Both variable)

Arrôba. 14.75 kilograms.

Bandeira, Bandeirante. See pages 21-23.

Braça. 2.2 meters.

Catinga. Scrub forest, especially in Brazil's arid Northeast.

Donatário. Donatary, or proprietor of a captaincy in colonial Brazil.

Emboaba. Outsider. See note, page 143.

Entrada. Entry, or expedition into the interior. See page 22.

Fazenda. Plantation.

Fazendeiro. Planter; proprietor of a fazenda.

Fidalgo (Port.), *Hidalgo* (Sp.). Nobleman; gentleman.

League. Generally about four miles.

Mameluco. Offspring of white and Indian.

Mocambo. Village of runaway Negro slaves.

Quilombo. Community of mocambos.

Sertão (pl. *sertões*), *sertanista, sertanejo.* See note, page 23.

Currency

vintem (pl. vintens)	20 réis
tostão pl. tostões)	100 réis
pataca	320 réis
cruzado	400 réis
milréis	1,000 réis
oitava	1,600 réis

(One milréis is written 1$000. In about 1700 one hundred réis were worth perhaps eight pence in English currency.)

Bibliographical Note

A useful conspectus of colonial Brazilian history will be found in Bailey W. Diffie, *Latin-American Civilization* (Harrisburg, 1945), chaps. 28-33. For more detail on selected topics the following three books, which deal with the 16th, 17th, and 18th centuries respectively, are recommended: Alexander Marchant, *From Barter to Slavery* (Baltimore, 1942); C. R. Boxer, *Salvador de Sá and the Struggle for Brazil and Angola 1602-1686* (London, 1952); and *The Golden Age of Brazil 1695-1750* (Berkeley and Los Angeles, 1962). Robert Southey's classic *History of Brazil* (3 vols.; London, 1810-1819), though partly obsolete, is still of importance.

There is little in English that relates directly to the bandeirantes beyond some of Boxer's chapters and some solid articles by Manoel Cardozo: "The Last Adventure of Fernão Dias Pais (1674-1681)," *Hispanic American Historical Review*, XXVI (1946), 467-79; "The *Guerra dos Emboabas*, Civil War in Minas Gerais, 1708-1709," *Hispanic American Historical Review*, XXII (1942), 470-92; and "The Brazilian Gold Rush," *The Americas*, III (October 1946), 137-60. One phase of bandeirante colonization is dealt with in Rollie E. Poppino, "Cattle Industry in Colonial Brazil," *Mid-America*, XXXI (1949), 219-47. Magnus Mörner studies the bandeirante offensive against the Jesuit missions of Paraguay in *The Political and Economic Activities of the Jesuits in the La Plata Region* (Stockholm, 1953), chaps. II, III. Clodomir Vianna Moog's *Bandeirantes and Pioneers* (New York, 1964) impressionistically defines the significance of the bandeirantes for Brazilian history and compares them to the American pioneers. Further bibliography in English on colonial Brazil will be found in R. A. Humphreys, *Latin Ameri-*

can History, A Guide to the Literature in English (London, 1958), pp. 65-69.

There is no need to give a full listing of works in Portuguese and Spanish, for an excellent bibliography with a critical essay and annotations was compiled by Alice P. Canabrava under "Bandeiras" in *Manual bibliográfico de estudos brasileiros,* William Berrien and Rubens Borba de Moraes, eds. (Rio de Janeiro, 1949), pp. 492-526. Nélson Werneck Sodré gives a shorter guide, also annotated, in *O que se deve ler para conhecer o Brasil* (2nd ed.; Rio de Janeiro, 1960), pp. 68-73, 82-108. Aureliano Leite's lengthy, uncritical Paulista bibliography in *Subsídios para a história da civilização paulista* (3rd ed.; São Paulo, 1954), pp. 401-558, contains much that is relevant to the bandeirantes. A series of bibliographical essays on the beginnings of Paulista expansion, presented at the Seminário de Estudo das Fontes Primárias para a História de São Paulo no Século XVI, was published in 1948 by the Instituto de Administração of the Universidade de São Paulo (Publications Nos. 21-31). See also José Honório Rodrigues, *Historiografía del Barsil, Siglo XVII* (Mexico, 1963).

The dean of bandeirante historians was Afonso d'E. Taunay. Two of his many works deserve particular mention, *História geral das bandeiras paulistas* (11 vols.; São Paulo, 1924-1950) and the short version, *História das bandeiras paulistas* (2 vols.; São Paulo, 1954). Other leading historians of the bandeirantes and of Paulista expansion include: João Capistrano de Abreu, Washington Luís Pereira de Sousa, Basílio de Magalhães, José de Alcântara Machado, Alfredo Ellis Júnior, Francisco de Assis Carvalho Franco, Sérgio Buarque de Holanda, and Jaime Cortesão. Quantities of material on the bandeirantes, both studies and documentation, have appeared over the years in the *Revista do Instituto Histórico e Geográfico Brasileiro,* the *Anais da Biblioteca Nacional do Rio de Janeiro,* and in the numerous regional journals of Brazil, particularly the *Revista do Instituto Histórico e Geográfico de São Paulo,* the *Anais do Museu Paulista,* and the *Revista do Arquivo Público Mineiro.*

Basic documentary collections include *Actas da Camara Municipal de S. Paulo* (São Paulo, 1914—), and *Registo Geral da Camara da Cidade de S. Paulo* (São Paulo, 1917—), which are sources for Paulista administrative

history, and *Inventários e Testamentos* (São Paulo, 1920—),
which contains colonial Paulistas' inventories and wills.
*Documentos Interessantes para a História e Costumes de
S. Paulo* (São Paulo, 1895—) has documents of various
sorts which bear upon the later phases of bandeirismo.
Other important documentary collections include: Pablo
Pastells, ed., *Historia de la Compañía de Jesús en la provincia del Paraguay . . . según los documentos originales
del Archivo General de Indias* (8 vols.; Madrid, 1912-1949);
Prefeitura do Município de São Paulo (Divisão do Arquivo
Histórico), *Bandeirantes no Paraguai. Século XVII (documentos inéditos)* (São Paulo, 1949); Afonso d'E. Taunay,
ed., *Relatos sertanistas* (São Paulo, 1953), and *Relatos
monçoeiros* (2nd ed.; São Paulo, n. d.); and Jaime Cortesão,
ed., *Manuscritos da coleção De Angelis* (6 vols.; Rio de Janeiro, 1951-1955).

Francisco de Assis Carvalho Franco, *Dicionário de bandeirantes e sertanistas do Brasil* (São Paulo, 1954), is an
excellent biographical dictionary of the bandeirantes. Contemporary maps of interest for bandeirante expansion are reproduced in Afonso d'E. Taunay, *Collectanea de mappas da
cartographia paulista antiga,* Vol. I (São Paulo, 1922),
while Taunay's *Ensaio de carta geral das bandeiras paulistas*
(São Paulo, 1926) gives a historical map which locates numerous bandeiras. Belmonte (pseud. for Benedito Bastos
Barreto) attempts a pictorial reconstruction of the world of
the bandeirantes in *No tempo dos bandeirantes* (2nd ed.;
São Paulo, 1940).

DATE DUE

JUL 2 5 1970			
GAYLORD			PRINTED IN U.S.A.